PRAISE FOR
Under an Afghan Sky

"Richly detailed." —*The Globe and Mail*

"Engrossing. . . . What makes this book so affecting . . . is not any Hollywood-style drama or tension, but a rather unexpected and touching relationship [Fung] builds with one of her abductors." —*Winnipeg Free Press*

"It's a powerful, warts-and-all study of how someone stays together in an unimaginable situation rife with incessant self-questioning and 'what-if' scenarios: Could she strangle her sleeping captor while he snores? Would she be able to get out of the hole under her own steam? . . . Fung invites us into her worst nightmare, providing honest reflections on her own strengths and limitations. . . . [A] courageous contribution to the written history of the past decade." —*Quill & Quire*

"There's a wonderful tension in *Under an Afghan Sky* between the wide-eyed curiosity, innocence, decency, resilience, and compassion of the narrator and the reader's sense of peril in the suffocating confinement, the ever-present likelihood of murder, and the backdrop of a fundamentally irrational conflict. I came away feeling that anybody but Mellissa would probably have perished and that she survived because of the strength of her character, which certainly surprised some of her kidnappers. I was totally captivated." —Linden MacIntyre, author of *The Bishop's Man*

"Grabbed at gunpoint, stabbed in the shoulder, knifed in the hand, thrown in an underground hole for twenty-eight days, and yet Mellissa Fung never stops being a reporter. Fung puts you in that awful, dark, rancid hole with her and lets you listen in as she never stops confronting her kidnappers. Vivid in its detail, dramatic in its conversation, *Under an Afghan Sky* is riveting journalism, and guess what? There's even an endearing love story that runs throughout the book." —Peter Mansbridge

"When I reached Mellissa Fung by telephone in Kabul, shortly after her release, we spoke at great length, like two sisters. The account she has written about the twenty-eight days of captivity is striking, because it gives us the full measure of her strength, which was put to the test, and her humanity." —Michaëlle Jean

"Mellissa Fung's vivid portrait of the soul of a journalist even in the most terrifying of circumstances is a recognition of the never-yielding human spirit. When we follow our calling it can save our lives. Her experience is an example of this." —Sandra Oh

"In *Under an Afghan Sky*, Mellissa Fung touches on some difficult issues and does not divide the world into the two realms of good and evil. As she tells of the long days and nights she spent with her captors in a hole in the ground, we get to know them as the flawed human beings that they were, desperate individuals who had been pushed to the edge by war, poverty, and political and religious extremism. This is an important book that can lead the reader to a better understanding of a very complicated country." —Marina Nemat, author of *Prisoner of Tehran* and *After Tehran*

Under an Afghan Sky

Under an Afghan Sky

A Memoir of Captivity

MELLISSA FUNG

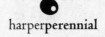

harperperennial

Under an Afghan Sky
Copyright © 2011 by Mellissa Fung.
Excerpts from the diaries of Paul Workman © 2011 by Paul Workman.
Reproduced by permission of Paul Workman.
All rights reserved.

Published by Harper Perennial, an imprint of HarperCollins Publishers Ltd

First published by HarperCollins Publishers Ltd in a hardcover edition: 2011
This Harper Perennial trade paperback edition: 2012

HarperCollins books may be purchased for educational, business,
or sales promotional use through our Special Markets Department.

HarperCollins Publishers Ltd
2 Bloor Street East, 20th Floor
Toronto, Ontario, Canada
M4W 1A8

www.harpercollins.ca

Library and Archives Canada Cataloguing in Publication
Fung, Mellissa
Under an Afghan sky : a memoir of captivity / Mellissa Fung.

ISBN 978-1-55468-681-0

1. Fung, Mellissa—Captivity, 2008. 2. Hostages—Afghanistan—
Biography. 3. Hostages—Canada—Biography. 4. Journalists—
Canada—Biography. 5. Afghan War, 2001– —Personal narratives,
Canadian. I. Title.
DS371.43.F86A3 2012   958.104'7092   C2012-900726-9

Printed in the United States of America
RRD 9 8 7 6 5 4 3 2

For my parents

Under an Afghan Sky

"I am Talib."

I looked up from where he had me pinned to the floor of the car. It had all happened so fast. My heart was pounding, and I still wasn't sure what was going on, except that I was staring up the barrel of a Kalashnikov. There were two men in the back of the car with me and one in the front, in the driver's seat. The men in the back tried to cover me with my black scarf, which I wore over my head whenever I ventured out into the real streets of Afghanistan. I struggled, but it was useless. They were pressing my camera bag in my face in an attempt to cover me up, in case we passed any police while the car sped away from the refugee camp. I tried to look out from underneath the scarf. I wanted to see where we were going.

I suddenly noticed I was bleeding. Huge red bloodstains spread over my blue-and-yellow flowered kameez. Blood was pouring out of my right shoulder and my right hand. One of the two men in the back—the tall one—was on a cell phone, speaking loudly and rapidly to someone who was barking back in Pashto, the language spoken in the south of the country. I had no idea what they were saying, but I knew deep down that it wasn't good.

"What's your name?" asked the man.

"Mellissa," I answered, and he demanded to see my passport. I didn't want to give it to him, but he started to search me. I had it in the left pocket of my hiking pants and fished it out for him.

"Canada. You not from America? Or Britain?"

"No. Canada," I replied as another warm gush of blood oozed out of my shoulder—though I felt no pain.

The man made another phone call and, between bursts of Pashto, I could hear him say "Canada."

I looked up at the door handle and instinctively reached out with my right arm to pull it, only to feel the pain of a worn leather shoe smacking down my hand. The other man, who had curly hair, pointed his bloody knife at me, glared at me with angry black eyes, and shouted, "No!"

"Where are we going?" I asked.

"We are almost there. Ten minutes more."

Ten minutes earlier, I had been working in the relative safety of Charahi Qambar refugee camp, just northeast of Kabul. My fixer, Shokoor, and I had gone there on a sunny Sunday morning, October 12, 2008, to interview people who had fled the fighting in Kandahar and other southern provinces of Afghanistan.

I'd arrived in Kabul the day before, flying up from Kandahar Airfield, where I was based for my second rotation covering the war, and in particular, Canada's military efforts in the south. As a journalist for CBC News reporting on mostly Canadian stories, I had been excited by the prospect of travelling again to Afghanistan. There are few opportunities for domestic reporters to get a taste of conflict zone reporting, and I was determined to make the best of it. I was fascinated by the country and the Afghans I'd met the year before on my first assignment there, and I wanted another chance to tell their stories. The fighting in the south had intensified over the past several months, and thousands were forced to flee their homes in Kandahar, Helmand, and Uruzgan provinces to set up temporary shelter in the safer areas of the north. This camp just outside Kabul was one of them.

It was only eleven o'clock in the morning when I arrived but already unbearably hot. A thick stench, emanating from the open sewers that ran through the camp, filled the air.

We'd spent just about an hour there, no longer. Shokoor was very careful about taking me around the city, knowing there is always a risk when foreigners in Afghanistan venture out. I tried to blend in as much as possible and always kept my head covered with a scarf. We'd interviewed several families that had recently arrived at the camp. One woman told me she'd lost her husband, two sons, and a daughter to a suicide bomber. She told me her life story as we sat outside her makeshift shelter where she lived with her remaining children—three little boys and a girl—as well as her puppy and another dog. She said she was maybe forty years old (Afghans don't celebrate birthdays), but the lines that creased her brown face made her look at least twenty years older. She had kind eyes, though, and a soft smile. I couldn't help but stuff a few hundred afghanis in her hand as I was leaving.

Her family shared their small space with another family from Kandahar province, a family of six or seven, and as I left her, I saw everyone gathering around a small fire—fifteen or sixteen people, waiting for a tiny pot of white rice to cook. It would be their meal of the day. Little did I know then how much of a luxury white rice would become for me.

After we'd finished our interviews, Shokoor and I ran into a group of people from the Office of the United Nations High Commissioner for Refugees (UNHCR) who'd been visiting the camp. The United Nations provided some assistance to the people who lived there, but the refugee situation in Afghanistan and neighbouring Pakistan was becoming critical. Tens of thousands of people had been displaced by the fighting, and there was nowhere for them to go. We made arrangements to stop at the UNHCR office next, to talk to the director about the plight of the refugees. The UN car left, and we made our way back to Shokoor's white Toyota Corolla. His brother was our driver that day, and he was waiting for us just outside the entrance to the camp.

The sun was beating down on us, and I was eager to get going. The UN interview would round out the story. And then we were going to visit a school in the centre of Kabul, funded in part by the Canadian International Development Agency (CIDA), for children who had been orphaned by the war. It was a busy day. But I was going to be in Kabul for only three days and I had four stories to shoot.

"That was good," I said to Shokoor as we walked on the dirt road leading out of the camp. He was holding the small digital camera we were shooting with, while I carried the camera bag and the knapsack with my radio equipment. Everything was going well. I knew I had an important story with the refugees—very few Western journalists had been to this camp.

Just then, a blue car sped toward us from the camp entrance and squealed to a stop next to us, kicking up a small dust storm. Three armed men got out and pointed guns at us. The shortest of them grabbed me and tried to push me head first into the car. "Shokoor!" I screamed as I struggled with the man. In a reflex action, I swung my right fist at his nose. I noticed a glint from the end of a knife and then felt something stick into my shoulder. My heart was racing, but I didn't feel pain, and I wasn't scared for myself. Rather, my overriding fear was that they would kill Shokoor. I saw him covering his head with his arm as one of the men pointed a gun in his face. I squeezed my eyes shut to brace myself for the inevitable sound of a gunshot.

"Shokoor!" I shouted again as I was shoved into the back seat of the car. "Call Paul! Don't go to the police!"

The car sped away, kicking up another dust storm in its wake. From the back window, I could see Shokoor running to the road, the camera still hanging on his shoulder. I continued to struggle in the car, swinging my fists as the men shoved my head down to their feet with the butts of their guns. The car smelled of gasoline and sweat. I tried to look up to see their faces but one of them held my scarf to my face and the other kept his foot on my back, not allowing me to move.

"Stay there," ordered the tall man, shoving a foot into my face. He was wearing dusty black leather shoes which he had flattened at back and wore like sandals.

Two of the men started going through my knapsack. There wasn't much in it.

"What's this?" the tall man asked, pulling out some wires.

"Who are you? Where are you taking me?" I asked, pushing the scarf off my face.

"I not going to kill you," he said in reply. "I am Talib."

Oh my God, I thought, *this is bad. This is really bad.* We had all considered the possibility of being taken hostage by the Taliban but never really believed it would happen. We took so many precautions every time we went out to shoot a story.

"Where are we going?"

"Do not speak."

His cell phone rang and he took his foot off my back. I sat up a bit. I could hear a loud, anxious voice on the other end of the line, speaking in Pashto. The men were looking out the window furtively, watching for police roadblocks, I guessed. I could feel the car turning and speeding, turning and speeding as the driver changed gears, stepped on the gas pedal, and then hit the brakes hard. The tall man, who wore a long black shirt, kept yelling at the driver.

The men continued going through my things. They rifled

through the small red case where I kept some powder and lipstick, then tossed it back into the knapsack. They pulled out my notebook and boxes of AA batteries, which I kept for the radio equipment. My camera bag was empty, save for a lens cap and some batteries. I was thankful that I'd left almost everything else in my room at the Serena Hotel in Kabul. Especially several thousand American dollars—money I'd brought from Canada to pay Shokoor and to take care of other expenses.

"Where is your laptop?" the tall Afghan asked.

"It's in my hotel room," I told him. "Why don't you take me back there and I'll give it to you."

He laughed and said something in Pashto to the curly-haired man. They both laughed. "Where is your cell phone?" he asked.

"It's in my bag," I answered. As the men searched my knapsack, I managed to take my second, spare cell phone out of my pants pocket and slip it down the front of my hiking pants without them noticing.

"Do you have money?" the tall one asked as I watched him take my cell phone apart. He took the battery out, and then the SIM card from the back of the phone, putting them along with the phone and back cover into his breast pocket.

"Money?" he repeated. I was carrying a few hundred afghanis and about two hundred US dollars in my pocket. I pulled it all out and offered it to them.

"If I give this to you, will you let me go?" I bargained. I think deep down I knew they wanted a lot more, but that didn't stop me from trying—maybe I would be able to persuade them to take me back to Kabul. The tall one laughed again and translated for his friend. They both laughed and split the money between them, giving a little to the driver as well. "If you take me back to Kabul, I will give you my laptop. And I also have some money in the hotel safe there."

"How much money?"

"A few thousand dollars, maybe."

This seemed to intrigue him, and he conversed in Pashto with the curly-haired man for a while. Finally, the tall one—apparently the only one who spoke a little English—said, "No, a few thousand dollars buys us nothing. It won't even buy a gun."

"You have a gun," I said, gesturing at the weapon on his lap. "Why do you want another?" I wanted to keep them talking.

"To kill Americans," he answered, as if it was obvious.

The curly-haired Afghan reached behind him for a bottle of neon orange–coloured pop. He took a swig and then offered the bottle to me. I shook my head.

"Where are we going?" I asked again. It felt like maybe half an hour had passed since they had ambushed us at the entrance of the camp.

"We're here. Get out." The car had stopped at what looked like the edge of a small village. I could not even see Kabul in the distance anymore. A large mountain stood in front of us. It all looked strangely fuzzy to me, and I realized I had lost my left contact lens. It must have been knocked out in the struggle to get me into the car. I felt slightly dizzy and off-balance as I looked around.

"Don't look back."

"Where are we? Where are we going?"

The two Afghans grabbed their stuff from the car—two bottles of the orange pop, a few boxes of cookies, my knapsack and camera bag—and the car backed up and sped off.

"Start walking," the tall man ordered. I followed, the curly-haired one behind me. Both men wore their Kalashnikovs over their shoulders.

We were climbing the mountain. The rocky ground was covered in stones and short grass. I looked back and saw the village in the distance. Except that now that I could see it from farther away, I realized it might not be a village after all. It looked more like a cluster of houses. Maybe a suburb of a suburb of Kabul.

"Don't look back," the tall man repeated, while the other glared at me again with his angry dark eyes and pointed his gun forward, as if to tell me to keep moving.

"What's your name, anyway?" I asked the tall one.

"Khalid."

"Calid? Say it again?"

"It's like Ha-lid."

"Khalid."

"Yes, that is right."

"And your friend's name?"

Khalid turned to the curly-haired man and said something in Pashto. Curly-hair turned to me and said in broken English, "My name Shafirgullah."

"Sha . . . say that again," I told him.

"Sha-feer-gull-ah."

"Shafirgullah."

"Yes."

Shafirgullah pulled a package of cigarettes out of his pocket and offered me one. They were Pines, the same brand I had smoked at the Kandahar Airfield base. I shook my head. Khalid took one, licked the end of it—I discovered later that this was so the ashes wouldn't flake off—lit a match, and then both men took turns taking long puffs.

"Your head," Khalid said to me, making a motion with his hand. "Keep covered." I realized my scarf had been hanging around my shoulder, and I lifted it with my left hand to cover my head.

We continued walking. Everything around us seemed brown and grey, save for the blue sky. The afternoon sun remained fiercely hot, making me sweat. I looked down. Huge drops of blood fell at my feet with every step I took. The blood was dark red and pouring out of my shoulder, running down my body in rivulets. I could feel my undershirt soaked and sticking to me, and there was also a gash in my right hand. I vaguely remembered Shafirgullah sticking his knife into my hand after he shoved me into the car. I must have lost a fair bit of blood, and I was starting to feel faint. I wasn't sure if the two men noticed me bleeding, but after a while they stopped.

"Sit down," Khalid said. I was glad to rest, and we all sat down on the rocky ground, a break in the middle of the uphill climb. The two Afghans pulled my scarf away to reveal the gaping wound in my shoulder. They spoke in Pashto to each other and studied the wound for a bit.

"Does it hurt?" Khalid asked. I nodded, though it felt more numb than anything. He unwrapped the black scarf that was wrapped around his neck and slipped it under my right arm, tying it in a tight knot at the shoulder. My kameez was ripped and soaked in blood. Shafirgullah offered me the bottle of orange pop, and this time I reached out and accepted. I took a few sips.

"Good?" Shafirgullah asked. I nodded. He opened a box of cookies. They were sandwich-style—two vanilla wafers with chocolate cream in the middle. "Biscuit?" he offered. I took one and ate it. And then another. It must have been mid-afternoon and I'd last eaten around seven that morning—a poached egg and toast in the café at the Serena Hotel. I loved having breakfast at the Serena. There was always a buffet with fresh fruit and juices, and breads baked that morning. You could have eggs any way you wanted, and the coffee was rich and dark. I could still taste the coffee. I'd had two cups.

"Get up," Khalid ordered suddenly.

We continued walking. The mountain was getting steeper. In the distance, I could see another village. Or maybe that was Kabul?

I really had no idea where I was in relation to the capital, or where we were going. Khalid and Shafirgullah kept looking up to the sky, and I could hear the faint rumble of airplanes.

"Do you have a GPS?" Khalid asked.

"No," I said, "why?"

"Airplanes. They tracking us." He led us into a ravine where the ground was covered with shale-like rocks. It was hard to walk and keep my balance. "Shh. Sit down."

Again, we sat down. The men took their Kalashnikovs off and put them on the ground. We waited. The airplane sound got louder, then faded. The two of them started searching my knapsack again. They pulled out my wallet and this time went through all my cards.

"Credit cards," Khalid said.

"Yes," I told him, "but they're only good in Canada. You can't use them here." He nodded and put them back in their compartments.

"Where this money is from?" He pulled out several denominations of Canadian bills.

"Canada."

"How much is this?"

I reached out and he put the bills in my hand. I counted.

"About a hundred dollars," I answered. He took the bills back and stuffed them in the pocket of his pants.

The men seemed convinced that I had a GPS, and they were determined to find it. Instead, they found my Nike wristwatch, which Khalid held to his ear as if to listen for the ticking. Then he took a sharp rock and smashed it into pieces. And then he smashed the pieces some more.

"That was my watch, not a GPS." I scowled at him. He had moved on already, pulling out my camera from the bag. I had a little Canon point-and-shoot that I'd bought—it was basically brand new—to take with me to Beijing while I was on assignment at the Summer Olympics only two months before. I watched as they took it out of its case and found the on switch.

"Camera," Shafirgullah said, proud that he knew how to say the word in English.

They scrolled through all my pictures, asking questions. "Who is that?" "Where is this?" "What were you doing?"

Khalid pointed the camera at me, motioned to Shafirgullah to sit next to me, and took a picture of us. Then Shafirgullah picked up his gun and pointed it to my head. He said something in Pashto and laughed—and click, the pose was captured.

The two men traded places. Khalid showed Shafirgullah which button to push, and it was his turn to hold the gun to my head.

"Stop this," I said to them, "it's not nice." They laughed. "And it's not funny."

Suddenly there was a *beep, beep, beep.* It was coming from my crotch.

"What is that?" Khalid asked. "You have GPS!"

"No," I lied, "that's coming from your phone." I pointed to his pocket.

Beep, beep, beep.

"Where is that? It is your pocket! Give to me!" Khalid was angry now. I had no choice but to pull my spare phone from my pants and hand it over.

"You lie to me," Khalid said. "You say you no have GPS."

"I don't. It's a phone. I forgot I had a spare one."

He grabbed the blue-and-white Nokia cell phone from my hand and did the same thing he had done with my other phone: he took the battery and the SIM card out and put them and the phone in his pocket.

"What else in your pocket?" he demanded.

"Nothing," I lied.

"I want to see." He stuck his hand in one pocket and then the other, and pulled out a small one-decade rosary. I'd bought it in Italy that summer when three of my girlfriends and I were in Tuscany for our friend Maureen's wedding. It was made of rose petals, and at one time had a nice rose smell, but the scent had long worn off. I'm not super-religious but I am a practising Catholic, and I'd kept the rosary in my right pants pocket since I bought it. *Never know when you might need it, Mellissa.* Khalid threw the beads to Shafirgullah, who tossed it onto the gravel.

"Let me keep that," I said, reaching my hand out. Shafirgullah picked it up and gave it back to me, and I put it back in my pocket.

"Get up," Khalid ordered. He said something to Shafirgullah in Pashto and the curly-haired man pointed his gun at me, pushing me forward. We started walking—up, up, up, and over, it seemed. I assumed we were headed west, since the sun was starting to set in that direction. We hadn't gotten very far when I heard voices in the distance.

"Shh. Stop! Sit!" Khalid ordered.

Shafirgullah and I sat down and watched as Khalid cocked his Kalashnikov and walked off.

"Biscuit?" Shafirgullah asked as he opened another box of sandwich cookies. He took four of them and handed the box to me. I took one and munched. I was more thirsty than hungry, but the bottle of orange pop was empty.

Soon, Khalid was back. After the two men exchanged a few words, Khalid took out his cell phone. He walked around until he found a signal and then made a phone call. I could vaguely hear an agitated male voice on the other end. When the call ended, Khalid made another. The second call lasted only a few seconds.

Shafirgullah pulled out the smokes again and waved the package in my direction. I said no, but Khalid took one and they both lit up.

"Get up," he ordered, and the three of us started walking again.

The sun was really setting now, and a cool wind was blowing as we reached the top of the hill.

"You are cold?" Khalid asked me.

I nodded and he took off his large black coat, about two sizes too big for him, and put it on my shoulders. I'm on the small side, and the coat was much, much too big for me and kept slipping off. He motioned for me to put it on, and then sighed as I struggled with it. Exasperated, he grabbed my left arm and stuck it in the sleeve of the coat. My right arm was still tied up in the scarf, and he held out the right sleeve as I gingerly tucked my arm into it.

"Okay?" he asked. I nodded. We were heading downhill. The air was cool, and the sky had become an amazing canvas of pinks, purples, and blues. I could see other mountains around us and a stream to the left, and for a minute, the beauty of the rugged land made me catch my breath. There were birds flying overhead, swooping down occasionally to pick at some tall grass on the hillside.

"Where are we?" I asked. "What's the name of this mountain?"

"You do not know," Khalid answered. I knew he wouldn't tell me. He didn't want me to know where I was, or where I was going. We continued walking for another hour. Dusk had fallen, and I was starting to feel a little faint again.

"Stop here." Khalid reached for his cell phone and made a call. More Pashto. I wished I understood it. Shafirgullah again offered me a cigarette. This time I took one. The matches were damp and he had trouble getting one to light up, going through match after match after match. Finally, I took the box from him, struck two matches together against the side of the box; both ignited. I lit all three cigarettes and passed the men theirs. I took a drag of mine and felt a head rush.

It had been more than a year since I'd smoked a cigarette. During my first stint in Afghanistan, we had gone off the main base at Kandahar Airfield to camp out at Ma'sum Ghar, one of the forward operating bases. It was about fifty degrees Celsius at the time, and the tent we were sleeping and working in had no air conditioning. There was no breeze, and the air hung heavy over and inside the tent. My cameraman, Sat Nandlall, had started smoking as soon as he arrived in Afghanistan, and now he and Richard Johnson, an artist/photographer for the *National Post*, were basically chain-smoking in the tent while we waited to head out on operations with the Canadian soldiers. I vowed I wouldn't start. Besides the obvious reasons, I didn't want to start smoking because I'm a runner, and it hampers my ability to run long distances. The second-hand smoke in the hot tent was so bad that it drove me out, and so I went to hang out with the soldiers in the common tent across the way. That tent was at least open.

It turned out that all the soldiers smoked—or at least the ones I was sitting with. One of them offered me a cigarette and that was it. I smoked like a chimney during my six weeks in Afghanistan and then stopped as soon as I got on the flight back to Canada. I hadn't had a puff since.

We were smoking the last puffs of our cigarettes when Shafir-gullah pulled out another.

"Why are we stopped here?" I asked.

"We waiting," Khalid answered.

"For what?"

"You like motorcycle?" he asked.

"What?" I wasn't sure what he was asking.

"Motor-cycle," he enunciated, so I might understand better. "You ride?"

"I have before. Why?" I replied.

"We wait. Motorcycle."

I didn't understand. "Where are you taking me?"

"We go to my home," he said. "It is nice place. You will like."

I asked him if had family there—a mother? A father?

"My girlfriend there."

"Your girlfriend," I repeated.

He nodded and smiled. "I not kill you. We just want money." Of course they wanted money. I knew how this worked.

"How much money you want?" I asked. I was beginning to speak like they did—in broken English.

Khalid lit another cigarette. "Two people. Last two people we take. They from Germany and Britain. We get . . . how you say . . . ten hundred—"

"Ten hundred?" I asked.

He was trying to do the math in his head. "Ten thousand hundred . . ."

He pulled out my notebook from my knapsack. He wrote a one, and five zeros after it: 100 000.

"A hundred thousand dollars," I said.

"Yes. Each one," he replied.

"That is what you want for me," I asked, "a hundred thousand dollars?" My heart sank. The idea of my network or someone having to negotiate with these guys didn't sit well with me. I'd heard of hostage-takers demanding millions from other governments and organizations.

Khalid looked at me closely, as if studying my face. "No, for you, maybe we ask two. Two hundred thousand."

"But you won't kill me?" I wanted to be sure.

"No, I no kill you."

"Promise?" I asked.

"Yes."

"Shake my hand. Promise." I reached out my hand. He took it and held it firmly.

"I no kill you. I promise you."

I hung onto his hand for a second longer to make sure he had shaken on his promise, then reached for another cigarette. Shafirgullah, who had been fixated on his cell phone and was text-messaging on it during this entire exchange, took a smoke out of the package and handed it to me, along with the matches.

I lit it and inhaled deeply. The nicotine must have emboldened me. I asked Khalid if I could use his phone.

"Who you want to call?" Khalid asked in reply.

"My friend."

"Why?"

"To let him know I am okay. He will be worried about me."

"It is a boyfriend?"

"Yes. Just one call. He will be worried."

Khalid and Shafirgullah conferred in Pashto for a minute.

"Okay, one call."

Khalid reassembled my phone and handed it over to me. It was the phone I had hidden and that had beeped earlier. Now I saw that there was a text message. It was from Paul. Paul Workman, the CTV correspondent with whom I'd developed a close bond since we met in Kandahar the year before. "What can you tell me?" it read. I knew then that he knew what had happened to me. With trembling fingers, I pulled up his number on speed dial. It rang twice.

"Hi, it's Paul."

"Hi, P. It's me. I'm okay, don't worry, I'm okay."

"Where are you?"

Khalid motioned to me. "Tell them you are with the Taliban."

"I'm with the Taliban," I said into the phone. "But I am okay."

"Oh, Mellissa."

"It's okay. I'm fine."

Paul asked me if I had any idea where I was, and if my captors were listening in.

"Yes, they're listening. They are treating me well. I'm being looked after by a very nice man. His name is Khalid. He wants to speak to you."

At that moment, Khalid took the phone from me. "Hello. Everything is okay. She is with us. We looking after her." Suddenly he looked spooked and abruptly ended the call. He took the phone apart again and put it in his breast pocket.

"What's wrong?" I asked. I hated that I didn't have the chance to say goodbye. I couldn't imagine what was going through Paul's mind.

He pointed up to the sky. "Planes. They are tracking us." *What paranoia,* I thought. I could hear the faint noise of an airplane flying somewhere, but it was nowhere near us. The sound faded after a few minutes.

"I never got to say goodbye to him," I said. "Can I make one more call?"

"No, enough," he replied.

"Please? One more call. Just to finish and say bye. Please?"

Khalid looked at me and sighed. He reached into his pocket and took out the components of my phone. Battery, SIM card, back cover. He handed them and the phone back to me. I dialed Paul's number again.

"Hello, it's Paul."

"Hi, it's me again. I'm just calling to say goodbye."

"What?!"

"I didn't get to say bye before. I'm okay. They're treating me well. Don't worry. They just want money."

"How much money? Ask them, where do we send the money?" Paul said. The line was crackly. But I was surprised that there was even cell phone service where we were—it was Afghanistan, after all, and we were in the hills.

Khalid interrupted. "Say goodbye. Now."

"I have to go now. Bye, P. I'm okay. They're treating me well."

"Thank them for me, for taking care of you."

"I'm sorry about everything. All the trouble I've caused everybody," I said.

"There's nothing to be sorry about," he replied.

"Bye. Love you."

"I love you, M."

Dearest M,

This is the only way I can keep in touch with you, writing letters, even if they won't get answered. I just hope that one day you'll be able to read them. I wanted you to have a record of what went on. I'm at the Gandamack Lodge on day three of our nightmare. I woke up before seven, waiting anxiously for the phone to ring. I have imagined every horrible scenario and I shake with fear. I cannot begin to understand what you are going through. The simplest of things: what they've made you wear, how they've transported you around the countryside, what you're eating, drinking, how you're going to the bathroom.

It's now been twenty-seven hours since your last call, and I look at my phone every minute to make sure it's on. I wonder if I made mistakes when I spoke to you, and that I wasn't reassuring enough, or didn't give you enough information. Everybody says it's very unusual that you were allowed to contact me directly, and that gives us a huge deal of hope that we're dealing with guys who are merely criminals, looking to make money, and not the Taliban.

I was on the way to the PRT when Shokoor called to say four armed men had grabbed you and taken you away. He was very distraught. That was about ten minutes after it happened. He said they roughed him up and threatened to kill him. At first I didn't believe or couldn't quite grasp what he was saying, and then it hit me. Al was sitting in the front seat, and immediately knew something awful had happened.

Al and I immediately went back to the Airfield, not really sure what to do, but already I was thinking about trying to get to Kabul as soon as possible. Shokoor said the kidnappers did not look like Taliban, and that gave me an initial sense of hope.

Your first call came at about 1645, I think, and my hand was shaking as I answered. You can't believe the relief when I heard you say, "I'm okay, don't worry, I'm okay." I think I asked if you knew where you were and if they were listening, and you said "yes." That's when you handed the phone over to this guy Khalid and the line went dead.

I was back inside the work tent when your second call came through. I couldn't believe they would let you call again, but I have to say, M, your first words scared the hell out of me. "I just phoned to say goodbye." I thought, *Oh my God, they're going to kill her.*

"Now what?" I asked.

"Waiting," he responded, and lit another cigarette. Shafirgullah and I each took one as well. I puffed hard and blew out long streams of smoke.

Suddenly, I heard the rumble of an engine in the distance. The two Afghans stood up and looked into the valley below. The noise got louder and louder, and soon I could see a figure on a red motorcycle approaching us, a cloud of dust trailing behind. The vehicle stopped, and an Afghan man got off. He greeted Khalid with a kiss on both cheeks and shook Shafirgullah's hand. They spoke for a few minutes, and then Khalid came back to where I was still sitting.

"Put this on," he ordered, unrolling a pair of light brown "man jams," as Western journalists called them. In Pashto they are called "salwar kameez"—a long, uncollared tunic with baggy pyjama-like pants. This pair must have been made for an overweight Afghan man. I stepped into the pants and was swallowed up by one leg.

"No," Khalid said. He made me take out my left leg and put it through the right way. The pants fell off immediately. He laughed and cinched the drawstring tightly around my waist. "Now this," he said as he put the kameez over my head. It smelled rank—as if the Afghan it belonged to hadn't washed it for a year. I wrinkled my nose.

"It stinks." My protest fell on deaf ears. They wrapped a kaffi-yeh around my head and put a pair of sunglasses on my face. Khalid got on the motorcycle first. He motioned for me to get on behind him, and I climbed onto the banana seat. Shafirgullah climbed on behind me and the man who had driven the bike up waved us off. I wondered if I would ever again see my knapsack, which we had left behind.

The road was rocky and hard to navigate, especially with three people sitting on the one seat. Khalid slowly steered the bike over rocks, but he sped up as soon as the path straightened out. It was bumpy, and I hung onto the sides of the seat as we sped down the hill. Shafirgullah kept reaching over to make sure my scarf and sunglasses were secure on my head.

I could see a farmer herding a flock of sheep next to the road. It was getting dark, and I could make out the shadow of what might have been his home a few metres away. It looked like a shack, and there were sheep everywhere. We zoomed past him as we continued down the bumpy road. Ahead, I could see what appeared to be a village. Few lights in the area indicated that there was probably little or no electricity. A slightly wider road led toward the village, and I could make out the headlights of a few cars. We sped down a dirt road, past mud walls and houses. It was a clear night. I could see stars above and a new moon, a bright little crescent that hung high, lighting up the branches of the trees below.

The road narrowed; we were now in the village. I saw a woman in a burka walking with her boy, a bag in her hand. We flew past parked cars. I saw the red tail lights of a minivan, about to back out onto the road. *What if I just jumped off the bike and started yelling?* My kidnappers would have no choice but to leave me or risk arrest. I turned my head and peeked over the dark sunglasses as we turned a corner where several women in burkas were gathered. As if he were reading my mind, Shafirgullah pushed my head down and forward, and repositioned my sunglasses to try to block my view. I kept my head down but tried to look over the glasses. I could see more people walking down the road: men and women and children. They looked at us as the motorcycle sped past them.

Soon, it seemed, we'd left the centre of the town, and there were fewer people on the road.

"Where are we going?" I asked. "Where is your house?"

"Just maybe ten minutes more," Khalid answered.

We drove over a mud bridge, ducking to avoid some low-hanging branches. There were more trees than houses now, and the road seemed desolate in the dark. We drove up to what looked like an abandoned white house, and Khalid parked the motorcycle across the road from it.

Two men came out of the house and approached us. They both had Kalashnikovs slung over their shoulders. They greeted Khalid and Shafirgullah with kisses on both cheeks and then they spoke rapidly among themselves in Pashto. I heard Khalid say my name a couple times.

One of the men came up to me. "Hello, Mellissa. I am Zahir," he said.

This was strange. It was as if I were being introduced to someone I was interviewing—in Afghanistan or anywhere else. "Hi, Amir (or Mike or Don or anyone else), I'm Mellissa, and it's nice to meet you." Except it wasn't so nice. I was meeting my kidnappers, the men who had just taken me from everything I'd known, who had taken away my freedom. "Hello, Zahir," I replied.

"Come with me," he said, taking my hand.

He led me across the road where the motorcycle was parked and into the house, the three other men following. Zahir had to guide me over the threshold in the darkness. We entered an empty room with a dusty dirt floor. There were windows facing the road, and windows on the side. It wasn't quite the "house" I'd imagined when Khalid said he was taking me "home." I sat down cross-legged on the wide ledge of the window facing the road. Out of the window, I could see the crescent moon, which was casting an iridescent glow over everything beneath it: the trees, the tall grass, the dirt road, and the red motorcycle. It seemed impossible that a bit of light could illuminate so much. I tried to take in as much as I could through the window. We were definitely on the outskirts of whatever town we had just driven through.

"Cigarette?" Shafirgullah offered his package and a lighter. I accepted and watched as he licked the end of his and lit it. As the flame illuminated the room for a brief second, I noticed the walls were riddled with bullet holes. I inhaled and watched as the four Afghans checked their rifles and conversed in Pashto. Khalid came over to me with the fourth man, whom I hadn't yet been introduced to. He was a shortish, fat man, and all I could make out from the light coming through the window was that he had curly hair and a beard.

"This my uncle, Abdulrahman," Khalid said.

"Hello," I replied.

"We are not going to hurt you," Abdulrahman said, as if to assure me. His English was better than Khalid's. His breath reeked of garlic and onions.

"You want money," I replied, "just tell my friends how much."

"Once the money comes," he said, "you go. Back to Kabul."

"How soon?" I asked.

"If the money comes tomorrow, you go tomorrow."

"I can't stay here," I said. "I have to go home."

"Where are you from, Canada?" he asked me. "I have been to Canada."

"You have? Where in Canada?" This was a surprise to me. How was it possible that this Afghan, dressed in man jams and armed with a Kalashnikov, could ever have been to Canada? As what? A tourist?

"I was there a long time ago. Before I was in New York. You know New York? I have friends there. I was with them."

Did I know New York? Of course I did. I'd gone to graduate school there and had returned at least once a year since graduating. It was only my favourite city in the world. I felt a pang in my stomach. New York was as far away from where I was now as you could possibly get.

"I've been to New York," I told the fat Afghan.

"I learn English there," he said proudly. "My English better than Khalid. I learn in America. Khalid learn from here."

I leaned back toward the window as I caught another whiff of rancid garlic. "Where are you from?" I asked.

"Here, Afghanistan," Abdulrahman answered.

"Where in Afghanistan?"

"Close to here."

"Where? Kabul?"

"Close by."

I figured he wasn't going to give me anything more, so I changed the subject and asked him if this was where we were spending the night.

"No, somewhere else," he answered. "A better place. You will like it."

"What's wrong with being here?" I asked.

"It is not safe here. The windows, people will see you. There are a lot of Taliban in this area," Abdulrahman said. I'd thought these men were Taliban, and showed my surprise.

"We are Taliban, but we not all together. You don't want other Taliban find us. We waiting here while other place getting ready," he said. "Very close to here." He then walked off to speak with

Khalid. I noticed two other men were now in the room, but no one bothered to introduce them to me.

"Cigarette," I said out loud to the room. Khalid came over with his package.

"You should not smoke much," he told me. "Cigarette bad." I pointed out that both he and Shafirgullah were also smoking.

"It is bad—smoking," he said as he took out a cigarette and lit it. He handed it to me and lit one for himself after licking the end.

Abdulrahman came over. "The house is ready. Come."

"Where are we going?" I asked.

"Don't worry, Mellissa," Khalid said. "I will stay with you tonight."

"I have to go to bathroom," I said.

"You go bathroom first. I take you." He took my hand and led me out of the house and around a corner to what looked like a large open room with mud walls and some kind of corrugated roof over it. "In there," Abdulrahman motioned. "Go there." I went into the corner of the room. The hard ground smelled like dung. I undid the drawstring of my pants and squatted in the dark.

"You finished?" Abdulrahman asked from outside.

"Yes."

"Come. Hurry."

"Where are you taking me?" I asked.

"I am not going to hurt you," he said, not answering my question. "We are friends now."

"Friends?" I said, the anger rising like bile in my throat. "Friends don't kidnap each other."

He laughed. "We are not going to hurt you. We are all friends. Mellissa and Abdulrahman are friends." He took my arm and led me around the back of the house, up a small hill, and around a mud wall.

"Sit here," he ordered. We sat in a corner, with mud walls on either side. I could make out what looked like another abandoned house to the left of us, a few metres away. Was that where we were headed? I heard a noise coming from the ground. It was Zahir. His head popped out of a hole next to where we were sitting. The opening was about the size of a manhole cover, maybe slightly smaller. He had a flashlight and he spoke briefly to Abdulrahman in Pashto before disappearing back into the hole.

"Okay, it is ready," Abdulrahman said to me. He pointed into the ground from where Zahir had appeared. "That is your room."

I looked down at the hole. It was dark, except for a little glow from Zahir's flashlight. My heart stopped for a moment, and for only the second time that day, I felt afraid. I had a bad feeling in the pit of my stomach that was quickly making its way up to my throat.

"Go," Abdulrahman ordered, taking my arm and pushing me toward the hole.

I looked down into the darkness again. "No," I said, "I am not going down there."

I have never been afraid of the dark. When I was a little girl and played hide and seek with my sister, Vanessa, and our friends, my favourite hiding place was the crawlspace in the basement of our house, in East Vancouver. It was a pretty large storage space, about four feet high, with my mother's shoes scattered on the floor. My father stored boxes of oranges in the crawlspace because the temperature was much cooler there than anywhere else in the house.

I would always crawl through the shoes and into the darkest corner of that dark little room, underneath the stairs. It was the best place to hide because everyone else was scared to go there. I was almost inevitably the last one to be "found."

Now, looking into this crude opening in the rocky ground, I realized that my kidnappers wanted to hide me in this hole. And I wanted to be found.

"Go," Abdulrahman ordered again, "it is a good room for you there."

"No," I said. I sat down again with my back against the mud wall. "I am not going there. I will stay up here tonight. I've slept on the ground before. I'll be more comfortable here."

"You must go," he said. "You will not stay here."

"Mellissa." I hadn't heard Khalid's footsteps, but he'd joined Abdulrahman and was now sitting next to me. He said my name with four syllables instead of three—it sounded like he was saying Me-llis-si-a.

"Khalid, please don't make me go in there," I pleaded. "I am afraid of the dark."

"Zahir stay with you," he told me. "I come tomorrow to see you."

"Can't we stay back in that house? It was better there."

"No," Abdulrahman said, "it is not safe there. Taliban are in this area."

"I thought you were Taliban."

"Other Taliban."

The two of them spoke in Pashto and then Khalid got up.

"I go now, see you tomorrow," he said.

"Wait, Khalid, you said you would stay with me." I looked hard at him.

"I see you tomorrow. Zahir stay with you tonight."

"No, you promised you would stay with me," I argued.

"Zahir my brother. He stay. I come tomorrow. I promise."

And he was gone.

Abdulrahman stood up and pushed me roughly toward the hole. He was fat and strong; I tried to resist, but there was no way to struggle, even though I really did not want to find out what was down there.

"Go," he said.

He grabbed my arm and yanked me to my feet and over to the hole. I looked down and saw the faint glow from Zahir's flashlight.

"I don't want to go in there," I repeated. Abdulrahman was getting impatient. He reached and grabbed me underneath my armpits and threw me down the shaft—which was maybe eight feet deep and two feet wide—and into the hole, feet first. I landed on my butt.

"Go through!" Abdulrahman ordered from above.

I felt Zahir's hand on my running shoe. "Come, this way," he told me, and I saw that there was a tunnel running off one side of the hole. I inched my way forward, but the tunnel was no more than about two feet high. My head hit the hard mud ceiling. I crouched down lower, slowing moving forward, following Zahir, who was crawling backward. The tunnel, about twelve feet long, opened up into a small space.

I looked around at the mud walls. The ceiling was made of old pieces of dark grey ceramic tiles and held up by two vertical wooden beams painted a bluish grey. There were hooks on the beams. The entire space was no more than six feet long, three feet wide, and just over five feet high. Two blankets were spread out, covering the dirt floor. The blankets, beige with coloured stripes, were woven from a thick canvas-like material. Two pillows bookended the hole on either side—one was a dark red velvet, the other a dirty white. A black metal bucket stood close to the entrance. In the middle was an old car battery, jerry-rigged to a light bulb attached to one of the hooks near the ceiling. A small plastic alarm clock sat on the battery. I noticed a white grocery bag to the side, a red plastic watering can, and my camera bag and knapsack in a corner. There was also a wooden door-like panel leaning against the wall next to the entrance.

Zahir sat cross-legged in the far corner.

"Sit," he said. Abdulrahman was shouting down to us in Pashto, so Zahir crawled back over to the shaft and spoke to him for a few minutes. Soon he was back. He wrapped his kaffiyeh around his head and face, motioning for me to do the same with my scarf. He then covered the entrance with the wooden door. "Cover your mouth," he told me. I was about to ask him why when I heard a noise at the top of the shaft. Someone was covering the opening with a board or some other object. I could hear digging. A cloud of dust came rushing through the entrance, filling the room. I tried to hold my scarf over my mouth but it was too late. I started coughing and looked up. That's when it dawned on me that they were covering the hole with dirt. No one outside would ever suspect there was a room underneath. After a few minutes, I heard footsteps above us, then there was silence.

I looked around. Everything was covered in a layer of dust. I tried brushing some of it off with my scarf but succeeded only in turning off the light bulb when I knocked the wires off the battery. Zahir turned on his flashlight and reattached the wires. The light came back on.

I sat with my back to the wall facing the entrance. I took off the coat Khalid had given me on the mountain. The inside was covered in blood. Zahir crawled over to me and pointed to my wound.

"Let me see," he said. His English was as good as Abdulrahman's and better than Khalid's. I took off the smelly kameez, but the odour of stinky Afghan man stayed with me. I took a deep breath through my mouth. Zahir unwrapped the scarf that was tied around my shoulder. The sleeve of my own shirt was caked with blood. The blue-and-yellow flowered cloth was ripped, and I watched as Zahir lifted it from my shoulder. It was stuck to the wound, glued on with blood. I winced as he pulled it off. He reached for the white plastic bag and pulled out a roll of dark pink toilet paper. Ripping off a few sections, he wetted the paper with water from the red can and held it to my shoulder.

"Does it hurt?" he asked. I hadn't felt pain from the wound until that moment. I nodded, watching from the corner of my eye as he wiped the wound. I didn't realize until now how deep the cut actually was. It was still oozing dark red blood. Zahir shook his head and continued to wipe the bloodstains off my shoulder. After he was satisfied it was clean, he ripped a few more pieces of toilet paper from the roll and pressed them into the wound to staunch the blood.

"Let me see your hand," he said next. I held out my right hand

and he examined the small stab wound. The blood had caked over, but the wound hurt when he touched it. My index and middle fingers were numb. Again, Zahir bandaged me with the pink toilet paper. Finished, he sat back.

"It is better?" he asked.

I stared at him and nodded. I was feeling a little dizzy, and realized I was still wearing just one contact lens, so everything looked blurry to me. Then I remembered that I always pack an extra set of disposable lenses when I travel, so I reached for my knapsack and opened the side pocket. I took out the package and peeled back the cover to take out the lens.

"What is that?" Zahir asked.

"It's like glasses, in my eyes, to help me see."

He watched as I poked the lens into my left eye with my dirty index finger. Finally, I could see properly again. I looked at my captor and blinked.

Zahir had dark eyes, set apart by a thin nose. He wore a beaded skullcap on the back of his head, like many Afghan men I'd met before. His kameez was a light green, with matching baggy pants. He'd left his brown leather sandals by the door.

"Where is Khalid? Where did they go?" I asked. I wondered if they had homes in the village. If they had beds, bathrooms, electricity, lights.

"They go home," Zahir answered.

"A house?"

"Yes, a house."

"Do you live there too?" I asked.

"I live there sometime," he said. "I live in Pakistan. You know Peshawar?"

I'd never been across the border. I had been close to it with the Canadian troops, and I knew that Peshawar was just the other side of the Khyber Pass. At one time it was a major supply route for NATO forces in Afghanistan. Over the last year, it had become more of a haven for insurgents. I remembered hearing that there had been a suicide bombing there just a few weeks before. I asked Zahir if his family was from there, and he told me they had a house in Peshawar.

"How many of you are there? You, Khalid, do you have other brothers?" He told me he had three brothers and one sister.

"And you travel back and forth between here and there?"

"I go back there tomorrow," he said. "We come to Afghanistan in summer. Peshawar in winter."

"What do you do there?" I asked.

"I go to school," he answered.

"School? How old are you?"

"I maybe nineteen or twenty."

"How old is Khalid?" I thought Zahir had to be younger, since Khalid seemed to be the one in charge.

"He is maybe nineteen. Maybe eighteen. He is youngest."

"Do your other brothers and sister come to Afghanistan too?"

"No," Zahir said, "Khalid and I come with our father. Our work is here." I asked him what he meant by "work."

Zahir gestured with his hand. "This work."

That's nice, I thought. *A kidnapping family! Why would he even bother to go to school when you can make a good living robbing people of their freedom?*

"Your father is here now?" I asked.

"No, he back in Peshawar. I go tomorrow."

"How do you get there?"

"My friend, have a car. We drive. It takes about six hours," he said. Then he stared at me. "You are okay?"

Was I okay? I'd been kidnapped, stabbed, thrown into a hole, covered in dirt, and he wanted to know if I was okay?

"I'm thirsty," I said. "Do you have water?"

Zahir reached for the red plastic can. "We drink this water," he told me. I looked inside. The water was murky, and brown sediment had settled on the bottom of the can. I looked at him, unsure of what to do. He picked up the can and told me to open my mouth. I was skeptical but thirsty, so allowed him to pour a small stream of water into my mouth.

"More?" he asked.

I shook my head. "Enough, thank you."

"Now we sleep," he told me.

Zahir laid his head on the dirty white pillow and stretched his bare feet out so they were next to my pillow. He sat up and detached the wires from the battery. Before the light went out, I noticed on the small clock that it was only eight-thirty. It was pitch black without the light on. I covered myself with the coat I'd taken off and put my head down on the red pillow. The ground was very uncomfortable. Even through the blanket, I could feel the bumps and sharp edges of the hard ground. I shifted to my side, only to have a rock dig into my hip. I shifted again. I just couldn't get comfortable. I sat up and leaned my head against the wall, but that was even worse. I folded up the coat to sit on top of like a cushion. That was a little better, but then there was nowhere to put my head. I lifted the red pillow and propped it against the dirt wall.

"Mellissa." Zahir's voice seemed loud in the darkness.

"Zahir."

"You cannot sleep." It was more of a statement than a question.

"No," I answered. "It's not comfortable. The ground is hard."

"Yes," he agreed. I heard him reach for the alarm clock. He used the light on it to find the black and red wires and reattached them to the battery. The light came back on.

"Zahir, I cannot stay here," I said. "Please let me go home."

He looked at me and nodded.

"It will not be long. I go to Pakistan tomorrow. My father will fix the money. Then you can go."

"What do you mean 'fix the money'?"

"We have your phone. We call. When money comes, you go to Kabul."

I asked how long it usually took, already dreading the answer.

Zahir thought about this for a while, then said, "The last two people who was here—they here for two weeks."

"*Two weeks?* I can't stay here that long!" I looked around the hole. There was no way I could stay here for more than a night. Or two at most.

"Two weeks very fast. Not a long time," Zahir said.

"Who were these people?"

"From Germany or somewhere Europe, I think," he answered. "Money was fast coming. They leave two days ago."

"Is that why you kidnapped me? Because you don't have anyone else now?"

"No, we have more places like this."

"Are there people in them?"

"Yes."

"How many?"

"Maybe two or three."

Two or three. Two or three other people, taken from wherever they were, sitting in holes like this one. I wondered who the others were. Where were they from? What did they do? And the kidnappers had just released two others. My mind was doing the math. A hundred thousand for each hostage! These guys could make half a million dollars in a few weeks. What a great business. Except that they use the money to buy guns so they can kill people.

"That's a lot of people," I said. "What happens if you don't get money? Do you kill them?"

Zahir didn't answer. He pointed at my knapsack. "Give to me."

I reached behind my pillow and passed him the black-and-red pack. He unzipped it and went through my things, just as Khalid and Shafirgullah had earlier in the day.

"What is this?" he asked, pulling out some cables.

"It's wires for my computer," I answered.

"Where is your computer?"

"In my hotel room in Kabul."

He pulled out my wallet and went through all my cards again.

"You have no money here?" he asked.

"Your brother took it. Ask him for it."

He took out my driver's licence and my citizenship card and put the rest back.

"I will take these tomorrow to my father," he said.

I thought about what an arduous process it was to replace my citizenship card. I'd had to do it once before, when my wallet was stolen from my workstation at the CBC in Toronto. I had to send my original birth certificate out to somewhere in Newfoundland, and then cross my fingers and hope that it would come back within six months. I reached for the wallet and pulled out my CBC identification card and my press card.

"Take these instead," I told him. He gave me back the citizenship card and put the others in his pocket.

"Now we sleep," Zahir said, and again detached the wires from the battery.

Darkness enveloped us. I struggled again to find a position that might allow me to sleep, but I couldn't get comfortable. A million thoughts ran through my mind. It had been about ten hours since I was taken from the refugee camp. Had Paul called the CBC in Toronto? Did my editors know what was going on? Surely by now the military had been told. Maybe the Department of Foreign Affairs would have had to be informed. The media liaison at the embassy in Kabul had been expecting me at the CIDA-sponsored school that afternoon. Had the Afghan authorities been informed? It all seemed so surreal. I was supposed to be at my hotel in Kabul, ordering room service and screening my tapes, preparing for an interview the next day with Afghan election officials. Even though the election was about a year away, they were beginning early registration of voters outside Kabul. That was to be my third story off the base.

And then I'd been invited to the Canadian embassy for Thanksgiving dinner. And I was to fly back to Kandahar on Tuesday—in time to watch the Canadian elections back home. We had sent video of soldiers voting in advance polls the week before, and Canada's mission in Afghanistan was somewhat of an election issue. And then . . . and then . . . and then . . .

I struggled with the pillow and tried to lie on my side, but felt a rock in my back. I started to think about my family. Who would tell them? I had put down my sister as my emergency contact on the forms for the military embedding program I had filled out before I'd set off for Afghanistan. It was very early Sunday morning Pacific time, and I didn't want to think about my sister getting a call from someone in the middle of the night. The thought of my family and my friends being woken up to find out that I had gone missing made me feel sick to my stomach. As a journalist, I had interviewed countless family members of people who had gone missing—from the missing women of Vancouver's Downtown Eastside, to hikers who had taken a wrong turn, to snowboarders who had gone out of bounds. The families always suffer tremendously when something bad happens, and I didn't even want to think about mine back home in Canada, wondering where I was in this strange and dangerous country that had drawn me and so many other journalists, with its beautiful landscapes, stunning people, and always imminent dangers.

I had called my father from Kandahar just the night before. When he asked if it was safe, I told him, "Yes, Dad, though Kabul has always been safer than here in the south. Don't worry. It will be okay. I'll only be away for three days." Now someone was going to have to call him and tell him I'd been kidnapped. I felt guilty, sad, and worried. I know it may sound strange to say I was worried about my parents being worried about me, but I couldn't help it. The last thing they needed at their age was stress and anxiety about one of their kids.

My parents immigrated to Canada in 1976 when I was four and my sister was barely two. We settled in East Vancouver in the spring of 1977, and my father started his own business, the first travel agency in Chinatown, with his former colleague Joe Pong, from Hong Kong. He worked six days a week. My mother continued working with Qantas, the Australian airline, as a ticket agent in its Vancouver office. It was essentially the same job she had been doing in Hong Kong, where my sister and I were born. I remember how hard they both worked. They left early in the morning and came home late in the evening, while my mother's parents—my beloved grandparents—took on the job of raising small children for the second time in their lives. We already had family in Canada, as my father's brothers and sisters had all moved to Ontario for school and were now living in Mississauga and working in Toronto, but after spending six months out east, my father decided to settle on the West Coast.

We were renting a house near Southeast Marine Drive, and I went to kindergarten at a school close by. My parents love to tell me the story of their first parent–teacher meeting. My kindergarten teacher, a kind woman by the name of Mrs. Dirksen, feared that she had a mute child in her class. For the first three months there, I didn't speak a word. Not one. I didn't respond to questions; I just stared at her and the other children and studied their interaction. Mrs. Dirksen told my parents, Kellog and Joyce, that if they didn't start speaking to their daughter in English at home, I would never learn the language and my development in school could be delayed irreversibly.

Now, I'd already been to kindergarten in Hong Kong, where children start school at the age of three. I'd learned how to add and subtract and I knew my times tables in Cantonese, my first language, which I still use when I'm doing math in my head. My parents figured that I would learn English on my own, but they were afraid I'd lose my Chinese, so they continued to speak to me in Cantonese.

I continued to be mute in kindergarten for the next couple of months, and then one day I bravely found my English tongue. I raised my hand. "Can I please go to the bathroom, Mrs. Dirksen?" She couldn't believe her ears when I started speaking in complete sentences, in unaccented English, asking questions about everything and anything. I suppose that's how it started, my constant asking of questions, and my mother says I've never stopped.

My parents brought us up with an expectation that we would go to university, since neither of them did, and they stressed academics above anything else. Like many parents, they dreamed their daughters would grow up to be doctors or lawyers, or in my father's case, accountants. "It's the most reliable profession," he used to tell me. "Everyone needs an accountant, whether they're getting rich or going broke, and so you'll always have work."

They got a lawyer out of my sister, but I don't think they ever dreamed their eldest would become a journalist, covering a war in a crazy and dangerous place half a world away. And now the profession I'd chosen, and the job I loved, was about to shatter their comfortable world.

Lying in the darkness, I blinked back tears and tried hard to convince myself that they would be okay. My parents are pretty strong people; they had, after all, moved their young family to a foreign country, where they were forced to speak a language that was not their mother tongue, to meet new people, and raise their children in a different culture. They knew that I was strong and stubborn and a survivor.

I pulled out my rosary, which was buried deep in the pocket of my hiking pants.

Hail Mary, full of Grace, the Lord is with thee.
Blessed art thou amongst women, and blessed is the fruit of thy womb, Jesus.
Holy Mary, Mother of God, pray for us sinners
Now and at the hour of our death, Amen.

I closed my eyes and repeated the Hail Mary nine times, running my fingers over each of the beads.

Glory be to the Father, the Son, and the Holy Spirit.
As it was in the beginning, is now, and ever shall be,
World without end, Amen.

And then I repeated the rosary again and again and again. It was the only thing I could think of to do and the only thing I thought might help. It gave me something to focus on. I turned those beads over and over and over in my hand. My mother raised us Catholic (my father would probably call himself an atheist). She had even gone to the archbishop of Vancouver to get me admitted to an all-girls' Catholic high school, after I failed the admissions exam—on purpose—by not writing the final essay. I was determined to go to the public high school with my friends, where I could play hockey and travel with the orchestra (I'd been taking violin lessons for years). But it was not to be. My mother's plea to the archbishop was successful, and gave me entrance to a high school education guided by nuns and a few great teachers who inspired me to achieve and pursue my dream to be a journalist.

Still, I try to go to church every Sunday, and it was only a week before that I had attended Mass with the soldiers in a small make-shift chapel at Kandahar Airfield. Canadian priests led the service every Saturday night, and I had been invited to go by Lieutenant Colonel Alain Blondin, the public affairs officer who worked with the Canadian journalists on the base. It was the first time I'd ever been in a church where people brought their guns and laid them at their feet while singing hymns and listening to scripture. I wouldn't call myself a devout Catholic, but rather a person who has faith and believes in God, and going to church was my way of spending some quiet time with God once a week. Now, as I lay awake on the cold, hard ground, I realized that if I were ever going to get out of this hole alive, and see my family again, I would probably need a miracle. And I had better start praying.

Hail Mary, full of Grace, the Lord is with thee.
Blessed art thou amongst women, and blessed is the fruit of thy womb, Jesus.
Holy Mary, Mother of God, pray for us sinners,
Now and at the hour of our death, Amen.

Dearest M,

A few more details about what happened in the hours after you were taken. I've had a lot of calls and messages from your friends, and I spoke to your parents and your sister late on Sunday night. They were upset, but in control. We're trying to keep this as quiet as possible, but we work for TV networks, and secrets spread furiously. I had a late call from [your girlfriend] Jen, who was almost hysterical. There was little I could do to calm her down. Everybody is very worried.

I spent what seemed like hours on the phone with people from CBC and CTV as the military started making plans to get us to Kabul. This was Sunday night. At first they said there was no chance of a military flight, but then a couple of hours later, we were told to pack up and be ready to go at nine.

As the night wore on, the flight kept being delayed. First it was nine o'clock, then eleven o'clock, and finally we were told we would be leaving at 2 a.m. We were getting frustrated, but too worried and anxious to feel tired. Al and I went back to the sleep tent to pack our clothes and I grabbed a few things of yours as well. It's all with me now, and I'm waiting to give it to you, M. Please don't disappoint me.

We finally loaded up the vehicle around 2 a.m. and drove to the other side of the airfield, where a Canadian Hercules was waiting, just off the road where we used to run in the mornings. I thought of that as we were pulling into the loading zone. I knew it would be a while before we would run around the base again. If ever. And that made me incredibly sad.

There were a lot of soldiers on the tarmac, all loading big knapsacks onto the back of the plane. I saw one of them putting on what looked like a portable ladder, and I began to think of them scaling walls to rescue you. Al and I were the only civilians on board, and just before we took off, one of the soldiers introduced himself and pulled a couple of sheets of paper out of his pocket. "Can you tell me if there's anything missing from this," he asked. On one sheet was a printed copy of your biography, and on the other, a couple of photographs downloaded from your Facebook page.

There was a spot of light on the wall behind Zahir's head. I turned to see where it was coming from. There was a small opening—a pipe leading up to the ground to let air through, and a trickle of light. The opening on the outside was, I presumed, covered with rocks to hide it. Clever, I thought. Then I noticed a second pipe on the opposite side of the ceiling.

It was just after seven in the morning. I must have dozed off after all. I suddenly remembered that I had been holding my rosary. I felt around for it and found it underneath my leg. Breathing a sigh of relief, I tucked it back into my right pants pocket.

"You sleep?" Zahir was already awake.

"Maybe a little, yes," I answered.

Zahir rubbed his back and grimaced. "Hard to sleep. Not good floor." He sat up and reattached the wires to the battery. The light bulb buzzed and a dim glow illuminated the room.

I nodded. "When is Khalid coming back?" I asked. "He said he would come today."

"They come—around twelve o'clock," he answered. "They come, and then I go."

"Zahir," I pleaded, "I cannot stay here. You must help me. You must tell your father to call Canada and ask for the money soon. I cannot stay here. Please, Zahir, you must help me." I must have sounded slightly hysterical. I could certainly feel myself becoming hysterical.

Zahir adjusted his skullcap and reached for the watering can by the wooden door. He poured some water onto his hands and washed his face, then motioned for me to do the same, which I did. When we were finished, he readjusted his position on the blanket and stared at me with his dark eyes.

"Yes. I will help you, Mellissa," he said, "but my father is the boss."

"Is he a nice man?" I asked.

Zahir shook his head. "He is . . . how you say . . . boss. We afraid of him."

They were afraid of their father. *This does not bode well for me*, I thought. The mastermind in charge of this criminal operation, and the person who would ultimately be responsible for my release, for my life, was probably a mean and nasty person. I was not surprised, but I still felt slightly deflated.

"Two weeks here is even too long." It was my turn to stare at the Afghan. Zahir held my gaze.

"I know, Mellissa. I am sorry for the trouble. I will ask my father. I will tell him to do this soon."

"As soon as possible. I cannot stay here," I pleaded again. "You must promise me."

"Let me see," he said, pointing at my shoulder. I nodded and he shuffled over to my side of the hole, then gingerly lifted my scarf and pulled away the collar of my bloodstained shirt to check the toilet-paper bandage he had put on my wound the night before.

"You have pain?" he asked, gently touching the tissue with his index finger.

"A little," I said. The pink toilet paper was now hardened with dried blood. "Still bleeding?" I asked.

Zahir patted the wound. "We leave this," he said, as if to say that it was okay.

I nodded, not even thinking about the risk of infection, and he sat back on his blanket. He reached for the plastic bag at his feet—beside my pillow—pulled out a box of chocolate sandwich cookies and offered it to me. I shook my head and watched as he opened the box, unwrapped the package, and took out four cookies for himself.

"Your English is very good, Zahir," I said. "Where did you learn?"

"I went to school in Pakistan."

"In Peshawar?"

"No, in the south, when we were younger. We learn Pashto, and Farsi, and English. You no understand Farsi?"

Farsi, the dominant language in Iran, is Persian and similar to Dari, the language most prevalent in the northern part of Afghanistan, while Pashto—the language of the Pashtuns—is more commonly spoken in the south. Most Afghans understand both. If my kidnappers were from the northern part of Afghanistan, running back and forth between here and Pakistan, it made sense that they would speak Dari as well.

I shook my head no in answer to his question.

"You speak English only?"

"I speak Chinese too. And a little bit of French."

"You are from China?" he asked.

"I was born there. In Hong Kong. But I am from Canada."

"Canada." Zahir paused for a moment. "I never go Canada. Is it good place?"

"Yes," I said, "it is a great place. You should go there someday. You would like it."

"If it is good place, why you come to Afghanistan?" he asked me.

"I come to report on the war. I am a journalist."

"You are journalist. Tell me, why your soldiers are here? Why your soldiers come to our country and kill our people?"

I wasn't sure exactly how to respond. Canada's role in Afghanistan was being debated enough at home. The prime minister had just promised to pull our troops out in 2011. And the rising toll of civilian casualties as a result of the fighting between the Taliban and coalition forces was something even the United Nations said had to stop. Canada was in Afghanistan to fulfill its commitment to NATO, but that's not something I would have expected Zahir to understand.

"We are here to help your people," I said instead.

"Help?" he scoffed. "You kill our people. You, and America, and Britain, you kill our people."

"We are here to try to help."

"You not helping. Taliban is only help for my people. Taliban is good for my people. Taliban help people of Afghanistan."

The same Taliban, I thought, who recently bombed a school for girls in Kandahar. The same Taliban who used young boys as suicide bombers, strapping explosives to their little bodies and then detonating them by remote control. I remembered the sadness and shock in the voice of a Canadian battle group commander when he told me of arriving on the scene of a bombing, to find a boy's shoe that had been wired. "The Taliban," he had said, "will stop at nothing. And there is nothing that is beneath them, even if it means blowing up their own children."

"You are not really Taliban," I challenged Zahir.

He looked at me. "No, we are all the same. Taliban is Afghanistan. Afghanistan is Taliban."

"The Taliban have done bad things to your people. Their bombs have killed people. They have killed children and beaten women."

Zahir laughed. "You wrong. America kill people. Your soldiers bomb our homes. Why you not go back to America?"

"I am from *Canada*," I corrected him.

"Canada, America, Britain, you all same. No different. You come, you fight in my country and kill my people."

"Canada and America are different," I argued, even though I knew it was useless. I had heard this sentiment before from other Afghans. I had interviewed a mother who had lost her children to a Taliban bombing. She blamed Americans, Canadians, the British, and all the NATO forces. Most Afghans don't differentiate between Western countries. They see us all as the same, as one homogenous foreign force, yet another invader in a country that has suffered countless invasions since its birth.

"You all same." Zahir would not be convinced. "Why you no leave Afghanistan?"

"We are leaving," I told him. "In 2011, Canada will be leaving."

"You are lying," he accused.

"No," I answered. "Canada's prime minister says he will bring our soldiers back. Canada will be gone from Afghanistan."

I thought that by trying to make Zahir see that there was a difference between Canada and the United States, I could make him realize his captive wasn't a sworn enemy of the Taliban the same way an American might be. I realized that I needed him, if any negotiations around my release were to be expedited. He was going home to speak with his father in Pakistan, and his father was probably the one in charge of all the decisions. Perhaps Zahir could influence him, and if I could get him on side, I just might be able to get out of this hole a little quicker.

"Two years still long time," he said. "Very long time."

"It's not that long," I argued, trying to make him think that Canada was already on its way out. "A year and a half, really."

Zahir shook his head and changed the subject. "Why you not Muslim?"

Wow, I thought. What the hell? From politics to religion in a single breath! I suppose nothing's too personal when you're trapped in a hole with someone, and no subject off limits when you're a prisoner and completely helpless.

"Why do I have to be Muslim?"

"Muslim good. You must be Muslim. You no go to . . ." He pointed up at the ceiling.

"Heaven?" I asked.

"Yes. *Jannat.*"

"Why do I have to be Muslim to go to heaven?"

"Koran say! Allah say!" He seemed shocked that I didn't know this obvious truth.

"I believe in Allah," I responded, "except I call him God. And I'll go to heaven if I am a good person."

"No, you no go heaven. You not Muslim! You Muslim, you go. Not Muslim, you not go."

"Do you think there is just one heaven?" I asked.

Zahir nodded. He pointed up. "When I go . . . I have girl-friends." He smiled a wide smile at me. I noticed his teeth were clean and straight.

"Girlfriends? You think heaven is about getting a girlfriend?"

"Not one girlfriend. Many girlfriends."

I had heard many interpretations of the houri, which in Arabic translates roughly as "lovely eyed" and generally refers to beautiful heavenly creatures. One interpretation, which is widely discounted by religious scholars, involves seventy-two houri being in heaven to greet a Muslim man who has been martyred.

I couldn't resist. "Seventy-two girlfriends?" I asked.

"Yes! Seventy-two girlfriends!" he responded happily.

"You don't think Allah would be upset with you because you have taken me?" I asked.

"We do for Allah."

"You think Allah wants you to kidnap me and keep me here?"

"We do for Allah. You must study Koran. You know Koran?"

"I know about the Koran. The Koran doesn't tell you to kidnap people and keep them in holes under the ground."

"Koran good. You study Koran. You be Muslim. You go heaven." He pointed up at the ceiling again.

"Why do I have to be Muslim to go to heaven?"

"You no Muslim, you no go heaven."

I sighed. There was no point in arguing with him. I was reminded a little of a friend I had in my Catholic high school. She was a born-again Christian and was worried for my soul because I didn't believe in God the same way she did. She wanted me to study the Bible with her at lunchtime so that I could better understand why Catholicism wouldn't lead me into heaven—and this was before and after Catechism classes with the nuns! I never understood it. I will never understand why we can't just accept that not everyone believes in God or in Allah the same way we do, or believes at all, and why some people desperately feel their mission in life is to evangelize and convert. To me, it showed a great deal of disrespect. Religious fundamentalism puts us at war with ourselves and is at the root of many of the world's problems and conflicts.

"I will study the Koran when I get back to Canada," I said to Zahir. "I want to see for myself if you are right."

He nodded. This seemed to satisfy him for the time being.

I looked at the alarm clock. It was barely nine o'clock—three more hours until Khalid was to come back, though I'm not sure I believed that he would. I thought that maybe they would move me somewhere else, maybe to a bigger hole, maybe to a house somewhere nearby. I wasn't sure I could spend another night here like this. The ground was hard, and the air was damp and full of dust. I wondered what was going on outside, whether my kidnappers had called anyone with my cell phone, whether my parents and my sister had been told. And I wondered how Shokoor was doing. Would my kidnappers try to hunt him down? The thought filled me with dread.

Shokoor was the CBC's fixer in Afghanistan and had worked with many journalists in some very crazy and dangerous circumstances. We all liked him, and trusted him with our lives. The term "fixer" really wasn't adequate or fair to describe what Shokoor did for us, or how much we depended on his help. He would set up interviews and then translate them. He shot videotape. He arranged transportation, which he liked doing—before working for Canadian television, he was an attendant on Afghanistan's national airline, Ariana. His English was excellent, and he could earn more money, in American dollars, by working with us than with Ariana, so eventually he became our permanent employee in Kabul.

Whenever we needed something, Shokoor was there. He was our eyes and ears outside the confines of the military base, our guide whenever we stepped off. On my first assignment to Afghanistan the summer before, he introduced me to nan-i-Afghani, the long flat sheets of Afghan bread, and had taken me shopping in Kabul for my first kameez. He knew I liked to eat and he knew I liked to shop. He had picked me up from the airport and taken me straight to the shopping district in the heart of the city—Chicken Street. It was the main shopping street, lined with little stores where shopkeepers sold carpets, scarves, purses, and jewellery—mostly to foreigners. I'd bought scarves and a beautiful carpet there the year before, and I wanted to go back for a few more of the lovely patterned silk scarves as gifts for friends in Canada.

Shokoor was always worried about the safety of the journalists he worked with. Every time I left the relative safety of the NATO forces base to go into Kandahar City, he would caution me to put my scarf over my head and to not stay in one place for any length of time. He had been looking forward to my coming to Kabul for a few days, and we were going to split the work of shooting video-tape, since the cameraman working with us had decided to stay in Kandahar. Shokoor had gone to the refugee camp a few days before on a "reccie"—a reconnaissance mission—to assess the security situation and to pre-interview some of the people there. Reports out of Kabul indicated the security situation in the city was rela-tively stable that summer. It was less secure in Kandahar and the south because of the increase in fighting.

Before coming to Afghanistan, I had read the security assess-ment by AKE, or Andrew Kain Enterprises, a security company hired by the CBC to train journalists who would be travelling to danger zones. I had spent a week outside of Atlanta, Georgia, the year before, learning about combat first aid, and being put through various scenarios, like what to do if the car you're riding in is pulled over by armed militants. It was extremely useful training and helped prepare us for the possibility that something, anything, might hap-pen in a war zone. One of the things we were taught: always have a location checked out before a shoot.

"It is safe," Shokoor told me on the phone from Kabul when I was still in Kandahar. "It is a good story, Mellissa."

We were not going to spend a lot of time at the camp, and he had already chosen a few families, as well as the camp spokesperson, for me to interview. He knew I liked doing stories about women and children, and what the war was doing to the everyday Afghan in his country. We'd done a story on a girls' soccer team the summer before, and another story about how the government was taking care of all the children who had been orphaned by the war.

Shokoor was so happy that Canadians could see what life was really like for Afghans. Like me, he believed it was important to tell the stories of those most affected, the homeless, the refugees, the children. Shokoor was young, in his late twenties. He was tall and soft-spoken. Only once had I seen him get angry, when he raised his voice at a guard who refused to let me into a government office even though we had an appointment. He lived mostly in Kabul with his family but would come down to Kandahar if we had stories to do in town and off the base there. That's where I first met his wife, Zarlashta, the year before, and their new baby. Now he had a second son, and I was supposed to meet him on this trip and go to his home for supper while I was in Kabul. Since I had already been invited to the Canadian embassy for Thanksgiving Monday, we had planned to have dinner with his family on the Sunday night, after our shoot.

I knew that wherever Shokoor was now, he had to be devastated by what happened. I hoped that in my absence someone would be able to reassure him that none of this was his fault. I just knew he would be blaming himself because he felt so responsible every time we went out with him. I hated the thought of Shokoor calling my foreign editor, Jack Nagler, in Toronto to tell him what had happened. I wished I could get on the phone and call him myself. "Jack, I'm okay. This wasn't Shokoor's fault. It wasn't anyone's fault. We had a good story at the camp. It's an important story."

Dearest M,

Had our first meeting at the Canadian embassy. The ambassador is away and won't be back for a week, but they're assembling a team as quickly as possible. We found out Shokoor and his brother are still in custody and are both considered suspects. The Afghan police believe they sold you to the Taliban, but you and I both know that's preposterous. Why would he do that when he makes a lot of money from the CBC and has done so much work for them over the years? They say there are "discrepancies" in his story. They were among the fourteen or fifteen people who were arrested in the hours after you were taken. But as things go in Afghanistan, Shokoor was allowed to keep his mobile phone in jail and I've spoken to him three or four times. He was crying. He blames himself for what happened.

We had to go to the Afghan interior ministry to meet the national police chief and then had a second session with another police "general." They wanted to make sure your calls were direct and not taped, or relayed through a different location. I don't understand how it works, but apparently the kidnappers hold two phones together and make the call that way. Seems like pretty farcical police work to me. This "general" told us they had arrested a number of people from the refugee camp and were looking for a guy named "Malik," who they said was very anxious to get you to visit his tent. He also told us they found the car that was used, and discovered the kidnappers' weapons at the bottom of a water barrel inside a house. There have been a lot of kidnappings, mostly rich Afghans, and we have serious concerns that the police are deeply involved. The Americans suspect the chief of police.

I also saw some of the videotape you shot in the camp, before they grabbed you, including some of your on-camera. It was hard to watch, M, knowing that just a few minutes later a bunch of thugs threw you into a car and took you away. We're all wondering if they were watching you, or if they were tipped off, or were they just there looking for a foreigner to kidnap?

I just got distracted by another call from Shokoor inside the prison. They took away his mobile, but he bribed some cop to use his, and essentially called to say he's still there. I don't suspect Shokoor at all, but there are stories that his brother lives somewhere near the camp and was having money problems. Who the hell knows, but I can't see them releasing Shokoor soon.

It's getting dark here, M, and it makes me shudder to think of you getting ready for another night in the dark and the cold. I'm very, very frightened.

I heard the familiar ring of a Nokia cell phone and instinctively reached into my left pocket, only to find it empty. It was Zahir's cell phone, and I was shocked there was a signal down in the hole. I watched as Zahir pulled the phone from his shirt pocket.

"As-Salaam Alaikum," he answered with the Arabic greeting used by Muslims. It was one of the first phrases Shokoor taught me on my initial trip to Afghanistan, so that I could say hello to the people we were meeting and interviewing. Translated, it means "Peace from Allah be with you."

I listened for several minutes, not knowing what Zahir was saying—I assumed he was speaking Pashto, but then I thought it might be Dari. Pashto is spoken mostly in the eastern and southern parts of the country, and also by a significant number of Pakistanis, especially those living in the tribal areas close to the Afghanistan border. When Zahir finished his call, I asked him who he'd been speaking to.

"That is Khalid."

"When is he coming?"

"This . . ." He was searching in his mind for the right word. "Afternoon."

"I thought he was coming at noon."

"Later." I asked him if he'd spoken to his father, and he said he'd see him the following day. I asked him to tell his father that I needed to go home to Canada, and he agreed.

Zahir shuffled over to the wooden door. "I go bathroom," he said, motioning for me to turn around. I turned and faced the wall opposite the door as he crouched behind it to urinate into an empty plastic water bottle. There isn't much privacy when you're trapped in a space smaller than many closets. Zahir finished and reached for the watering can to rinse his hands, pouring the water onto the dirt floor just outside the door.

"You go bathroom?" he asked me.

I hadn't gone since before I was thrown into the hole, and I wasn't really feeling the need, and I also wasn't sure how it worked. I assumed the dirty black bucket was my toilet. I looked at it and shook my head, delaying the inevitable for a little longer. I've peed in worse places—in a rice paddy in China when our family's minivan broke down; in a hole in the ground when I was out with the Canadian battle group the summer before, though that was better than the porta-potties the military used on its forward operating bases; and in a farmer's field in southern Saskatchewan, where I'd been posted for the last two years, trying to avoid the sting of mosquitoes when I pulled down my pants. This dirty bucket was nothing in comparison, but the idea of having to pee in front of my captor bothered me a lot. It sounds silly, but I felt somehow that by using that bucket I would be surrendering in a physical way and resigning myself to being a prisoner, and that was something I wanted to put off for as long as I could.

It wasn't that I was in denial about what was happening to me. Rather, I wanted to maintain as much control over the situation as I could, even if it meant holding it in for another hour or two.

I looked at the clock again. It wasn't even noon. Time is amazing. There's never enough time when you're in a hurry, with a deadline looming, and you have a zillion things to do. If I were at home in Canada and awake at six in the morning, on a Sunday like this, I would have already gone to Mass, gone for a run, showered, changed, and barely had time to meet my friends for Sunday brunch. Here, in the darkness of a hole in the ground, with nothing to do, time couldn't have passed more slowly.

Zahir was playing with his cell phone. I pulled a pen and my notebook out of my knapsack and flipped it open to an empty page. It was one of those thick spiral-bound stenographer's notebooks, divided into five or six sections. I'd started the last section a few days before, taking notes at the refugee camp, the names of the people we'd interviewed, and details about their background, which I planned to weave into my script on the refugee camp.

I started to write.

Dearest P,

I can't imagine what you're thinking right now, or what you're going through, and I don't even know where you are, so I just wanted to write and tell you that I'm okay. It happened so quickly—Shokoor and I were just leaving the camp when this car drove up and these men grabbed me. I have two small stab wounds because I threw a punch at one of them when they were trying to get me into the car, but I'm okay. They say they are with the Taliban, but I'm not sure I believe them. They don't seem entirely organized, and they just keep talking about money.

"What you writing?" Zahir interrupted.

"A letter," I answered. He shuffled over, grabbed my notepad, tried to read what I'd just written, and handed it back to me.

I think these guys are a bunch of kids with guns, darling. Don't worry. I'll be fine and I'll come home soon. Please tell everyone at home that I'm okay. They're not hurting me, although I'm not sure where we are. We walked up and over a mountain to get here. I think I'm somewhere outside Kabul. It's dark here, but I am not afraid. So don't you be afraid either. I'm just so sorry for all the trouble I'm sure I'm causing everyone. I'm so sorry I ruined our plans. I miss you so much, P. I hope you know how much I miss you and I'm thinking about you. It will be okay. I know you don't really believe, but if you have that little rosary I gave you the last time you came to Kandahar, and say a prayer for me, I'm sure that will help. I'm so sorry for everything you're going through. I'm with you, and I'll be back. I promise.

I put down my pen and blinked back the tears that were threatening to roll down my face. I couldn't help but imagine the panic that must have already set in. Paul is one of the calmest and most level-headed people I know. The consummate foreign correspondent, he'd reported from every war zone over the last two decades and had been to Afghanistan more times and knew the country better than most journalists in Canada. We'd met in Afghanistan the summer before, and spent five weeks together on the base, jogging around the airfield together, working out at the gym together, and meeting up in Kabul for a few days, on different assignments for our respective networks. We'd kept in very close touch over the past year, exchanging emails and chats almost every day. We'd grown very close and cared about each other deeply, and we both knew we had to make some hard decisions about our personal lives. With a little editorial organizing, we'd arranged another five weeks together in Kandahar.

I started doing the calculations in my head. *If Zahir gets to his father by tomorrow, and if it's really money they want, and not very much money, it could be over in a week. I could arrange to borrow some money when I got back, and repay whoever put up the funds. If Zahir would plead my case to his father, I could be back on the base by next Monday—since there were no flights to Kandahar on Sundays—and we could still catch our scheduled flight out to Dubai on Wednesday.*

I picked up my pen again.

It will be okay, P. We'll still get there. I know we will. I'm here and I'm okay. I just miss you so much it hurts.
xox

The spot of light behind Zahir's head had faded, a sign that it was getting dark. I wasn't sure how we'd managed to spend an entire day sitting in that one spot, but I'd been praying the rosary (although I'm not sure rote recitation constitutes real prayer) over and over and over while Zahir napped. I found out a little more about him as we talked on and off throughout the day. He had a girlfriend and he liked listening to music—two admissions, which, as a young devout Muslim, he was both giddy and sheepish in telling me. He told me his mother liked the girl, but he had to wait for his father's approval before marrying. We talked about marriage and family, and he told me he wanted seven children, one girl and six boys, because he had grown up with only three brothers, but one sister was enough. He asked about my family and seemed surprised to hear that I only had one sister and no brothers. "No boy in your family?" He was incredulous.

I had also caved and peed in the dirty black bucket. Zahir covered his head with his blanket and turned his back while I pulled down my hiking pants. It wasn't as bad as I thought it would be, but the can had obviously been used before and was very dirty and smelly.

The alarm clock read five-thirty, and I had my rosary in my hand and was about to start another decade of Hail Marys when I heard digging overhead. Zahir pointed up.

"Khalid," he said before covering his mouth and face with his kaffiyeh. It sounded like the digging was being done with a shovel, and billows of dust swept down the tunnel and into the hole. I closed my eyes and covered my head with my scarf. Dust rained down on us for several minutes, and then I could hear something being dragged off the opening of the hole.

"Goodbye, Mellissa." Zahir moved the wooden door to the side and hiked up his pyjama-like pants to crawl up the tunnel.

"Zahir, please tell your father to hurry," I implored.

He took my hand and looked into my eyes. "Yes, I promise. You go home soon."

And then he inched his way into the tunnel and up. I could hear voices speaking in Pashto outside. A few minutes went by and I heard a thud. I could see a pair of worn black leather shoes at the end of the tunnel.

"Hello, Mellissa!" It was fat Abdulrahman from last night, with two white plastic shopping bags.

"Hello, Abdulrahman," I replied.

"How are you? Do you like your house?"

"No. It is dark and uncomfortable. I want to go back to Kabul."

"You will go, you will go," he assured me.

A second pair of leather shoes appeared at the end of the tunnel. It was Khalid.

"Mellissa." He held out his hand as if to shake mine. I took his hand and he held it tightly. "How are you, Mellissa?"

"I am okay, Khalid. When can I go home?"

"You not like here? I make this house."

"I want to go home."

The two Afghans spoke to each other in Pashto, then Abdulrahman reached into one of the big white plastic bags. He pulled out a kameez and matching pants, nylon and the colour of rust, with vertical beige stripes.

"Here," he said. "This for you. You wear."

I picked up the outfit and ran my fingers over it. It was better than the smelly men's kameez they had put me in for the ride through town on the motorcycle.

"Are you hungry, Mellissa?" Khalid asked.

I shook my head. The only things I'd managed to eat all day were two chocolate cookies. Khalid reached inside the plastic bag and pulled out several sleeves of cookies—mango cream, orange cream, strawberry cream. He also pulled out two apples and several boxes of mango juice.

"You must eat," he told me.

"Not hungry," I answered.

He took a juice box, stuck a straw in it, and handed it to me. "You must," he said.

I took it from his hand and took a sip. It was syrupy thick and sweet. Still, it was probably better than the water I'd been drinking from the red plastic can. I noticed there was also a full green plastic can of water, no cleaner than the water in the red can.

"It is good?" he asked. I nodded.

"I come tomorrow," Khalid said, moving toward the opening of the hole.

"Wait," I said. "Where are you going?"

"I go home. I come tomorrow. My uncle stay here tonight," he said.

"When can I go home?" I asked.

"Inshallah, soon," he said. "I go now. I see you tomorrow." He crawled up the tunnel and back out, leaving me with fat Abdulrahman. I heard something that sounded like a heavy wooden board being dragged over the hole and then the sound of shovels. I covered my face with my scarf as dust swept in. Abdulrahman did the same. The whole process took about five minutes and at the end of it, after the dust had settled, Abdulrahman looked up and stared at me with his beady little eyes.

"You no like your house," he laughed at me.

"No, I hate it here. I want to go home," I said to him.

"What? It is a very good house," he smiled. "I help make this house."

"I thought Khalid said he made this place."

"Yes, Khalid and me. We build. Very nice, you no like?"

"No, it's dark and not very comfortable. It's hard to sleep."

"You no like your clothes I bring for you?"

I didn't say anything. I was perfectly happy in my bloodstained clothes.

"You wear." It sounded like an order.

I took the top and put it over my head, over my ruined flowered kameez.

"No, you take off," the fat Afghan said.

"It's okay. I'll keep it on. It doesn't matter, it's just a little blood."

"No. Off."

Reluctantly, I pulled my bloodied kameez over my head, leaving my once-white undershirt on. I noticed that it, too, was now brown with dried blood. I felt self-conscious with Abdulrahman staring at me, so I quickly slipped the clean rust-coloured kameez on and adjusted the sleeves. It was too big, but at least it was clean.

"Pants," he said. I stood up, my head almost touching the ceiling, and pulled the baggy pants over my hiking pants. They immediately fell off. Abdulrahman laughed and shook his head.

"You too thin," he said, pointing at my waist.

"It's not me; the pants are too big," I said, sitting down. "Where did you get these? Who do they belong to?"

"A friend of Khalid," he replied. "A girl."

"Khalid's girlfriend?" I asked.

"No, friend."

I sat back on my blanket, leaning my back against my knapsack and camera bag, and stared at him for a while. Abdulrahman was short, with a round stomach that stuck out, frizzy dark hair under his skullcap, and small dark eyes. He pointed to my knapsack and said, "Give to me." I did as instructed and watched as he, like Zahir, and Khalid, and Shafirgullah before him, went through all my belongings, pulling out one credit card at a time from my wallet, one item after another from my makeup bag.

"What is this?" he asked, producing a compact.

"Makeup," I answered.

"I take for my wife." He put the black compact in his pocket.

"Where is your wife?" I asked.

"She is in Kabul. With my son."

"How old is your son?"

"He is two year old. He look like my wife. She very pretty."

"How old are you?"

"You ask many questions, Mellissa. Why?"

"I am a journalist. I always ask questions. How old are you?" I repeated, knowing I would probably get only an approximate answer from him.

"Maybe I am twenty-seven or twenty-eight."

"You only have the one son?"

"Yes. My wife, she want more. We have a few more. There is time." He paused for a second. "I call her." He took his cell phone out of his breast pocket and held it up to the ceiling, as if to find a signal from the highest point of the room. Then he dialed a number and put the setting on speakerphone so that I could hear. A woman's voice answered on the third ring.

"As-Salaam Alaikum." I could hear her voice loud and clear. You would hardly know we were in a hole.

"Salaam," Abdulrahman said, and the two proceeded to chat for a few minutes, their conversation punctuated by laughter. Then I heard a baby's voice. Abdulrahman pointed at the phone and looked at me. "My son. Do you hear him?"

I nodded and forced myself to smile. It hardly seemed fair that he was freely able to call his family and laugh and smile with them, while I was cut off from my loved ones, who were probably sick with worry about me.

"It's not fair," I said after Abdulrahman had said goodbye to his wife and son.

"What is not fair?" he asked.

"You can talk to your wife, and I can't talk to anyone."

"Yes, it is not fair," he laughed again, his laugh high-pitched and piercing.

"Let me make a phone call," I suggested. "That is fair."

"No," he answered. "You cannot."

"Please? My family and friends are very worried about me. I just want to tell them I'm okay, and that you are taking good care of me."

"No," he answered.

"Please?" I pleaded. "It will only take two minutes to call them. One minute. Just to say hello."

He appeared to think about it for a while, then shook his head. "No."

"Maybe tomorrow? Think about it."

"Maybe."

Abdulrahman reached again for the white bag and pulled out an apple. He offered it to me but I shook my head. He bit into it, finishing the entire thing in about four big bites, the juice running down into his beard. He wiped it off with the sleeve of his light green kameez.

"It is good. You need to eat," he told me, reaching next for a package of orange-flavoured cream-filled cookies. He ripped open the sleeve, grabbed a handful, and tossed the rest to me. I took one and bit into it. The sweet artificial orange taste spread between my teeth. If this was going to be my diet for a while, I was sure I'd develop serious cavities, and going to the dentist is not something I enjoy, even on a good day. In fact, I'd gone to great pains to avoid the dentist over the last three years, making sure I brushed and flossed at least three times a day. Now I wasn't sure when I'd get to brush my teeth again.

Defiantly, I grabbed another cookie and stuffed it into my mouth, as if to say, *Fuck it. If this is my fate, I may as well go all out.* I chewed the cookie and imagined all the sugar molecules getting into every crack and nook of my teeth.

"You like biscuit," Abdulrahman said to me, not really asking a question.

"It's okay," I said.

"I tell Khalid to bring you rice tomorrow," he suggested.

"I want to go home tomorrow."

"You go home, maybe three days."

"Really?" This was the first time I'd heard a timeline from any of the kidnappers. I didn't believe him, but I really, truly, desperately wanted to.

"Money come, you go." Abdulrahman made a gesture with his hand as if brushing me off. "Money come, you go."

I asked him when the money would come, how it would come, and when I could go.

"If money come—tomorrow, you go. Tomorrow, Monday, you go Tuesday," he replied.

"Why can't I go on Monday if that's the day the money comes?"

"Maybe."

"Maybe what? Maybe I can go?" I was starting to get impatient.

"Maybe you go back to Kabul."

I sighed. I wasn't getting any straight answers.

"Abdulrahman. This kidnapping racket. How does it work? You kidnap someone and then what happens?"

Abdulrahman scratched his crotch and readjusted his skullcap.

"We ask for money—from your father, friend, your company. We get money, you go back to Kabul."

"How long does this take?" I could feel a burning anger inside my stomach.

"Few weeks."

"A few weeks? How many?" I was beginning to treat him like an interview subject who was being deliberately evasive, like so many politicians I'd tried to get straight answers from over the years. He was no different.

"Last two people, they go last night."

"You have other hostages?"

"'Hostage' bad word," Abdulrahman admonished me. "You are our guest." He grinned.

"Guest?" I almost spat out the word. "You stab your guests and throw them in holes in the ground? Is that your idea of hospitality? How many other 'guests' do you have right now?"

"The two are gone. You are only guest now. Khalid going to look for more."

"That's nice. Hopefully you treat them better."

"You are lucky. You are woman. We no leave you here yourself," he said, ignoring the anger that was flashing in my eyes. "The two men—we leave them alone. We tie their hands, feet . . ." He motioned with his hands that they were handcuffed and tied to the ceiling. "We give water, biscuit; no one go there to stay with them. You are woman, we have to stay with you."

"Why?"

"Muslim law."

I shook my head. Here we go, I thought, another discussion about Islam. I had no appetite and no interest, but it wasn't like I had much of a choice.

"Where does it say in the Koran that it's okay to kidnap a woman and stab her?" I challenged.

"Tsk, tsk." Abdulrahman shook his head. "You no understand. We do this work for Allah. You must read Koran."

"I read the Bible. But I would like to read the Koran, so I can see where you get this from. Because I don't believe Allah would be happy that you're holding me as a prisoner."

"You Muslim, we no keep you here. You no Muslim, you are our guest." He grinned again. I noticed he had a crooked set of top teeth.

"You think Allah says it's okay for you to kidnap me and throw me in a hole?"

"This is very nice house, you are guest," he said. "Allah happy."

Allah might have been happy, but I was getting frustrated and annoyed. "I don't think Allah would like what you're doing to me," I argued. "Allah would want me to go back to Kabul, and then back to Canada."

"You no understand Koran. You must study Koran," he replied, echoing Zahir. "You will understand Allah if you study Koran."

"I want to study the Koran. I want to know where it says in the Koran that it's okay to do this to someone. You probably also believe that this will help you get to heaven and your seventy-two waiting girlfriends."

Abdulrahman smiled. "Yes. Seventy-two girlfriends."

"What about your wife? What happens to her when you have girlfriends?" I was getting angrier.

"My wife is my wife. My girlfriends are my girlfriends." He grinned again.

"You can't have a wife and seventy-two girlfriends at the same time."

"Why not? Allah say okay!"

"That's the most ridiculous thing I've ever heard. Allah wouldn't want you to ignore your wife while you're entertaining your girlfriends. What kind of God does that make him?"

"Allah say okay! Allah is great!"

As with Zahir, I realized the conversation had reached a dead end and I didn't want to pursue it any further. Even though the Koran says women and men are equal under God, I knew that the Taliban and other Muslim fundamentalists believed in applying traditional laws to women. Women have to be covered up; they have to wear chadors or hijabs, to hide any trace of their sexuality in public. They even pray separately in mosques. Men and women are anything but equals in a Taliban-ruled Afghanistan. Women are stoned for infidelity; men are allowed to have up to four wives. No wonder they're promised seventy-two virgins when they get to heaven.

"You must be Muslim!" Abdulrahman said loudly. "Allah is great!" He glared at me. "This," he gestured with his hands at the hole, "is Allah's will. We no kill you. Inshallah, money come, you go."

"You're saying that kidnapping me, and holding me like this, is God's will?"

"Yes. Inshallah, money come, you go."

"Inshallah," I said. The light bulb attached to the ceiling flickered. I had noticed it was getting dimmer and dimmer throughout the day. Abdulrahman noticed it too and pointed to the battery. He said he'd ask Khalid to bring a new battery the following day. I told him I didn't want to still be in the hole by then. Abdulrahman laughed. "Maybe day after tomorrow. Why you go to Kabul?" he asked.

"So I can catch my flight back to Canada," I answered.

"Canada. I know Canada," he said. "I have been to Canada."

"Yes, you told me. Where in Canada did you go?" I knew he wouldn't be able to tell me. "Eastern Canada or western Canada?"

"Do not . . . remember. Close to New York." I asked him why he was in New York, and he told me he had friends there and was learning English. I remembered he had told me that on the first night, when we were in the bullet-ridden white house.

"And then you visited Canada?" I asked.

"Yes, very close to New York. But Canada—Canada is not a country like Afghanistan or Pakistan."

"What do you mean?" This was a very strange thing to say.

"Afghanistan, Pakistan—this country been hundreds of years. What is Canada? How old?"

"One hundred and forty-one years," I answered. I knew that because I had been in Italy during Canada Day in July, when my girlfriends and I had been invited to the Canadian embassy for Canada Day celebrations.

Abdulrahman scoffed. "That is nothing. Other countries are hundreds of years old. What is a country that is one hundred years? It is nothing. Not a country."

This bothered me a lot. Just like I wouldn't say I'm a devout Catholic, I wouldn't call myself as an unduly patriotic Canadian. I'd gone to graduate school in the United States, and I'd travelled the world in search of other cultures and history. But everywhere I went, I was pretty proud to be a Canadian, proud of everything Canada stood for internationally in the tradition of Lester Pearson and Pierre Trudeau. I had recently been in Beijing for the Olympic

Games, where I'd been lucky enough to see Canadian athletes win medals in their sports. I wasn't embarrassed to say my heart would skip a beat every time I saw the Maple Leaf raised and the anthem played.

"Canada is a great country," I told the fat Afghan. "You don't know anything."

"Why you think it is so great?" he asked. "It is not a country."

"It is a great country. You don't have to be old to be great. It's a young nation, but we are a peaceful nation, and Canadians care about other people," I said.

"You send your soldiers here to kill Afghan people," he said.

"We send our soldiers here to help the Afghan people." I must have sounded a bit like any one of the Canadian military commanders I'd interviewed about the war and their struggle with the Taliban. "The Afghan people do not want the Taliban to rule here. The Taliban are bad for Afghanistan. Our soldiers are here so young girls can go to school, and women can feel safe outside their homes."

"Women no work, girls no school," Abdulrahman spat. "My wife, she no work."

"Does she want to work?" I asked.

"No. She happy. She work at home. She cook, she have baby."

"What if she wanted to work?"

"She no work. She work at home."

"That's fine if she doesn't want to work. But some women like to work outside the home," I argued. "And they should be able to. And girls should be able to go to school."

"Why you work?" he asked.

"Why wouldn't I work?" I answered.

"You no husband, you must work."

"I like my job. I like to go to work. What is wrong with that?"

"Women should not work."

"That's your opinion." I was getting tired of this. If we were having this conversation anywhere else, I would have walked away. Unfortunately, that option wasn't open to me. I didn't need to worry, though. Abdulrahman reached over and disconnected the cables.

"Sleep time," he said.

I looked at the clock and saw that it was after ten. I'd spent at least three hours arguing with him and now welcomed the silence. The ground was hard and uncomfortable. I pushed my face into the red pillow and forced myself to shut my eyes.

I was finally drifting off when I felt Abdulrahman's hand on my leg. He was inching closer and closer to me. I sat up with a start and fumbled to reattach the wires to the battery. The light came on, but it was definitely fading. "Don't touch me," I warned him.

"I must fuck you," he said matter-of-factly.

"Fuck off," I told him. My blood felt cold as it coursed through my body. I told myself to calm down, but more than anger now I was feeling fear, something I'm not used to.

"I must fuck you," he repeated.

"No." I was willing my voice not to shake. "Allah will punish you. You will not go to *jannat* if you dare touch me." I pulled my legs up to chest and hugged my knees together. "You're married, you have a wife, and the Koran says you must not touch a woman who is not Muslim. You will go to hell." I spoke slowly and firmly.

There was silence for what felt like hours. Abdulrahman reached over and touched my leg again. I shuddered and shook his hand off me. "Do not touch me," I repeated again. "Allah will kill you. *I* will kill you."

At this, he laughed. "You cannot kill me! You are a woman!" He undid the string on his pants.

"I can and I will. I know karate. And you will be dead. And Allah will send you to hell." The karate thing was a half-truth. I know tae kwon do, a martial art intended for practising self-discipline and control, but I had no problem using it for self-defence or murder at this point. "You will go to *jahannam*." I used the Muslim word for hell, which I had learned from an imam in Toronto a few years before when doing a story on the arrest of eighteen men for allegedly plotting terrorist attacks on Canadian targets like the CN Tower and Parliament Hill.

"Allah will send you to *jahannam*," I repeated.

Abdulrahman scratched himself and pulled down his pants. I inched closer to the wall next to me.

"Stay away from me," I warned again. Then I saw the glint of a knife.

"I must fuck you," he said, more menacingly, holding what looked like a small carving knife to my throat.

"Fuck off, go to *jahannam*," I repeated. He pressed the blade into my neck. I closed my eyes and started to pray.

Hail Mary, full of grace, the Lord is with thee, blessed art thou amongst women, and blessed is the fruit of thy womb, Jesus.

_____

When he finally moved away from me, he reached for the wires on the battery. "Sleep time," he said.

"No," I answered. "I want to sleep with the light on." He shrugged and turned his back to me. I left the light on for much of the night, even though I knew the bulb was dying, but I didn't sleep. I rocked back and forth in a fetal position, hoping that I would wake up and realize this was all a horrible nightmare. I repeated the

Hail Marys, looking at the clock and watching the seconds pass into hours, until I could see a faint spot of light on the wall behind Abdulrahman's head.

Monday, October 13, 2008, 7 a.m.

My dear P,

I hope wherever you are, you are sleeping on a soft mattress, your head resting on a sheeted pillow. I've spent the last two nights on hard ground, and I haven't been able to get much sleep at all. I can't imagine how worried you must be about me. I just need you to know that I am okay. My stab wounds have scabbed over and I'm not bleeding anymore. I've eaten a few cookies since my last breakfast at the Serena, but I'm not really hungry.

I'm in a hole somewhere outside Kabul. I don't really know where, or which direction we were going in, but we had to hike over a mountain and into a village.

I'm not sure where you are—whether you're on the base in Kandahar or maybe on your way to Kabul, but I'm sure you're sick with worry, just as I'd be if it was you who had disappeared. These guys just want money. I don't know how much, but I will take out a loan when I get back and repay whoever can put up the cash right now.

It's Thanksgiving today, and I'm supposed to be at the embassy for a turkey dinner, and even though I'm in this hole, I have a lot to be thankful for. This year, I'm thankful for you. I'm thankful for all the fun and laughter and happy times we've been lucky enough to share.

I'm not afraid to die, you know that and we've talked about it so many times. I don't believe in regrets and I like to think I've tried to live a good life.

But we shouldn't be talking about death. I'm coming back soon. And we can

get on with our lives and our plans. We have a lot to do, remember? Surfing in
Tofino to start.

xox

"What you writing?"

Abdulrahman hadn't moved all night, but now he was sitting up and staring at me. I didn't want to look at him.

"Give to me," he ordered, motioning to my notebook. I handed it over and watched as he read my letter to Paul, although I'm not sure he actually read it, or understood what he was reading, since he threw it back at me pretty much right away.

"I go bathroom," he said, pulling down his baggy pants. I quickly turned around as he reached for the pop bottle by the door. With my back turned, I could hear him rinsing his hands with the water from the green can, and then he burped.

"You hungry?" he asked me, unwrapping a sleeve of sandwich cookies and offering them to me. I shook my head, then watched as he ate one cookie after another until the whole package had filled his bulging stomach. He wiped his mouth with the back of his hand and reached into his pocket for his cell phone. Like Khalid, he also had taken the phone apart and was now putting in the battery, the SIM card, and then fitting on the back cover. He turned the phone on, pressed a few buttons, and then put it back into his pocket.

"You have cell phone?" he asked me.

"No, Khalid took my phone," I answered. "Can I use your phone to make a call?"

He shook his head.

"Please, Abdulrahman. Please let me call."

"No. They know you okay. We call."

"When did you call?"

"Khalid father call. He is boss."

"Has he already called?"

"I do not know. Yes. No. Maybe he call tomorrow."

"Khalid's father is your brother?"

"Yes. He is boss."

"Khalid is his son."

"Khalid youngest, but he is very brave." Abdulrahman seemed both proud and jealous of his nephew.

"So Khalid is number two. His father is boss, he is second. Yes?" I was trying to get an idea of the hierarchy of this family organization and figure out where this fat Afghan fit in.

"Khalid is boss here. Khalid father—my brother—in Pakistan."

"Your nephew is your boss?"

Abdulrahman twitched his nose, probably not liking the way that sounded. But he nodded.

"Yes, but he listen to me. I know things he don't know. You ask many questions."

"I'm a reporter. I'm supposed to ask questions."

"Okay. Ask me something."

"You want me to interview you?" This was a strange request, but Abdulrahman seemed to like the idea of being the subject of an interview. I reached for my notepad and flipped to an empty page. I pulled out my pen and took off the cap.

"Where are you from?" I started. "I mean, where were you born?"

"In Kabul."

"Is that where you live now?"

"Sometime. Sometime I live here. Sometime I live in Pakistan."

"Where are we? What is the name of this town?"

"Tsk, tsk." He waved his finger at me. "Not allowed to ask this."

"Are we north of Kabul? How far are we from Kabul?" I asked.

"Maybe we are north. Maybe we are west. About one hour to Kabul."

"Why can't you tell me where we are?"

"I cannot. My brother kill me."

"What do you do with all the money that you get from kidnapping people?"

"We buy gun. Kalashnikovs very expensive. We buy at market." I was surprised that there was a gun market and asked him where it was.

"You know Mazar-e-Sharif?"

I nodded. Shokoor had tried to persuade me to go to Mazar-e-Sharif the year before to do a story on a women's program in the city, northwest of Kabul. We never made it there because of time constraints.

"There is market in Mazar-e-Sharif. We buy gun there. Very expensive."

Mazar-e-Sharif, I scribbled on my notepad. *Guns, very expensive.* "How expensive?"

"For one, maybe one hundred thousand afghanis."

I did the math in my head. *US$2,000 for a used Kalashnikov,* I wrote.

"Is that all you buy with the money?"

"No, we also buy things to make bombs."

"You know how to make a bomb?"

"It is easy. You need only few things. We make many bombs."

"But you're not really Taliban, are you?"

"We are different but same."

"Is Mullah Omar your brother's boss?" I was referring to the man known as the leader of the Taliban.

Abdulrahman laughed. "No, we do not know Mullah Omar, but he is very good man."

"So, if you've never met or talked to Mullah Omar, you can't really be Taliban."

"We are all different Taliban."

"Either you're Taliban or you're not. If your boss is not Mullah Omar, you're not really Taliban."

"We are all different Taliban. And this area where we are—many Taliban."

"Is the Taliban the same as Al Qaeda?" I asked.

Abdulrahman smiled and looked at me. "Osama bin Laden is very good man. Very good person."

"So you are connected to Al Qaeda?"

"We do not know bin Laden. But he is a very good man."

It was becoming more and more obvious to me that my kidnappers were no more than a gang of thieves who seemed to espouse the same anti-Western philosophies as the Taliban and Al Qaeda, but they weren't real terrorists, or real members of those groups. The insurgency in Afghanistan was becoming fractured, more like a patchwork of disenfranchised groups that hate the central government and the presence of foreign troops in the country. My kidnappers were most likely just a group of thugs who hated the government and wanted foreigners to leave. Afghanistan is full of criminal gangs like these. Kidnapping is a big business, with a lot of money to be made on unsuspecting foreigners. I'd heard stories about hostages being bought and sold, and even if their kidnappers weren't Taliban, they eventually ended up in the hands of the Taliban, or other insurgents. Lives are measured in dollars, and in the desperation of the kidnappers to make a quick sale. I knew I did not want to be traded or sold to the Taliban.

"What do you do with the bombs you make?" I asked.

"We put them on roads. Americans come on road. *Boom!*" His laugh was now starting to sound more like a cackle.

"I thought the Taliban did that."

"We all the same."

"Why do you hate America?"

"They come, they kill our people. America very bad. George Bush—you know George Bush? He very bad man."

"I agree, I think George Bush is a very bad man," I said. This wasn't completely untrue, and I figured it was time we agreed on something.

"Yes, George Bush very bad person." He seemed to spit with every word.

Suddenly, the light went out. I jumped back and grabbed the alarm clock, pressing the button on the side to light up its face. Abdulrahman took it from me and held it by the battery. He detached the wires and then held the clock up to the light bulb at the ceiling. He unscrewed the bulb and screwed it back in again. Then he ripped apart the wires and rewired them together before reattaching them to the dying battery, after giving it a good shake. The light bulb buzzed and came on, but it was now even dimmer than before.

"Battery no good," he said, pointing at the grey slab next to me. He took the cell phone out of his pocket and scrolled through the numbers until he came to the one he wanted. Through his receiver, I could hear the phone ringing on the other end. A man answered, and after a brief conversation in Pashto, Abdulrahman hung up.

"He bringing light," he told me.

"Has he talked to your brother yet? Has he talked to Zahir?"

"Zahir going to Pakistan today. He talk to my brother."

"He better tell your brother to hurry up and fix this. I can't stay here any longer."

I was thinking about my comfortable room at the Serena Hotel, where many foreigners and diplomats stay when they travel to Kabul. The Serena had been the target of suicide bombers about ten months before I arrived. Several men entered and detonated a suicide vest. A Danish delegation was there at the time, and several foreigners were killed. The target was the hotel gym, where I had worked out on a treadmill the morning I met Shokoor to go to the refugee camp. Since the attack, the hotel had taken steps to tighten security, and Shokoor said it was a fortress, which was why he had reserved a room there for me on this trip. I thought about that nice comfortable room and wondered what would happen to my belongings. Would Shokoor call the hotel and tell them to pack me up if I couldn't get back in time to check out? My laptop, my BlackBerry (I said a little prayer of thanks that I'd left it in the room, because it was my phone book, my connection to everything, and I would have hated the kidnappers to go through it). I figured everything I'd brought with me to Kabul would still be there. And I hoped that Shokoor was okay—and that my kidnappers weren't now going after him.

Abdulrahman was unwrapping another sleeve of cookies. I watched as he put one after another in his mouth, wiping the crumbs from his face with his kameez as he offered me what was left—about three cookies. I shook my head.

"Why no eating?" he asked, shaking his head at me in return. "You must eat."

"I'm not hungry." This for me was a rare statement. Everyone who knows me can attest to how much I like to eat—and how much I eat. My friend Kas calls me the "human garburator," and every cameraperson I have ever worked with knows how much I like to stop at whatever fast food joint is on the road between shoots. I used to joke that I spend my life thinking about my next meal. I bring shopping bags to work full of food to last me throughout the day—salads, sandwiches, leftover pasta. When a bunch of us went out for dinner on a rare night off during the Beijing Olympics, we ordered plates of food—fish, chicken, and vegetables—all served family-style, as is the Chinese custom, and prompting the cameramen to joke that I must have a tapeworm: I ate more than they did combined. We ended up having to order more.

Whether it's a deep-fried fish, dripping with sweet and spicy sauce in a Beijing restaurant, or A&W onion rings on the road between Regina and Saskatoon, I love to eat. I also love to cook. And I don't discriminate when it comes to food, though in the past few years I'd been staying away from pork. I'd covered the Robert Pickton story—the pig farmer in British Columbia who killed prostitutes. Canadians know the details of this horrific mass murder very well. He lured prostitutes to his farm, tortured and killed them, and fed their bodies to his pigs before slaughtering the animals, which may have been processed for human consumption. I couldn't bring myself to put a knife and fork into a pork chop after that.

"You must eat." Abdulrahman was poking a straw into a carton of mango juice. I watched as he slurped it back in a few short gulps, the sound of the straw making a sucking sound as he searched for the last drop of juice in the carton. He stretched out on his blanket and went to sleep.

I took my rosary out of my pocket and silently started to pray again.

God, please help me. I don't know how I got here, but please help me get out. I am certain the people who kidnapped me are not evil people and they do not mean any harm to me. But you are the only one who can help me. I don't know why this is happening, but I am begging you, Lord, to help me. And please, if you can, help everyone at home who is worried and wondering about me. Give them some peace, and tell everyone I am okay. Lord, please help me. I know I'm not the best Catholic in the world, but I've tried hard to be a good and faithful person. Please help me get back to everyone who loves me and everyone I love. Please help me. Please.

I must have dozed off after a little while. I woke to see that the spot of light on the wall behind Abdulrahman's sleeping lump was fading. I looked at the clock. It was just after four-thirty in the afternoon. I could hardly believe that I'd spent another day in the hole. I should have been back at the Serena, screening videotape from the shoot that Shokoor and I were supposed to go on that day. After that, I would have been getting ready for Thanksgiving dinner at the Canadian embassy. My contact at the embassy, Isabelle, had invited me the week before, when I was firming up my travel plans to go to Kabul. She wanted me to meet a Pakistani journalist who was embedding with the Canadian contingent in Kandahar for a few weeks. He would also be coming to dinner, and she hoped I could tell him a bit about the embedding program and what the south of Afghanistan was like.

I was really looking forward to turkey and stuffing and pie. I love Thanksgiving, and every year, I try to write a letter to someone in my life I'm thankful for. I got the idea from one of my teachers in high school, Sister Josephine Carney, who was the sister of the then-archbishop of Vancouver. I received a letter from her several years after I graduated, saying she was thankful God had sent me to her class and how she hoped I learned as much from her as she did from me. I'd called to thank her, and she told me it's her Thanksgiving tradition every year to thank someone for being in her life. I pulled out my notebook again and wrote to Paul.

Hi, darling P,

It's almost 5 o'clock in the evening. Thanksgiving, October 13. I should be going to the embassy now, but I'm still in this hole, as far away from turkey dinner and cranberry sauce and pumpkin pie as I can be. In fact, the only thing I've had to eat all day is a few chocolate sandwich cookies. I hope that if you're on the base, or at the PRT, that there's a piece of turkey on your plate, and lots of stuffing and gravy. An extra portion for me.

It's one of my favourite dinners and I wish I could be cooking it for you and everyone else. You'll have to try out my great stuffing someday. It's made with sticky rice and reconstituted dried shiitake mushrooms. You will love it. I also make a pumpkin-pecan pie that you'd love. It's the traditional pumpkin on the bottom, and the traditional pecan on the top. I started making it a few years ago because some people always prefer to have one or the other, and then you end up with two half pies at the end of the night. This way, everyone gets a bit of both, and they don't have to feel piggish about it. I serve it with whipped cream. I think you'd love it, and I hope I get to make it for you next Thanksgiving.

Please try not to worry about me. I'm okay. The cut on my hand is tingly to the touch, but it doesn't seem to be affecting my motor skills, since I'm still able to write. It's just not the most comfortable place here, that's all. But for the most part, my kidnappers have been treating me well. I'm just feeling a little homesick, missing Thanksgiving, and most of all, missing you.

xox

Dear M,

You'll love this, M. We've been given code names by the embassy. I'm Victor 7. Every time we need a ride somewhere, we have to call and use those names. They don't want us travelling outside the Gandamack without an escort. And, hey, yesterday was Thanksgiving Day. Al and I were invited to the embassy for turkey, but were too exhausted, and distraught. I just hope we can have Thanksgiving together next year. Please come back soon, M. I can't be disappointed. We can't let this end in Afghanistan where it began.

xx

I was finally getting hungry thinking about turkey and stuffing and gravy, so I opened a new package of chocolate cookies and stuffed one in my mouth. I could feel my back top-left tooth ache a little, and I shuddered at the thought of a cavity, but I kept chewing. Pumpkin-pecan pie it wasn't, but at least my captors were not starving me. I pulled out another cookie. The crunch of the bag and the cookie wrapper made Abdulrahman stir. He had been sleeping for hours. He sat up and yawned.

"What is the time?" he asked.

I handed him the clock. He looked at it and gave it back to me. The light in the hole was very dim, and everything looked a pale shade of green.

"When are they coming?" I asked.

Abdulrahman shook his head and rubbed his fat belly.

"I not feel so good," he said.

"What's wrong?"

"Stomach. Something I eat not happy." He moved past me to the opening of the hole. He took my garbage pail and my roll of pink toilet paper, covered the hole with the wooden door, and crawled to the end of the tunnel. A horrible stench soon filled the small space. I thought I might die from the fumes. I remembered seeing matches in the plastic shopping bag, so holding my breath for as long as I could, I fished around in the bag and dug them out. I lit one after another, and exhaled.

Soon, he was back. He left the garbage can a few feet away from the entrance to the hole and rinsed his hands with the water from the green can. I scowled at him, angry he was using up the clean water, and angry that he had stunk up the room.

He smiled. "Better, much better," he said, reaching for the plastic bag. "Why you use the matches?" he asked, looking at the burnt matches scattered around.

"So I could breathe," I replied.

He glared at me, and then pointed to the bracelet on my wrist. "Take this off," he ordered.

Fuck, I thought. I had been wearing my little charm bracelet so long that I forgot I even had it on. I don't wear much jewellery—my late Great-Aunt Eileen gave the bracelet to me when I was fourteen, and I hadn't ever taken it off. I also had on two small rings—one was my late grandmother's wedding ring, the other my sister gave me when I got my master's degree. It was silver, with the words *Semper Fidelis*—Latin for "Always Faithful" and the motto for the US Marine Corps—engraved on it. I took it to mean I would be always faithful to my morals and principles as a journalist.

"No," I said.

"I will kill you," he said, grabbing my arm.

"No! You've already taken enough from me," I yelled, remembering how he had rifled through my makeup bag the night before, taking things for his wife. He grabbed my arm and tore the bracelet from my wrist, almost burning my skin with the chain in the process.

"It is very nice," he said, smiling as he turned it over in his fat hand.

I removed both rings and stuffed them in my pocket while he was examining the bracelet.

"I see you," he told me. "Give to me."

"No, you can't have my rings."

"I will kill you."

"Kill me. What will your brother say? What will Khalid say? They will kill you if you kill me." This made him angry and he lunged at me.

"Stop!" I yelled. He had grabbed my long shirt and was trying to pull it off me. I stood up quickly and hit my head on one of the wooden beams. The rings fell out of my pocket. Fuck, I thought. I must have not stuffed them in deeply enough. Abdulrahman let go of my shirt and picked the rings up off my blanket.

"Give them back to me!" I yelled.

"Very nice," he said. "I give to my wife."

"You can have the silver one," I told him. "Give me back the other one. It means a lot to me." He stared at me for a while, then threw the silver ring at me, holding up my grandmother's ring. "I give this little one to my wife." He put it in the pocket of his baggy pants.

"You're disgusting," I spat.

"My wife will be very happy," he said, smiling. Then, as if nothing had happened, he reached for the cookies, opened the package, and starting stuffing them in his mouth.

"I don't think you should eat any more," I said angrily, "if you're not feeling well."

"I am hungry," he said. "I will have dinner soon."

"Dinner?" I asked.

"I go when they come." He pointed at the roof. "I go have dinner."

"That's nice. You think I'm not hungry? That I don't need dinner? I should be having a very nice dinner now in Kabul." My eyes were flashing with anger.

"You have biscuit," he said, pointing at the chocolate cookies beside me. "I no eat your food."

"Good, or you will be fatter," I told him.

He rubbed his stomach again, and I worried for a second that he was going to go back to the bucket.

"My wife very good cook," he told me. "She make rice."

I asked him where his wife was, and he said that she was waiting for him so they could go to Pakistan together. Abdulrahman and his family spent the winter in Pakistan and their summers in Afghanistan, where they did their "work." I knew that many insurgents—including the Taliban—head back to Pakistan in the cold months of the winter and return in the spring for the summer fighting season. I was pretty sure my kidnappers were not real Taliban insurgents, but it still didn't surprise me that they would "winter" across the porous border.

"We have home there. All together. My brother and his wife—Khalid father and mother. Khalid, other brothers and sister. My uncle and his wife."

"Your house is very big."

"Yes, it is very nice house. Twenty people—more than twenty people—live there, yes."

"Your wife must hate living with your family," I said sarcastically, unsure if he would understand. And he didn't.

"My wife like our house. We have room for us and baby."

There was a noise outside.

"Shh." Abdulrahman put his finger to his lips and looked at the ceiling suspiciously. I heard footsteps and voices.

"Abdulrahman." The voice came from outside. Abdulrahman stood up and leaned over me to speak into one of the pipes.

"Hezbollah," he said softly. The voice outside spoke back in hushed Pashto, and the two men conversed quickly. He turned to me. "Khalid," he said, pointing up.

I felt a wave of relief. I heard digging, and I covered my face with my scarf and hid the white plastic bag under my blanket.

When it was over and the dust had settled, Abdulrahman moved the wooden door to the side and crawled up the tunnel. Cold air blew into the hole. It was mid-October, and even though temperatures could get as high as thirty degrees Celsius during the day, it was often very cool at night. Shokoor had warned me of that before I came to Afghanistan.

"Bring a sweater, Mellissa," he told me via email. "It is not like July and August when you were here last. It can get cold in the evening."

The air carried with it the hushed voices of the men standing outside. I could hear them speaking softly to each other. Then more shuffling, and I was surprised to see Abdulrahman crawling back through the tunnel toward me.

"Where is Khalid?" I asked.

"He coming. I must do something first." He pulled out a cell phone from his pocket. He pressed a few buttons and held it up to me.

"What is your name?" he asked. It was clearly a phone with the capacity to record several minutes of video.

"Mellissa," I answered.

"What do you do?"

"I am a journalist," I said.

"What is your father name?"

"Kellog."

"Okay," he said and stopped the recording. He pressed a few buttons, and said something under his breath in Pashto.

"We have to do again."

He asked me the same three questions and I answered. I knew this drill. We had all seen so many videos of hostages, usually with guns pointed at their heads, answering questions and begging for their lives. At least I didn't have to do that. I remembered seeing Jill

Carroll from the *Christian Science Monitor* and Daniel Pearl from the *Wall Street Journal*, looking frightened as they begged for their lives and for their governments to leave the countries they were being held in. I felt terrible for their families. I wondered what it would be like to be forced to say something I didn't believe in, to have to beg for my freedom in such a public venue. I was relieved I only had to answer a few short questions. At least for now.

"What are you going to do with that?" I asked.

"We send to your family. Your company," Abdulrahman answered, glaring at me like I was stupid for not knowing.

"You taking to Pakistan? You give to your brother? Your brother send? How will you send? Email?" I asked, slipping back into broken English. I was full of questions that I knew he could not answer, and part of me was repulsed by the fact that I needed anything from this foul man who I hated.

"Yes, yes, yes," he said as he gathered his skullcap and brushed off his pants. "I go now. Goodbye." He crawled back through the tunnel and up through the hole. I waited again, and wondered what would happen if my parents ever saw that video. I was afraid of what it would do to them, how much it would frighten them. I wished the Afghans wouldn't send it, but at least then my family would know that I was alive. I pictured my parents sitting in their bright kitchen watching the video, sick with worry about me. I did not want anyone to see that recording because I knew how it would look. At least the men weren't pointing their Kalashnikovs to my head.

I heard more footsteps above me, and then a soft thump. A kaffiyeh-wearing figure was shuffling toward me, and there was someone behind him.

"As-Salaam Alaikum, Mellissa." It was Shafirgullah. He had come down with two plastic bags.

"Shafirgullah, salaam," I said.

"Hello, Mellissa. How are you?" Khalid was behind him and brushing off the dust from his black kameez.

"Khalid," I said. "You came back."

"I am back. I tell you I come. How are you?"

"I would be better if I was going to Kabul."

"You will go." He crawled back up to the entrance of the hole and handed Shafirgullah several things, including a kerosene lamp, a small bottle of kerosene, another white plastic bag, a small black pot, and a silver tin.

"Light," he told me, pointing at the lamp. He pulled a match out of his pocket and lit the lamp. Shafirgullah was dismantling the light bulb and old battery.

"Yes, that is good," I said. "There is no light down here."

"How are you? I bring you food," Shafirgullah said, pulling the covers off the black pot and silver tin. The pot was half full of what looked like a stew, and the tin was full of rice. I wasn't sure I was hungry enough to risk eating their food, so I shook my head.

"Not hungry," I said.

Khalid looked me in the eye and held my gaze for several seconds. "You must eat."

"I am not hungry."

"I bring for you. Food. It is good. You must eat."

As if to prove to me that it was edible, he stuck a spoon in the stew and ate big chunks of meat, which I assumed must have been lamb or goat. I shook my head. "I do not want any."

"Rice," he said, pushing a spoon in my hand and the tin toward me. Several grains fell on my blanket. I picked them up and put them in an empty plastic bag.

"Please eat a little little," Khalid said, digging my spoon into the rice. I truly had no appetite, but I figured white rice couldn't hurt. I brought a spoonful of rice to my lips and gingerly ate half of the rice that was on the spoon. It was flavoured with spices. And it didn't taste too bad. I finished what was on the spoon and pushed the tin away from me.

"Enough," I said. "I am not hungry."

He sighed, frustrated, and reached into the plastic bag, pulling out a flat of Afghan bread.

"You like bread?"

I shook my head again. "Maybe later," I said. "I am not hungry now."

Khalid shook his head and said something in Pashto to Shafirgullah, who looked at me, ripped off a piece of bread, and held it out to me. I waved it away with my hand.

"No, thank you," I said to him. He looked at Khalid, shrugged, and stuffed it in his mouth, chewing loudly and openly. Khalid sighed and ripped off more bread. He dipped it into the stew and within several minutes, he and Shafirgullah had finished most of the meat that was in the small pot. I was curious about the stew, so I ripped off a piece of bread and dipped a corner into the brown sauce at the bottom of the pot. It was cold and salty. I finished the piece of bread and sat back.

"I leave for you," Khalid said, pushing the silver tin at me. "You eat. I go now."

"Where are you going? I thought you were going to stay?"

"Shafirgullah stay. I come tomorrow."

"No." I realized that the only one I semi-trusted was Khalid. I did not want another repeat of what happened with Abdulrahman the night before.

"Why no?" Khalid must have read the fear in my voice. "Did my uncle touch you?"

I shook my head but did not answer.

"He touch you."

"I was afraid of him," I said quietly.

"You afraid from him," Khalid repeated. I nodded.

"He stole from me. My bracelet and my ring."

Shafirgullah looked at us, and Khalid put his hands on his head, translating our exchange for him. The two Afghans spoke in Pashto for a while. They seemed upset and angry, and Khalid sighed heavily several times. They were both shaking their heads and rubbing their temples with their hands.

Someone above us said something in Pashto. Khalid responded in kind, and soon we were joined by a third man I did not remember seeing before. He was wearing a white kameez and matching baggy pants. His head was wrapped in a white kaffiyeh, and I could see that he had a lazy left eye. The three Afghans sat in a circle next to me, speaking softly to one another, sometimes rubbing their heads with their hands, and often glancing furtively in my direction. I sat with my chin resting on my knees and my arms wrapped around my legs, wishing I could understand Pashto, since they were clearly discussing my situation.

After a few minutes, the third man left and Khalid and Shafirgullah turned to me.

"Mellissa," Khalid said, "I stay tonight if you want, but I not stay all the nights. Shafirgullah stay tomorrow. Or he stay tonight and I stay tomorrow."

"Why can't you just leave me here on my own?" I asked. "Why does someone have to stay all the time?"

"My father say," he answered. "You are girl. If you not a girl, you stay alone. You are man, you stay alone. We come only to bring food."

"I can stay alone," I said. I would rather be alone than stuck in a hole with a disgusting man like Abdulrahman. It was a small space anyway—barely enough room for one.

Khalid shook his head. "You no stay alone. Shafirgullah stay tonight. He no hurt you," he said, trying to reassure me. He looked over at his friend, and Shafirgullah nodded and smiled at me. "You no afraid from Shafirgullah. He no touch you. You are my sister. Okay, Mellissa? You my sister. We no touch you. You no afraid from us."

Shafirgullah nodded again and smiled as if also to reassure me. I looked warily at both of them and sighed. I didn't have a choice.

"Okay," I conceded. "Shafirgullah stay then."

"He touch you, I will kill him," Khalid said. "I kill him he touch my sister."

"Okay." I nodded. "When you coming back?"

"I come tomorrow or next day. We go outside maybe. For walk. You like yes?"

"Yes, I would like to be outside."

"Okay. Everything okay, Mellissa."

"Everything okay, Khalid. Except I want to go back to Kabul."

"Yes, inshallah. You will go." He took my right hand as if to shake it, but just held it for a while and examined the back of it where Shafirgullah's knife had ruptured the skin.

"It is hurt?" he asked.

"Yes, still hurting," I answered. This was no lie. The wound hurt, though I had no feeling around the base of my middle and index fingers.

"Tsk," he said, looking at his friend.

"I sorry," Shafirgullah said, probably using two of the few English words he knew. "I sorry, Mellissa."

"It's okay," I said. "It's no longer bleeding."

Khalid translated for him and Shafirgullah nodded. The two men spoke in Pashto quickly and then Khalid got up.

"I go now," he said. He was on his way out when he turned around. "My brother—Zahir—he touch you?"

"No," I replied. "Zahir was very nice." Khalid seemed pleased to hear this and nodded.

"Yes. Zahir good. Abdulrahman is bad man," he repeated. He must have said the same thing in Pashto because Shafirgullah shook his head and echoed him, "Abdulrahman bad. Bad, bad, bad."

"Abdulrahman no come anymore," Khalid told me.

"You promise," I said.

"Yes, he no come again."

"Okay."

"I go now, Mellissa. I see you tomorrow or next day."

"Okay."

"What else I bring? What you want? You are cold?" I said I was, and he promised to bring me another blanket. After saying a few words to Shafirgullah in Pashto, he crawled up the tunnel.

Shafirgullah reached for the wooden door and took his kaffiyeh off, using it to seal the edges. We both covered our faces as dirt and dust filled the hole. I could hear footsteps fading into the distance over our heads.

Dearest M,

I just looked at my watch and it's after four o'clock already, which means we'll soon be heading into darkness again and your fifth night with those bastards. I have a vision of you chained up to a wall and it scares the hell out of me. Between all the anxiety and the phone calls, the day passes very slowly.

It's now 10:15 p.m., darling, and I'm going to bed feeling distraught and grumpy. I'm having a lot of trouble getting through the nights. We went down to the bar before dinner—remember it?—and had a beer, but I couldn't stay. It was too painful being there without you. The place has been given a fresh coat of paint, but it will never, ever be the same.

Shafirgullah spent the night teaching me how to say various words in Pashto, which helped to pass the long hours. I'd learned how to count to ten, and the words for door, ceiling, blanket, hands, eyes, nose—and most other body parts we could point at. By the time he blew out the kerosene lamp, I could see from the alarm clock that it was almost midnight.

Shafirgullah slept soundly. I could hear snoring before too long, and once again, I was in the darkness alone. It was hard to get comfortable. The thin blanket that covered the dirt floor couldn't stop the hard ground from pushing into my back. Every way I shifted it felt like a piece of rock was pressing against some part of my body. I could hear Shafirgullah's steady rumbling. *If only I could sleep half as well as my captors,* I thought, *then maybe it wouldn't be so hard to pass the time.*

I've never really had trouble sleeping. But I usually need only about five or six hours a night. My routine at home, and even on the military base in Kandahar, with all the noise from trucks and airplanes, usually had me going to bed around midnight and getting up very early in the morning to hit the gym or go for a run, depending on the weather. I rarely had trouble falling asleep, but now, after three days of lying here wide awake, I was feeling weary. I closed my eyes and hoped I would drift off.

I clutched the rosary in my right hand. *Hail Mary, full of grace, the Lord is with thee.* I figured if I just said it over and over again, I would eventually lose consciousness.

Then I heard a loud boom. And another. It sounded like rockets landing, a sound I'd heard before but one I'd never get used to. In the last few weeks, there had been several rocket attacks at KAF—Kandahar Airfield—including one that seemed so close that we dove for the floor under our desks in the work tent, and another one that prompted the military to make us wear our body armour, even helmets, while working inside. None of us in the media tents wanted to, of course. The gear is heavy and hugely uncomfortable, but we had no choice.

BOOM. BOOM. Now it sounded very close. And then *tick, tick . . . tick, tick . . . tick, tick, tick.* Automatic gunfire, also not foreign to my ears, or to those of anyone who's ever lived through a war or travelled with soldiers fighting one. *Tick, tick, tick, tick, tick, tick, tick.* And the sound of more explosions. The noise went on for about an hour, and I didn't know what to think. I felt safe and afraid at the same time. Then the noises seemed to fade a bit, moving farther away from us. There were periods of silence, before they picked up again. *Tick, tick, tick, tick, BOOM!* Shafirgullah did not move, snoring softly.

This was simply the routine sound of night in Afghanistan. Who was shooting? And who were they shooting at? Were NATO soldiers close by? Were my kidnappers involved?

The rhythm of my prayers couldn't put me to sleep, but the rhythm of war finally did. It was past six when I woke up. I had slept for more than four hours, which for me was a small victory. I ran the beads of my little rosary through my fingers once again, a prayer for each bead, five times around. Day three. How many more would there be?

I stood up and stretched. If I had stood on my toes, my head would have bumped the ceiling. A small beam of light again shone through the pipe. I held my leg up behind me—left leg, right hand; right leg, left hand—until I could feel the stretch in my quads. I squatted and stood several times to try to exercise the muscles in legs that were used to getting a workout every morning. I kicked my right leg out to the side in the first of a set of side tae kwon do kicks, which I had learned years ago when working on getting my brown belt. Then the left leg. Then a few roundhouse kicks with my right, and then again with the left.

Finally, I sat down. It was almost seven, and I had managed to distract myself for an hour. Shafirgullah was still sleeping. He had stirred while I was doing my exercises but was now a snoring lump on the other side of the room. I stared at him for a while, wondering what would happen if I nailed the side of his head with one of my roundhouse kicks. I'd certainly knock him out. Perhaps I could take my scarf and tie it around his neck, cutting off the flow of oxygen and choking him to death. The idea of killing someone was a strange one. I wondered if I could. After all, people do it all the time, especially in this part of the world, where life and death are connected by barely a thread, where the value of a human life is often measured in afghanis and dollars.

I closed my eyes and tried to imagine what it would be like to kill someone with my bare hands. It was difficult. There was a part of me that was tempted to, but I don't think I possessed either the courage or the anger to actually do it. Besides, I'd strangle him, and then what? Would I be able to climb out of the hole on my own? I knew what was covering it. Dirt, and a board of some sort, and maybe a rock. But what if someone came by? What if someone was watching? Would he then shoot me for trying to escape? And what would happen if I couldn't get out? Khalid and his gang would come back by nightfall and they would find me alone, with Shafirgullah's dead body.

I realized that I was making a fist with my left hand, and the cross on the rosary was digging into my palm, a gentle reminder, perhaps, that I was entertaining some very un-Christian thoughts. I smiled at the absurdity of it, pressed the cross to my lips, and started to pray again. *Our Father, who art in heaven, hallowed be thy name. Thy kingdom come, thy will be done, on earth, as it is in heaven . . .*

Then, instead of moving on to the first Hail Mary, I kept my fingers on the crucifix, and said the Lord's Prayer again, this time stopping at *"as we forgive those who trespass against us, and deliver us from evil."* One moment I wanted to kill, and the next I was thinking about forgiveness and my own desperation. *Please, Lord,* I begged, *I forgive these kidnappers. They're only doing what they've been told. But please deliver me from this. Please deliver me home to the people who are waiting for me. They must be so worried, Lord. Please.*

I didn't even want to think about my family. Surely they'd been notified by now. My sister, Vanessa, was my emergency contact and she would have been the first person they called. I hated the thought that she'd have to break the news to my parents over the telephone from Los Angeles. I wondered what was happening at home. I pictured my mother going to church to pray the same prayers as me. I knew she had a great deal of faith in God, and I hoped that would sustain her until I was released. My father was a different story. Kellog was your stereotypical, stoic Chinese father who didn't say much but felt and kept everything deeply, and I was afraid of the stress on his health. I'd hardly seen my father show any emotion throughout my childhood, except when he was angry with us. I remember seeing him cry at his mother's funeral six years before. We went up to my grandmother's open casket together, and I felt him shaking with tears. It unsettled me because I wasn't used to any show of emotion from my father. I imagined it might be the same when he heard about my disappearance. He might be angry with me for venturing so far from home and into a place he didn't understand, wondering why I would put myself and our comfortable existence at risk. I was, in fact, much more afraid of my parents' reaction than of what my kidnappers might do to me.

Shafirgullah stirred again, but this time, instead of rolling over, he propped himself up on his elbows.

"Mellissa."

"Shafirgullah," I said. "You slept a lot."

He looked at the alarm clock and took a match out of his pocket to light the kerosene lamp. The flame flickered and cast a warm glow into the dark hole, but a small stream of black smoke was starting to pollute the air in such a confined space. He waved his hand around the lamp and turned the knob down to lower the flame. But the smoke still came out. He sighed and set the lamp down between us, then sat back and took a pocket mirror and comb out of his left breast pocket.

I watched as he took the can of water and washed his face. He took a small stick with some rope tied to one end and used it to clean his teeth—like you would with a toothbrush. Then more water onto his hands and onto his jet black hair. He combed it carefully and checked himself out in the mirror, rotating it several times to make sure even the hair at the back of his head was neatly combed. He put on his skullcap, and placed the mirror and comb back in his pocket.

"You," he pointed at me, "biscuit?"

"You, biscuit." I nodded back at him.

He reached for the plastic bag. "Me, biscuit." He took out a box of the chocolate cookies, unwrapped them, and proceeded to eat the entire contents, washed down with two boxes of mango juice. Satisfied, he sat back and stared at me. It was barely nine o'clock. I wondered how we would pass another day with nothing to say to each other, and a language barrier that was like a wall between two people, two genders, and two cultures.

Shafirgullah pointed at the door.

"Darwaaza," I said, remembering the Pashto word for door he had taught me the night before. He pointed at my notebook. *"Kitab,"* I said. He smiled and pointed at his hand. *"Laas."*

And we continued. *Nuk* was finger, *sar* was head, *stergae* was eye, *pssa* was foot. We counted to ten, first in Pashto for me, then in English for him.

Then he wanted to learn how to count in Chinese. I tried explaining to him that there are two kinds of Chinese—Cantonese and Mandarin. I told him that I spoke Cantonese, being from Hong Kong. But I knew how to count in both forms—so we went through the numbers. I wrote them down phonetically in English, and he in turn wrote them down phonetically in Pashto.

Cantonese first: *"Yut, yee, saam, say, mmm, look, tsut, bhat, gow, sup."*

"Mmm?" Shafirgullah was confused by the sound of the word for five.

"Pindza," I said to him, the Pashto word for five.

"Mmm!"

Then Mandarin: *"Yi, er, san, si, wu, liu, qi, ba, jiu, shi."* A little harder to get the tones right, but Shafirgullah was a determined linguist. Getting me to say the words slowly, he repeated them over and over, rolling his tongue around his mouth until the syllables fell out right.

"Very good," I said.

"Very good," he repeated. He sat back and reached into his pocket. "Cigarette?"

I took it from his hand as he reached for another. Smoking was probably the worst thing we could do in such a small space, but it was a good way to kill the time. The young Afghan lit a match, held it to my smoke, and then his. We both inhaled deeply. He blew the smoke out the doorway and into the tunnel, as if to clear it from our sleep space. I followed suit, and soon our cigarettes were nothing more than glowing embers. I put out the butt of mine in a small notch in the wall behind me. Ashes scattered over my knapsack and camera bag, and I brushed them away. Everything was covered in dust anyway, and I didn't even want to imagine what my lungs would look like after a few more days in the hole. At least, I hoped it would be only a few more days.

"Me, bathroom," Shafirgullah said. I turned around and waited for him to relieve himself into the plastic bottle by the door.

"Okay," he said. I watched as he took the can of water and poured it over his hands, scrubbing them hard over the metal bucket. When he was done, he adjusted his skullcap on top of his head and took off his kaffiyeh, spreading it over his blanket. Then he knelt down on top of it to pray.

Shafirgullah prayed for a good half hour, murmuring what I assumed were passages from the Koran and pressing his forehead to the ground several times.

I took out my rosary and fingered the beads again, starting to pray my own way. *Hail Mary, full of grace, the Lord is with thee.* I kept looking over at the Afghan in the skullcap, praying hard and looking as devout as some of the born-again Christians in the Deep South. This is where I had trouble. If we were both praying to the same god, like I'd always believed in—and Allah is God, God is Yahweh, Yahweh is Allah—then who was God listening to? Does the God I believe in have a split personality? Does Allah listen to Shafirgullah, and God listen to me? Is that why I was still here—because Allah had overruled my God? How could it be possible that we were praying to the same entity? I watched as Shafirgullah knelt and prayed, his eyes closed, his lips mumbling verses from the Koran, which he had probably learned by heart as a young boy, just as I had learned to pray the rosary when I was a little girl.

I looked down at the crucifix on my rosary and, instead of reciting the Lord's Prayer, found myself asking God a lot of questions. *Who are you? Who are you listening to? I know he's as much of a human being as I am, but if we both believe, how could you allow them to take me like this and keep me here, and create such chaos in the lives of my family and friends? I don't understand.*

The more I thought about it, the more upset I got, so I put the rosary away and took out my notepad.

Tuesday, October 14, 10 a.m.

Dearest P,

Another day and another long wait for something to happen. Shafirgullah, the one who stabbed me on the first day—is my guard today. He's teaching me some words in Pashto to help pass the time. He's a funny dude—very conscious of cleanliness and appearance. He must have combed his hair twenty times this morning. I've never met another Afghan man quite like him.

I hope that wherever you are, you're okay, and I think—if I know you— that you're in Kabul by now, trying desperately to find out where I am. If I knew, I would tell you, but I have no clue where this hole is and I'm starting to feel a little desperate.

Khalid said he would take me out for a walk sometime—I'm not sure what that means, but it would be nice to breathe some fresh air. So many things we take for granted that we don't realize until it's taken away or until we don't have it anymore. Even something as simple as fresh air and sunshine. And a bathroom, or a toilet. Or food.

It's funny, you know, I remember being at the refugee camp wondering how people live—how they pack their families into these small living quarters.

In my mind's eye, I could still see the camp and all the families crowded into it. I had spent a few minutes in a small mud hut covered with a makeshift roof of corrugated metal, a pile of blankets on one side. It was maybe twice the size of the hole I was sitting in. A father, mother, and their five children, ages approximately three to sixteen, were crammed inside. The father had told me he was a cobbler. He had made shoes in a shop in Kandahar City, and his eldest son was his apprentice. They described the life they had left in Kandahar as a happy one, even though they did not have a lot of money. The small business had brought in enough to feed his family, and he was happy that his son was able to work with him.

It all changed in the summer of 2008, when the fighting in Kandahar got worse. Not a day went by, he told me, without the rattle of gunfire, the explosions of mortars, and the constant threat of a bomb. I remembered the cobbler's feet. They were shoeless and so caked with mud that you could barely see his toes—it was hard to believe this man made shoes for a living.

The family had left with everything they had and were now trying to survive in this small space. Yet, he was more than welcoming to two journalists, insisting on making tea from his small black kettle and pouring it into small glasses for me and Shokoor—we were his guests in his small mud hut, and he treated us as such.

We drank the tea quickly, thanked the family, and left.

I'd never felt so helpless as I did during my time at that camp. All those families—widows, children, babies, puppies—with nowhere to go, victims of a war they wanted no part of. But that's why I was there. To tell their story, and hopefully make people see how much suffering there is among the innocent civilians caught in war. It might sound a little corny, but it's why I became a journalist in the first place. I thought that if we could understand each other a little more, the world might be a better place. (I remember watching stories about the famine in Ethiopia in the 1980s and then trying to convince one of my grade school teachers that we should all go on a fast for several days, so we might be able to understand what people in Africa are going through.) I've always believed that if even one of my stories could move just one person to think about something differently, understand something a little more deeply, maybe write a letter to the governor or premier, then I'd done my job and done it well. And that's what I was hoping to do at the refugee camp.

We have no idea in the West how much we have, I continued writing. *If people in the West could even get a glimpse of how most Afghans live, maybe we'd be a little more thankful for what we do have.*

"You hungry?" Shafirgullah had finished with his morning prayers.

I shook my head.

"Cigarette?" he offered.

I couldn't help it. Again he lit it for me and handed it to me, the smoke already beginning to fill the air. Then he pointed at my shoulder. It had been more than a day since I had dressed the stab wound. The pink toilet paper I'd used to staunch the bleeding was now glued to the wound by blood, becoming part of the scab that had formed.

"Hurt?" he asked.

"It's okay, a little pain, yes."

"I sorry," he said. It was maybe the third or fourth time he'd apologized for stabbing me. I wondered if a tenet of his religion was that one should not hurt women.

"It's okay. It will be okay." I wished I knew more about Islam so I could better understand where he was coming from, particularly because there was already a language barrier. I knew that women generally had fewer rights than men. The sexuality of a woman is veiled so as to prevent men from being tempted into committing a corporal sin. It's not for me to be critical of other religions. God knows there are enough problems with Christian fundamentalists in Western society, but it always struck me that the subjugation of women in Muslim culture was the root of many of that society's problems. Young girls are painfully circumcised. Then they're covered up and hidden from view, the property of a husband in an arranged marriage. Men are seen as owners of their women, whether they're daughters or wives, sisters or cousins.

So much has been written about the stifling morality that separates men and women. Some hold the view that sexual frustration of Muslim men is at the root of male aggression. Whatever it was, I didn't know how to reconcile the two religions, the two beliefs. Women in Islam are just viewed differently from women in Christianity. But yet, from what I could gather through conversations with my kidnappers, they were treating me differently, maybe better, than they would if I were a man. I didn't doubt them when they told me they would have left me alone in the dark for days without light or food. I believed them when they said they would have beaten me with their guns.

Shafirgullah's phone rang.

"As-Salaam Alaikum," he said. He spoke for a while in Pashto before hanging up.

"Khalid," he said to me.

"Where Khalid? He is coming tonight, yes?" I asked.

"Khalid, Kabul."

"Why Khalid go Kabul?" I asked. I was speaking in broken English, maybe subconsciously hoping he would understand me better this way. He just shook his head.

"So Khalid not coming tonight."

"No, he no come."

This was upsetting, only because it meant I wouldn't be able to ask Khalid everything I wanted to know. Had his father contacted the network? Had he called Paul? Were they talking about money? They had been so focused on money that it would have been naive of me to think they would release me for nothing. I know that my company had insurance for situations like this, but I felt guilty about all the money that was sure to be spent on gaining my freedom, whether it was for hiring negotiators like AKE or an actual ransom payment, which is something I felt very uncomfortable with. I was a hostage because others had paid these kidnappers. If they got payment for me, the vicious cycle would be perpetuated. I silently vowed that however much it cost, I could always take out a big loan and pay it back. I just wanted to know that there was movement, that talks were happening, and that maybe I would get to go back to my life soon.

"Why Khalid go Kabul?" I repeated. Shafirgullah responded in Pashto, speaking very quickly, and I didn't understand. I asked him what he was saying. He spoke in Pashto again and I shook my head. He looked at me and laughed.

"It's not funny," I said. "I want to go home. Don't you understand? Of course you don't. How would you know what it feels like to be a prisoner?"

He continued talking in Pashto and laughing. It began to feel like he was mocking me, and I was getting angry.

We fell into a long silence. I was tired of this. Tired of him, and tired of being stuck in a hole. I pulled the blanket over me and turned to the wall.

"You sleep?" he asked in English.

"Yes," I lied.

"I sleep." The Afghan lay down, and soon I could hear deep breathing.

I was a little relieved to be left alone, and I reached for my notebook and turned up the flame on the kerosene lamp, almost daring the smoke to fill the hole.

Hi again, dear P,

I miss you so much. I am so sorry for putting you through this, and I just want to come home. I don't know how much longer I will last here. I'm writing to you by the light of a kerosene lamp and I'm surrounded by smelly black smoke. It's dark and dank and I'm trying very hard not to feel sorry for myself and stay positive and think about the day I get to come home.

I hope that's soon. I figure if I'm out by the weekend, I can still catch the Kam Air flight to Kandahar and be back to pick up my stuff and we'd still be on schedule to leave KAF on Wednesday.

Please try not to worry about me. I'm okay. They're not beating me or anything. It's just boredom I'm fighting and the hard part is watching the clock. I've never known time to move so slowly. It's funny, because we're always on a deadline, fighting the clock. Do you remember we were just talking the other day about how time flies when we're together, even in the dustbowl of KAF. Now it seems like time is standing still, and not when I want it to.

I noticed that the lamp was fading, and I realized that the kerosene was running low. I reached for the plastic bag, where I knew there was a bottle of it. I blew out the flame and poured some more kerosene into the base, then lit a match.

I preferred the warm glow of this lamp to the harsh fluorescent light bulb of the day before. It reminded me of the fireplace at my best friend Kelly McClughan's house on Chesterman Beach in Tofino, on the north end of Vancouver Island. We'd come in from an afternoon of surfing, put a fire on, pour a glass of single malt, and sit in front of the fire and talk about the big wave we missed or the big wipeout—or rather, my big wipeout.

I might be an avid surfer, but I wouldn't say I'm a good one. I just get on my board, catch a wave from time to time, and feel transported. And it's a great escape for me, really one of the few times when I'm focused on just one thing. I'm cursed with an overactive mind, constantly thinking about one thing or another—but usually work related, whether it's a story or a person or something I should be doing. So to get out on the water and surf for a few hours is freedom from all of that.

I love the feeling of standing on water, propelled by nothing but the power of the waves. I think it's maybe because I was born on an island, Hong Kong, and grew up in Vancouver, next to the ocean, that I've always felt at home by the sea. It's a romantic idea anyway.

My last trip to Tofino had been the summer before—with Kelly and my friend Kas. I spent my mornings out running on the path leading into town, and the afternoons playing in the surf. It was Kas's first trip to Tofino, a small town populated by hippie environmentalists in the 1960s and 1970s but today a bit of a resort destination, drawing tourists from all over the world to fish in its salmon-rich waters and surf in its cold white waves. Despite this, the natural beauty of the place has not changed. Tall cedars, part of the old-growth forest, line the beaches and give grey owls a place to hide. Sometimes a thick fog blankets the beach, especially in the fall, and a heavy dampness settles in. Those are the days when you curl up by the fire and lose yourself in a book.

Kas told me how much she was blown away by the beauty of Tofino. One night, we took a walk on the beach after dinner with a few friends. The sand had a phosphorescent glow in the moonlight. It was a magical, happy place, and I desperately wanted to take Paul there. In my mind I could see us walking on the beach together, bundled up in big sweaters to shield us from the cold and the wind.

I opened my eyes and saw the dark mud wall in front of me. Fuck. I was as far away from my happy place as I could ever be. The lamp was flickering and black smoke was pouring out of it. I turned the knob down, and realized there was a draft blowing into the room from one of the pipes, and it was blowing the flame around. I stood up and stared into the pipe. I couldn't see much, as the opening was obscured by rocks. But there was definitely a draft.

The familiar ring of the Nokia phone woke Shafirgullah from his slumber. He answered and had a short conversation with someone in Pashto, then played with the phone for a while before looking over at me again.

"You, game?" he asked.

I wasn't sure what he meant, until he took the SIM card out of the phone and then handed the phone to me.

"Game," he said.

I scrolled through the phone and saw that it was set to Pashto or Farsi. I clicked on settings, switched it to English, then found the games icon. There was a soccer game and a game called Snake Xenzia. Shafirgullah pointed to the snake game, so I clicked on it and a screen with a big dot and a snake figure appeared. I realized that by using the phone's arrow buttons, I could control the snake. The goal is to "eat" as many of the balls as you can without running into the snake as it grows longer.

I played the game for a while, until I realized the phone battery was running low. I didn't want to waste the battery playing a game, especially if Khalid was maybe going to call, so I handed the phone back to Shafirgullah.

"You no game?" he asked.

I shook my head. "Maybe later."

He put the SIM card back in the phone and slipped it back into his pocket.

"You, biscuit?" he asked, reaching for the cookies. I shook my head again. He shrugged and pulled out two juice boxes and another sleeve of cookies. He opened the package and started eating, and sucking juice noisily out of the box. He held out the package to me and I took two cookies, and then a juice box. I was trying not to drink too much because it was a pain to have to use the garbage can as a toilet, but I was quite thirsty.

"Juice good." Shafirgullah reached for another box and drank it until the box caved in on itself. I nodded and thanked him.

The afternoon must have passed because eventually I heard footsteps up above. Someone called down to Shafirgullah and soon I could hear digging. I wasn't sure what was happening because I didn't think Khalid was coming, since he was in Kabul. Shafirgullah put the wooden door over the entrance and shrouded it with his blanket to protect us from the dust that was about to fill the hole. Soon I could feel cool air coming through the entrance. Shafirgullah removed his blanket, set the wooden door to the side, and scrambled up the tunnel.

Darling M,

I woke up at four o'clock and had a sense you were awake too. I wasn't restless, but couldn't get back to sleep. My mind was preoccupied with all kinds of crazy thoughts. What will you be wearing when they release you? Who will pick you up and where? How will they handle the media? Then I dozed for a while and had a dream about you coming home. You were wearing black and walking toward me down the dim hallway of a hotel. But it wasn't you, it was somebody short and heavier, somebody I seemed to know. I kept shouting, "Where's Mellissa? Where's Mellissa?"

There was a small earth tremor around 5:30 that I'm sure you felt as well. That was my first thought! "Did Mellissa feel it?" I think I dozed off again, but it was fitful, and I finally got up around 7:30.

The first thing I do now is throw on pants and go to the kitchen for a pot of tea. They know me well, and we always smile and shake hands. There's a young waiter named Jawad, who calls me "Mr. Paul." The cook makes croissants and fresh bread every morning, and it makes me think of you. Everything makes me think of you. I keep telling myself I cannot lose you now, I will not lose you.

xx

I like to eavesdrop. I think it's part of being a curious reporter, but I'm probably just a very nosy person. I remember as a kid trying to listen in on my parents' conversations, whether they were talking between themselves, or to their friends at family gatherings. We used to have big get-togethers, with our family of six, including my grandparents, and two or three other families, friends of my parents' from Hong Kong who had also made the move to Canada. Six or seven of us kids would play hide-and-seek through the house, while our parents drank and smoked and yakked until the wee hours of the morning.

I remember hiding in the pantry once, waiting to be found; but more to the point, I could hear the grown-ups sitting around the table in the kitchen—with drinks, of course—saying lots of things that seemed amazing to a seven-year-old. I learned a lot about what their lives were like before they moved to Canada, before they had children. They talked about the places they used to frequent as young adults in Hong Kong, their travels throughout Asia, the great adventures they had before kids came along. It was fascinating to think that my parents had a whole other life, one I couldn't possibly imagine, before I was born and before we moved to Vancouver.

As a journalist, I rather perfected the art of eavesdropping when I was assigned as the provincial political reporter for my former network, Global Television. Our office was just below the premier's at the legislature in Victoria, hidden behind the press theatre.

I headed up the stairs one day and overheard a conversation, loud and clear, between the premier and his press secretary about how they planned to handle a scandal that was about to hit the front pages. They had no idea I was listening.

I also learned how to stand behind politicians and their aides, just far away enough so as not to attract attention, while they were talking on their cell phones. I listened as I tapped away on my own phone to make myself look busy.

Now, I could hear voices outside the hole. The entrance to the tunnel was still unblocked. I crawled into the tunnel and strained to listen. Shafirgullah was speaking with one, maybe two other people. I think I heard three male voices in total. I knew they were smoking. I could hear the click of a lighter and then the sound of puffing on cigarettes. I heard the tones of dialing on a cell phone, and then the familiar greeting, "As-Salaam Alaikum."

I couldn't understand any of the conversation, since it was all in Pashto, but I assumed it was about me. What else could they all be talking about as they stood over a hole where they were holding me? I suppose they could just have been shooting the breeze about the weather, or what they had for dinner, but the conversation sounded serious and was not punctuated by laughter. So, I had to believe it was about me, and what they were going to do with me, and maybe what, if any, conversations they'd had with Paul, or the AKE person I assumed was by this time en route to Kabul.

Or maybe they were talking about my release, having realized they'd made a mistake, since I wasn't a European who worked for a company willing to pay hundreds of thousands of dollars for my freedom, or better still, an American whom they could keep out of a sense of moral and religious righteousness. I was a mistake, damn it! A Canadian working for a public broadcaster that had no money! And now they were wondering how they'd get me back to

Kabul before morning. Or at least that's what I desperately hoped they were talking about.

The crinkle of a plastic bag brought me back to the harsh reality of where I was. I knew instinctively that it held more supplies for the night—and the next day. There would be no freedom tonight.

I crawled back into the room and tried to brush myself off, but looking around, I wasn't sure why I bothered. Everything was coated in a thick film of dust. My knapsack and camera bag, my red velvet pillow, my notepad. I noticed that Shafirgullah had put his skullcap over the watering can, so at least we didn't have to worry that our water was getting contaminated, although I wasn't drinking water from that can anyway. I was at least glad for the fresh air coming through the opening of the shaft and down the tunnel. It also gave the black smoke from the lamp a place to escape.

I picked up the package of cigarettes from where Shafirgullah had left them, took one out, and lit it with the flame of the lamp. Then I heard footsteps, and a loud thud. Probably Shafirgullah making his way back to the hole with new supplies. But when I looked up, it was someone I didn't recognize.

"Hello, Mellissa, I am Abdullah."

Abdullah looked almost exactly like Shafirgullah, but he was a little bigger.

"I am brother Shafirgullah." Of course he was. He stuck his hand out.

"Hello, Abdullah," I said, and we shook hands, something not common between men and women in Muslim culture. I had never shook the hand of an Afghan man—except for Shokoor, who is more familiar with my Western customs.

"How are you, Mellissa?" Abdullah's English seemed to be a little better than his brother's.

"I am okay. I want to go to Kabul. I want to go home."

He laughed. "Yes, yes, you go Kabul."

When, I wanted to know.

"Soon, inshallah, soon."

I heard another thud and then Shafirgullah's voice in the tunnel, calling out to his brother. Abdullah turned away from me and handed him the plastic water bottle that was now full of urine, and the black garbage can. Soon, they were both returned, emptied. Then Abdullah gathered up the empty juice boxes and cookie packages, and a hunk of now-hardened Afghan bread. He put them into a plastic bag and handed it to Shafirgullah, who handed it to someone else, then crawled into the room with a fresh can of water and a bulging plastic bag.

"You, cigarette?" he asked. I had just had one, so I shook my head. He reached into the bag and pulled out a new pack of cigarettes. The brothers each lit one and puffed away, speaking in Pashto to each other. Now and then Abdullah would look over at me and smile. He was a nice-looking young man with a wide smile and good white teeth. He had dark eyes, set wider than Shafirgullah's, which made him seem friendlier, whereas his brother's smile could easily be seen as slightly menacing.

They spoke for a while, and then Abdullah turned to me. "Goodbye, Mellissa." He waved. "I see you again." He crawled up the tunnel and disappeared. Shafirgullah put the wooden door over the entrance, covered it with his blanket, and we braced ourselves for the avalanche of dirt. When it was over, we once again dusted ourselves off.

"You, biscuit?" he asked. I shook my head. He reached into the dust-covered plastic bag and pulled out a new sheet of Afghan bread and a silver pouch of juice, not in boxes this time. I peered into the bag and saw that the chocolate cookies had been replaced mainly with the cheaper fruit-flavoured creme-filled kind. There were six pouches of juice: cherry, apple, pomegranate. I took out a pomegranate pouch. It was tart yet sweet, and cold. Shafirgullah offered me some nan-i-Afghani. I tore a corner off and chewed. I wished I had something to dip it in—some dal, or hummus, or curry, anything with a little protein and a little more flavour. I loved Afghan bread, but eating it cold and plain, I realized it was because I loved everything else that usually came with it.

A few days before I left the base, a group of us had gone into Kandahar City to arrange my flight to Kabul. Paul was there, with his wonderful cameraman, Al; and their fixer, Jojo; and Sameem, who was the CBC's local driver and cameraman. I liked these trips to the city, since it was a chance to get off the base and talk to ordinary Afghans. And a chance to eat real food, which was always preferable to the bland stuff served in the cafeterias at the base, where we ate breakfast, lunch, and dinner almost every day. I suppose it was risky, but Jojo had arranged lunch in a local restaurant where he knew we'd be safe.

The restaurant was on a main road in the centre of Kandahar City. The facade of the building looked too rundown for me to imagine that it was a place that served food. I was wearing my headscarf, as I always did on these trips, and we hustled in, trying to be as inconspicuous as possible. Our Afghan fixers spoke to the managers and we were led into a small room at the back of the restaurant, empty except for pillows scattered throughout. Two waiters spread a tablecloth on the floor, and we sat down against the pillows. They brought us yogurt drinks and distributed a flat of bread for each of us, along with many dishes: radishes and peppers, a spicy and saucy meat stew, and rice. The stew was served on the bread. It was so delicious—the sauce subtly flavoured and the meat tender. Any concerns I had about cleanliness or getting sick soon disappeared.

Then the lights went out and my heart stopped. What the hell was going on? Nobody said a word, but we were all thinking the same thing, conscious—as always—that we were foreigners out in a city that wasn't safe. Just as suddenly as the lights had gone out, they came back on. I looked at Paul. He looked at me. Al continued to eat. It was just a brownout, typical in this part of the world, and especially this country, but for a few seconds, my heart had skipped a few beats.

Now, I was eating bread in virtual darkness again, except this time I had no stew to dip it in, and no friends to share it with. I felt trapped. This was not a restaurant in Kandahar. It was a cell. A hole in the ground. And I was a hostage.

I took a sip of juice and chewed on the bread. The arms of the alarm clock showed that it was just after seven. It would be another long night, and I wasn't sure—again—how we'd pass the time.

Shafirgullah had a solution. He reached into the bottom of the plastic bag and pulled out a book. He handed it to me. It was a school textbook, probably used to teach English to young Afghans in school.

I flipped through the pages and saw they were filled with short stories, followed by questions about the stories. An example: Salim and Abdul went to the store together on a sunny morning. They wanted to buy some ice cream. Salim wanted to have chocolate and Abdul decided on strawberry. They paid the store clerk ten afghanis and left to go home.

The questions that followed were along the lines of "What did Salim and Abdul want to buy?" "What kind of ice cream did Salim buy?" "What kind of ice cream did Abdul have?" "How much did they pay the clerk?"

There were about two dozen of these exercises in the book, and I read through them all in half an hour and handed it back to

Shafirgullah. He opened it and started reading out loud, pointing at words he didn't know how to pronounce. I was pretty sure he didn't know most of the words, or had no idea at all what they meant. After several words, he grew frustrated and pulled another book out of the bag. It was an English–Farsi phrase book.

"This is not Pashto," I said to Shafirgullah.

"No, Farsi," he replied. "Me, Pashto." I took that to mean that Pashto was his first language and that he had a limited knowledge of the other.

I was right. As he started reading phrases, he stumbled on many of the Farsi phrases, almost as much as he had stumbled on the English ones. But this was good. This was a way we could communicate.

"You are my friend," he read from the book. I pointed to the Farsi translation, and he read it out to me. I repeated the phrase.

We went on for a while longer, reading phrases out of the book—"I am hungry." "What is the time?" "I am angry." "Where do you live?"

We barely noticed that the flame in the kerosene lamp was fading until Shafirgullah started to cough. The smoke from the lamp was bothering him, and he removed the wooden door to allow the fumes to escape up the shaft.

"You sleep?" he asked. I looked at the clock and saw that it was close to nine. We had whiled away three hours with the books. That was good. But I wasn't sleepy yet, so I shook my head no.

"Cigarette?" he offered as he lit one for himself.

"*Tashakor*," I said, thanking him in Pashto. I don't know where I got the idea that smoking would help pass the time. A cigarette takes about five or ten minutes to smoke, depending on how many drags you take of it, so it's not as though it helps pass *that much* time. We finished and flicked our cigarette butts out to the tunnel.

"Me sleep," Shafirgullah announced.

"Good night," I said to him, glad to be left alone again. I picked up my notepad.

Hi darling,

I was thinking about our last meal in Kandahar City today. Do you remember the little room and the lights going out? I wish we were back there again. I almost wished today I hadn't come to Kabul, that I had just stayed at KAF and done some stories out of the PRT and the city. But we both know why I wanted to come. This was an important story I was working on, the refugees. And it's one I haven't seen in the media back home. My captors are treating me well, for the most part. I'm just so tired of being here, and I feel horrible about the pain and suffering I'm causing you and everyone at home.

Shafirgullah is spending a second night in the hole alone. We passed the time by reading phrases out of an English–Farsi phrase book and smoking cigarettes. I've been so good about the smoking since last summer, but there's not much else to do in here. I shudder at the thought of what all the smoke and dust, and kerosene fumes—is doing to my system, but I have no options.

I just hope you know that I'm okay. I know you must be so afraid for me, but I need you to know that I'm not afraid. I don't think these guys want to hurt me at all. I just think they're a bunch of young thugs with guns and a messed-up idea of Islam and the West. I'm not afraid of them, and you shouldn't be either. They're not bad people. They just don't understand tolerance, and probably never had a chance to learn when they were young.

I looked over at the sleeping Shafirgullah and tried to imagine him as a little boy. Did he grow up poor? Did he and Abdullah go to school? I imagined they were like the orphans I had met the year before in Kabul at a state orphanage for boys; girls were housed in a separate orphanage, which I visited later. Many of them had lost their parents in the war, and their prospects for the future were seriously limited. They slept in bunk beds in a dark and dirty building, twelve or more to a room. During the day they went to classes. The younger ones learned how to read and write, and the older ones learned a trade. The government official in charge of orphans told me they had to make sure children were given as many opportunities as possible because it was too easy for the Taliban to recruit young men, especially those who felt they didn't fit into society. I saw a young boy, maybe six or seven years old, his face scarred with burns that he'd suffered as a baby. I watched as he hung around the playground alone and tried to ignore the taunts of the older boys. I asked him his name. Sediq. He told me that his parents died because of warlords and that he missed them so much. He was happy to be in the orphanage because he was fed and given clothes, but he had no friends and he was lonely.

I couldn't forget the emptiness and despair I saw in his eyes. I could still see his sad, scarred face even now. He was exactly the kind of boy the Taliban would try to recruit. The director of the orphanage said as much. And he was one of so many in Afghanistan. I'd left the orphanage that day feeling utterly helpless. I could tell Sediq's story to the world, but who was listening? And even if people listened, what could they do to help him?

Maybe Shafirgullah and his brother grew up like Sediq. Maybe they grew up in an orphanage; maybe they were abandoned by their parents. They probably had a little schooling, since they could speak a bit of English, but I imagined they were probably young boys without a stable family life and without much to keep them occupied, trying to navigate their way in a country torn apart by decades of war. Why wouldn't they fall prey to criminal gangs and terrorist groups like the Taliban? That's where they could find a sense of community, a sense of belonging. It seemed perfectly reasonable to me, but it also left me feeling quite depressed to think that my kidnappers really had no choice. Why go to school when you can make hundreds of thousands of American dollars kidnapping foreigners? For young men who don't have much of an opportunity to succeed in the way we Westerners typically think of success—a steady job, good income, roof over your head, food on the table—criminal activity is often the only viable option.

It's like asking the Afghan farmer to plant pomegranate trees instead of poppies because stopping the heroin trade is how we in the West believe we can win against the Taliban. But for that poppy farmer, harvesting a pomegranate crop might yield only a fraction of the money he could get for a poppy crop. It might be wrong, and the farmer might even know that drug money is being used to fund the Taliban's activities, but at the end of the day, he's got a family to feed.

There are no excuses, P, for what the kidnappers have taken from me. My freedom. But all I can do is try to understand why they do this. It's not right, but it's their world, and all we can do is try to understand.

Night, night, darling. I hope that wherever you are, you're getting more sleep than I am. Love you. xox

I put the pen down and tucked myself back inside my blanket. It was so uncomfortable, and I could feel now that the ground was quite cold. I reached inside my pocket for my rosary and prayed.

Shafirgullah kicked me in the leg as he turned in his sleep. It was a hard jab, and it startled me. I sat up and looked at the clock. Six in the morning. *Damn,* I thought, *why couldn't you give me another hour of sleep? Another hour of unconsciousness, another hour of escape from this hole.*

The morning passed as it had the day before. The young Afghan woke up and did his ablutions and prayed for half an hour, then ate an entire package of cookies, washed down with two pouches of juice. I noticed there were only two left.

My stomach was hurting a bit, and I huddled myself into a fetal position, turning my back to Shafirgullah. I stared at the wall, hoping the feeling would pass. It did, but came back in waves throughout the morning.

"You okay?" Even my kidnapper knew something was wrong. I shook my head and rubbed my stomach in an attempt to tell him I wasn't feeling so good. "Ah," he said, looking concerned. He offered me juice, which I refused, and some cookies, which were the last thing I wanted. He also asked if I wanted to play the snake game again. I took his phone and distracted myself for a few minutes, until even the game got too boring. As soon as I gave it back to him, he put the SIM card in and made a call. The conversation was in Pashto, but I didn't even have to guess whom he was speaking with.

"Khalid still in Kabul?" I asked.

"Khalid no Kabul," he answered. He pointed his finger down. "Khalid come."

I was about to ask when, but my tummy rumbled with another wave of discomfort. I wondered what I would do if it got worse, and reached for my knapsack. I always carried pain medication because I'm plagued with migraines, so I have a constant supply of Tylenol, Advil, and beta blockers. I fished around. Fuck. They were all sitting in my toiletries bag back at the Serena Hotel. I looked into the side pockets, hoping to find something. My hand wrapped itself around a pill bottle. Cipro. Yes! It was supposedly the cure-all for anything that might come along, including a poison gas attack. I had brought it to Afghanistan the year before, thinking that I would need it if I drank bad water or ate bad food. And I'd been warned by my colleagues that the bad food would more likely come from inside the military base than out in the cities. I hadn't needed it, but I remembered doling out a few pills to my friend

Don Martin, who was there for the *National Post* before he left on what would end up being a very long trip off the base.

I opened the bottle and saw that there were five big white pills left. I bit one in two, then swallowed a half with a chug of cherry juice. The syrupy sweetness of the juice didn't stand a chance against the bitter pill. I gagged but got it down, the horrible taste spreading through my mouth and down my throat. I took another swig of juice and swished it around my mouth to wash out the bitterness. And then I waited for the ciprofloxacin to do its thing.

I must have dozed off again because I woke up to Shafirgullah poking my leg and pointing to the ceiling. It was about two in the afternoon, and I could hear footsteps and digging overhead.

"What's happening?" I asked.

"Khalid," he replied.

"Why is Khalid coming now?"

Shafirgullah covered his head with his kaffiyeh and I did the same, as again the dirt came down all around us. Soon, the sound of digging faded and I could hear the sound of a board being dragged away. Then a *thump*, and a figure dressed in black crawled down the tunnel.

"Hello, Me-llis-si-a." He was back to pronouncing my name with four syllables.

"Khalid, salaam," I replied. "Why are you here now?"

"I say I come today. I bring you blanket," he said. I noticed he was dragging behind him a thick baby blue duvet. It was big and fluffy and warm and I thanked him. Shafirgullah lifted my other blanket and my red pillow and shook off the dust. I folded the new blue blanket in half and set it down on my half of the hole, like a sleeping bag.

"It is good, yes?" Khalid asked.

"Yes, thank you."

"How are you, Me-llis-si-a?"

"I am okay. I would be better if I could go back to Kabul."

"Yes, inshallah, you will go."

"When?"

"It take . . . time. Three, maybe four days."

My heart sank at the thought of spending even another hour in the hole.

Khalid looked around the hole, then peered into the plastic bag. "You not eating, they tell me."

I shook my head and argued that I had actually eaten lots of cookies and drunk lots of juice.

"Shafirgullah say you sick," he said accusingly. I admitted that I'd had a little bit of a stomach upset but assured him I was okay.

He nodded. "If you not sick, we go out."

"Out?" I asked, pointing up to the ceiling. Khalid nodded again, and I looked over at Shafirgullah, who was nodding and smiling. I wasn't sure what to think. Maybe I was being moved to another location. Maybe they had fixed up the other house—the one from the first night—and that would be my new cell. It was a lot bigger and a lot more comfortable, and at least I wouldn't be in semi-darkness all the time. I looked up the tunnel and could tell from the light cast at the end of the shaft that the sun was shining outside. Khalid told me to take off my scarf, which was loosely draped over my shoulders. I removed it and handed it to him.

"I am cover your eyes," he told me, folding the scarf in half lengthwise and wrapping it around my head like a blindfold. Instinctively, I reached to pull the scarf from my eyes, but Khalid held my hand.

"No," he said. "You take off later. Come now." He led me by the arm to the entrance of the hole and gave me a gentle push. I heard the rustle of feet scampering ahead of me. I assumed it was Shafirgullah.

"Go up," Khalid said. I blindly crawled up the tunnel until the top of my head no longer hit the ceiling and I knew I was in the shaft.

"Stand up," Khalid ordered from behind me. I stood and was wondering how I was going to climb to the top when I felt the Afghan lift me up from the bottom of my legs. Two sets of hands reached down and grabbed me under my arms. I was lifted out and set down on the ground.

"Wait," came Khalid's voice from below. I heard him drag himself out of the shaft and felt him take me by the elbow. "Come, quickly."

We were walking forward, not off to the side, as I thought we would if we were going back to the abandoned house. I guessed that we were going to the other house that I'd seen, the one about fifty feet from the hole. I tripped as we went down some stairs, and Khalid steadied me, whisking me through what I assumed was the door to a house, around a corner, and through a hallway, until we stopped and he sat me down on what must have been a ledge.

"Turn around," he said. I followed his instructions, turning my head to face him so he could remove the scarf. We were in a large room with a window. My back was to the window and I was staring at a wall covered with peeling yellow paint and riddled with bullet holes. The cement floor was covered in dirt. A piece of scrap metal lay in the corner.

"Where are we?" I asked.

"Shafirgullah house," Khalid answered. He was sitting next to me on the ledge. I turned around to look out the window.

"Do not look," he ordered. I realized he didn't want me to see anything about where we were, which I hoped was a sign that I might be released soon. My kidnappers wouldn't want me to tell the authorities about any landmarks, whether they were mountains or a house or some trees, that would allow them to find this location.

"This is a nice room," I told him. "Why can't I stay here?"

"It is not safe," he said.

"It looks very safe to me." I could hear the roar of jets overhead, and I wondered where the closest military base was. I assumed it was Bagram, as we couldn't be too far from Kabul.

"Americans," Khalid said, referring to the sound of the jet engines. "Police come here. They have guns. You see?" He pointed to the bullet holes in the wall. "Not safe for us."

Shafirgullah appeared in the doorway and said something to Khalid in Pashto. He was followed by another man dressed in a white kameez and matching pants, and wearing a white skullcap. Looking closely, I realized he was the one with the lazy eye who had come down to the hole with the others on the second night.

"Stay here, don't look out," Khalid ordered and followed the others out, leaving me sitting alone in the empty room.

As soon as he left, I turned around and looked out the window. I could see two large hills, or mountains, on either side of the house. The sky was cobalt blue and cloudless, and I could feel the heat of the sun. Khalid was outside having a cigarette and speaking on the phone. I walked to the doorway and saw that there was a hall leading into another room in the obviously abandoned house.

Shafirgullah must have seen me, for he came back in, his eyes flashing.

"No!" he said angrily, and I took that to mean that he wanted me to sit back down on the ledge. I obliged, and he left the room again. I sat in the room alone for what felt like the better part of an hour. Shafirgullah was praying out in the hallway, and I could hear other voices coming both from within the house and outside. I walked around the room a bit, glad for the chance to exercise my legs.

Khalid came back and told me it was time to go.

"Where are we going?" I asked.

"Back," he replied, taking my scarf and blindfolding me again. He led me out of the house the same way he had led me in. I could hear voices. We had walked a few steps when suddenly Khalid pushed my shoulder down. "Sit down," he said.

"What?" I asked.

"Sit down! Do not move!"

I dropped to my knees and sat quietly. I couldn't sense anyone next to me, so I wasn't sure what was going on. I heard the sound of a jet engine in the distance. Perhaps they didn't want to be spotted and that's why we had stopped moving. A few minutes later, I felt a hand on my elbow.

"Stand up," Khalid ordered. I did, and he led me back—I assumed—to the entrance of the hole. I could hear digging and then felt myself being lifted and dropped. I tried to brace myself, but I landed on my ankles. A sharp pain shot through both of them. I shoved my headscarf off my eyes and looked up.

"Go!" Khalid shouted from above. "Go!" I crawled back through the tunnel and into the room. I shook off the dust from my clothes and sat back down on my new duvet. I looked at the clock—it was just after four in the afternoon. I could hear the Afghans speaking to each other above me, and I lit another cigarette as I waited.

Thump.

The shuffle of shoes, and soon Khalid's black kameez appeared in the doorway. He took off his faded black leather shoes and placed them carefully by the entrance, then brushed the dust from his clothes. I realized they had all been fastidious about removing their shoes. He rearranged his black skullcap on his head and sat down, staring at me with his wide-set eyes.

"You stay tonight?" I asked.

"I stay."

"Good."

Another *thump*, more shuffling, and Shafirgullah appeared with two white plastic bags: cookies, juice, cigarettes. He ripped open the package of smokes and offered them to me and Khalid. We each took one, and Khalid lit them with a lighter he fished out of his breast pocket. Inhale, exhale. Blue smoke filled the small cave, and I felt a head rush with each puff.

We finished our cigarettes, and Shafirgullah scampered up the tunnel and out of the shaft. The digging started again and dust rained down over everything.

Shafirgullah shouted down to Khalid, and then he—and the others—were gone. Khalid reached over and dusted off the duvet. Then he took my hand and placed it between his big palms.

"How are you, Me-liss-si-a?"

"How do you think I am?"

"You not happy."

"Of course not. You've taken me away from everything. My family, my friends, my life. You have taken everything from me. How can I be happy?" My voice was cracking. I didn't want him to see me cry, so I pulled my hand away from his and turned to face the wall. He didn't seem to know what to do. He put his hand on my shoulder and tried to tell me it would be okay, but I wasn't listening. He patted my back and kept telling me I would soon go back to Kabul.

"But I need to go back now!" I could hear myself almost yelling, but I felt almost as though I was out of my body, a spectator to this drama. "I have a family! I have a job! I need to go back to them! You don't know what you're doing to me!"

He turned my head to face him and stared me directly in the eye.

"Don't cry, Me-liss-si-a," he said.

"Mellissa," I finally corrected him.

"Don't cry."

"I want to go back to Kabul. Khalid. Please. You have to help me. You said I am your sister. You have to help me get back to Kabul. You're the only one who can help me. You have to talk to your father and tell him I need to go back." I was pleading with him, but I didn't care. He might be the only chance I had to make this nightmare end sooner than later. And he seemed sympathetic. He looked into my eyes and wiped away a tear I didn't even know was there.

"I am sorry for you, Mellissa. I am sorry you are not happy."

"Then please help me. Please, Khalid. You're the only person who can help me. You took me; you must help me get out. Please."

He nodded and readjusted his skullcap. "I will talk to my father."

"Talk to him now. Please call him. Now. I can't stay here any longer. Please."

Khalid shook his head. "I call tomorrow."

"Call him now. Please. Call him now."

"Tomorrow," he replied as he reached into his breast pocket for his cell phone.

I sat back dejected, as if all the energy had suddenly been sucked out of me. I picked up my notebook and began to write, seeing out of the corner of my eye that Khalid was punching in numbers on his phone. A loud voice, which I thought I recognized as his father's, came through the receiver. Khalid's voice dropped, sounding more apologetic, with none of the authority I'd come to expect from him as the leader of my motley gang of kidnappers. They spoke for a few minutes, and then Khalid hung up the phone.

"Was that your father?" I asked. "What did he say?"

"He say your friend must call him. They fix money and then you go."

"Give me his phone number and let me call my friend," I asked.

"No, I call."

"When?"

"Tomorrow. I not call from here. I call tomorrow, when I will go to Kabul."

"You're going to Kabul tomorrow?"

He nodded.

"For how long?"

"One day maybe. Maybe I come back Friday."

I had more questions. He told me he would take his motorcycle there and that he always stayed with his sister's husband, who had a small room somewhere in the city. His sister was in Pakistan with the rest of the family.

"What does her husband do?" I asked.

"He is Taliban."

"Is he really Taliban or like your type of Taliban?" I asked. I was curious how he saw himself.

"He is Taliban." Khalid made a gun with his hands. "He kill people for Taliban."

I must have looked a bit skeptical, so he went on to tell me about the time his brother-in-law got into a gunfight with some American soldiers and killed three of them, even though he was shot in the shoulder himself.

"He killed three soldiers?" I didn't believe him. "Where did this happen?"

"Ghazni. You know Ghazni." I nodded. Ghazni was just southwest of Kabul, a province away from the country's capital. But I still didn't believe him. It seemed highly unlikely that a Taliban fighter, even a true Taliban, could get away alive after shooting and killing three American soldiers.

"Why you going to Kabul?" I asked.

"I have work."

"What kind of work?" I imagined that he might be heading back to the refugee camp he had taken me from, trolling for someone else to steal. Khalid smiled at me as if trying to tell me that I didn't want to, or need to, know. It felt a little sinister to me, but it stirred my curiosity.

"You want to take someone else." It was more of an accusation than a question. He kept smiling, and I knew he wasn't going to tell me. I gave up and reached for the package of cigarettes.

We spent the night talking, not turning out the lamp until well after midnight, according to the alarm clock.

Khalid seemed especially happy to be able to speak openly about his girlfriend of six months, Shogufa, who was in fact his first cousin on his mother's side. He talked about going to her house all the time, and how she made the best bread and fried potatoes. She had long dark hair and brown eyes. She lived with her parents, and her mother was Khalid's aunt. His mother's younger sister, he told me. She was fifteen, maybe sixteen, but he wasn't sure.

"She is very *shayesta*," he told me. "Like you."

"*Shayesta?*" I repeated. Again, my Pashto was failing me.

"*Shayesta*—very pretty," he said again.

I asked if he had a picture of the very *shayesta* Shogufa, and he promised to bring me one.

"Does she know what you do?" I asked.

He looked at me and seemed to be thinking. "She know little, little," he said after a long pause.

"She knows you take people and keep them in places like this?"

He nodded. "A little."

"And what does she think? Does she know about me?"

Khalid looked down and cracked his knuckles. All ten of them, and then he cracked his toes. And then his neck.

"Did you tell her you took me?"

He nodded.

"And? What does she say?"

"She no happy." He lit a cigarette and offered me one. I took it and he held the lighter out. I took a long drag and we finished our smokes in silence.

Khalid blew out the lamp. "Sleep coming to me," he told me and he stretched his long body out next to me. His dirty feet were too close to my pillow for my liking.

I turned to face the wall and took out my rosary, fingering each bead and praying silently until I fell asleep.

I woke up the next morning with a kink in my neck. I reached for the lighter and lit the lamp. I glanced at the clock. It was way too early, and I was angry at myself for not being able to sleep more. Even another hour would have helped me get through the day faster. Another hour of escape. I lit a cigarette and inhaled it in a few long puffs before opening my notebook.

Dearest P,

Another morning, and another day in this hole. I'm holding up fine, but smoking a lot. Between the cigarettes and the dust, I'll be lucky if I can get out of here without some horrible respiratory disease.

Khalid stayed last night. He's interesting. I think he feels responsible for taking me, and responsible that this isn't being resolved as quickly as he told me. He's really not a bad person. We talked about his girlfriend all night—he's really in love! I mean, as in love as an eighteen-year-old kid can be, but it made the time go by. More than anything, I just miss talking to people. You, and my friends, and not having my BlackBerry or my phone is a really odd feeling. To be so disconnected from the world, from you, and from everyone I love. I'll feel even more cut off when Shafirgullah comes back tonight. At least with Khalid here, there's someone to talk to.

I've said this before, darling, but try not to worry about me. I'm fine. Really. I'll get out of here soon enough.

Good morning, P. I hope that wherever you are, you're having a good hot cup of tea and a croissant—or two. One for me. I miss you so much. Do you know?

xox

Khalid slept for twelve hours, not waking up until about noon. I can't remember the last time I slept that late, not even when I was hungover, which didn't happen often. When he got up, he told me to turn around while he crawled up to the entrance of the hole and relieved himself into the water bottle.

After opening another sleeve of cookies and drinking three boxes of juice in a row, he grew talkative again. I decided to pick up where we had left off last night.

"When can I meet Shogufa?" I asked.

He laughed. "She want to see you. I say no. She no happy."

"Of course she's not happy. How would you feel if someone had taken her? And put her in a place like this?" I gestured around the hole. "This is no place for her, or me, or anyone. Especially a woman."

"She want to see you," he said. "I no let her."

"I would like to meet her too," I said, even though I knew that would never happen. It would be a disaster for Khalid to have his girlfriend see exactly what he does. I imagined she was a typical Afghan girl, like so many I had met in this poorest of war-torn countries: big eyes and a shy smile, half hidden under a headscarf until she married, and then put into a burka, where she would remain hidden from the world for the rest of her life.

I thought of the young girl I'd met just a few weeks before in Kandahar, outside the gates of the camp where the Canadian Provincial Reconstruction Team was based. The PRT was where the military and the civilian components of the country's mission in Afghanistan met. More than twenty-five PRTs were set up throughout the country to provide services to the Afghan people. It was where officials and staff from other government departments and agencies were based—sort of an outreach outpost—and where they could deal directly with Afghans who needed help. It was the centre of Canada's civilian–military cooperation program, providing assistance to the Afghan people while fighting a war in their country.

We were at the PRT early one morning because it was Eid, the celebration of the end of the month of Ramadan, and the Canadian military was giving out gifts to families in Kandahar: jugs of cooking oil, bags of rice and sugar and flour, tea, and scarves for women—an Eid package that would feed many of them for the weeks to come. We were told in advance that the handout was by invitation, that only a few hundred families had been invited to come to the PRT that day to receive gifts, families that had been identified by outreach workers in the weeks before.

We arrived early, and the front gate of the compound was already swarmed by a sea of humanity: women, children, all without invitations, all clamouring to get in. Word had spread that the Canadians were handing out food, and it seemed that everyone in Kandahar wanted—needed—something. There were women with children on their backs, and many older children just standing on the street and tugging at the sleeve of every foreigner who walked by. I felt a pull on my headscarf and turned around. A little girl, maybe five or six years old, in a pink headscarf—stared back at me. She had big deep brown eyes and a wide smile. As I took a picture of her, she turned away. Shy, I thought, but then she looked up at me again. I took another picture, and she reached out to look at the screen. I showed her the picture. She beamed and grabbed the camera to show her friends.

Soon I was surrounded by a group of girls. I took pictures of all of them and turned the camera over to show them. The little girl in the pink scarf clung to my side. An older boy joined the group. His name was Zhalil, he told me. He spoke pretty good English and was able to act as my translator.

I turned on my recorder and held the microphone to his mouth.

They wanted food, he told me. They wanted to know if I could help them get through the gates of the compound. They knew that food was being given out and had been sent by their parents. The little girl in the scarf said she had an older brother who was in a wheelchair, his leg blown off in a bomb. The boy pointed, and I saw a young man, a teenager, in a wooden wheelchair.

"That's her brother?" I asked. The girl nodded and tugged at my sleeve again.

Just then, two women in dirty blue burkas came rushing toward me, pointing their fingers at the gate and yelling something in Pashto.

"They say it's not fair that only the rich people, friends of Afghans who work here, got chosen to receive gifts," my young translator told me. The women continued to yell and point, standing so close to me that I had to step back with the microphone or the sound would be too loud, too hot, to use in editing.

Now a third woman came up to me. I could see through the screen of her burka that she was crying. She grabbed my arm and said something in Pashto.

Zhalil translated. "My son is sick and he is dying in the hospital. Please can you help me get through the gate?"

I felt helpless. "Tell her I'm sorry, there's nothing I can do." Zhalil translated, but she only tightened her grip on my arm and continued talking. Her husband was dead, she said, and there were no other men at home. She wanted me to help her.

"We have to go!" It was an Afghan soldier posted at the gate. "Now!"

We'd been out there for only about half an hour. I could see Paul and his cameraman, Al, a few feet away—Paul was shooting an on-camera. But we all knew that it was not safe to be outside like that for any length of time. We were an easy target for a suicide bomber, or kidnappers.

"We have to go!" the soldier repeated. The little girl was still clinging to my side, her grip on my shirt sleeve tightening. I asked Zhalil to explain to her that I had to go.

She looked up at me with pleading eyes and clung to me with both hands. Zhalil had to peel her off. She started to cry. I wanted so much to pick her up and take her with me. But I knew I couldn't. And before I knew it, I was being ushered through the gate, and she was lost in the crowd.

"You can't save them all," Paul told me later that day when we were back at the base. "She'll be married off in a few years, and put in a burka."

"I don't want to save them all," I said. "Just her."

I asked Khalid if Shogufa wore a burka. He said no, because she was still a girl. She would start wearing a burka, he told me, after they got married.

"When is that?" I asked. He shrugged. Maybe in a year. Or two.

"Are you sure she wants to marry you?" I raised my eyebrow at him and he laughed.

"Yes! We are in love!"

It was so unusual to hear an Afghan man speak openly about love and feelings, and I realized quickly that it was because these subjects are so often taboo among Afghans themselves. Islam, at least in this part of the world, dictates a kind of discretion when it comes to talking about men and women and relationships. With me, Khalid probably felt safe talking about affairs of the heart, so I found myself in the odd position of being a new-found confidante to my captor.

He was full of questions. Was it okay to kiss her when other people were around? How was he going to tell his father about this relationship? Should he just let his mother speak to him? What if his father didn't approve?

"It's your life," I told him. "It doesn't matter if he doesn't approve. You have to do what's right for you."

"But I am afraid from him," he kept saying.

"You're afraid *of* him," I corrected. "He's running your life. You do everything he tells you to do. He can't tell you not to fall in love with someone. Love is something you can't control."

Khalid nodded. Yes, he told me, it was something he couldn't control. He loved Shogufa and he wanted to marry her, and it was as simple as that. His mother was supportive, he told me, so maybe she could speak to his father. His father liked Shogufa, he was certain, but he just wasn't sure if he'd approve of them getting married so soon.

"It *is* soon," I told him. "You're young to get married." But I knew that in developing countries like Afghanistan, people get married very young, and have their children very young; indeed, the average life expectancy in this cruel and underdeveloped part of the world is about thirty years shorter than in North America. Even though they were much younger than me, I would outlive Khalid and his young bride by many years.

But then he surprised me.

"We get married; then I will die."

"What are you talking about?" I asked.

"I die. I bomb." He made a motion of putting something around his waist, and I knew instantly what he was talking about.

"You want to be a suicide bomber."

"Yes. My father say."

I wanted to understand why he would want to get married, then blow himself up, so I pressed for answers. Why would you do that to Shogufa? Don't you know there are many innocent Afghans who would die in a suicide bombing? What do you think you might accomplish?

"I die. I go *jannat*."

"What do you think is in *jannat*?"

"There, I have girlfriends."

"But what about Shogufa?"

"Shogufa my wife, but I will have girlfriends in *jannat*."

"I'm not sure Shogufa would like that very much. I don't know of any woman who thinks it's okay for her husband to have girl-friends."

My arguments fell on deaf ears. Khalid said she would under-stand and that, in fact, she also wanted to be a suicide bomber because then they could die together. Their parents would look after their children if they had any. They planned to do this in a year or two. They'd be martyrs and go to *jannat* together.

I wasn't really surprised that Shogufa would say that, make that kind of marriage vow. The majority of suicide bombers are still male, but an increasing number of women have been willing to suit up to kill—in Chechnya, Lebanon, Iraq, and recently Afghan-istan. Many follow their husbands, who espouse fundamentalist ideologies; others seek revenge and are ripe targets for extremists. I'd always thought that was an interesting subject—the mentality of the female suicide bomber.

Shogufa isn't going to blow herself up, I told Khalid, just so she can go to *jannat* and watch you parade around with a bevy of girlfriends.

He laughed. "She love me. She is my wife."

"So you die together," I said, "and what have you accomplished? You might kill a lot of people, but what good is that if you're killing other Afghans and not foreigners?"

He told me that his father wanted to have a son who was a martyr. "He would be proud if I die as a suicide bomber. You watch. You will hear of something . . . big . . . you know it is me, going to *jannat*."

I wasn't sure if any father could accept his child dying like that, for no reason. I thought about my own father and imagined he might be thinking the same thing right about now. He would be angry that I had put myself in this situation, causing so much trouble to so many people, when he had spent most of his life being very cautious, after having risked everything to move his young family to a foreign country where he barely knew the language.

My father is the most risk-averse person I know. Don't run before you can walk; take everything slowly and safely—that was his constant advice to me. I was, of course, the opposite, always in a hurry to do everything, with no patience to wait. The first time I told my parents I was going to Afghanistan, the summer before, I could sense over the phone my dad's unease. He wouldn't tell me not to, but I could tell it was the last place on earth he wanted his daughter to go. It's an important story, I told him. Canadian soldiers are dying there, and Afghans are suffering, and that's why reporters need to be there. To tell those stories and help people at home understand why it's happening.

I think my parents, like those in most immigrant Asian families I knew, still wished I had been a doctor or a lawyer. Journalists, in their culture, are considered bottom-feeders, a step above used-car salespeople. Yet, I had grown up watching the news because it was all my parents watched when I was little. They were news junkies, and we grew up extremely well informed about the world around us. As new Canadians, it was important for them to make sure we knew what was happening in our community, our country, and around the world. I remember the federal election in 1980, when Pierre Trudeau regained office. There was an all-candidates meeting at my elementary school, and after the debate, the local candidates for our riding took questions from the audience, and I was the first one to stick up my hand. My question was about immigration policy, and I wanted to know where each of the parties stood and what they would change. I think I was seven years old at the time.

In recent years, I think my dad had finally come around to understanding that journalism was like a calling for me. They've followed my career closely, from the early days when I was doing godawful live reports for a local station in Vancouver to covering the Olympic Games in Beijing for my network. It took a while, but I think he was finally proud to be able to tell people I was a journalist.

I couldn't imagine what he was thinking now. Khalid seemed to read my mind.

"Your father," he asked, "where he is?"

"In Canada, and probably worried sick about me. You have to let me go, Khalid. It's not fair to my parents. They will be sick wondering where I am. Imagine if Shogufa was taken, how would your aunt and uncle feel? How would you feel?"

He calmly told me that if Shogufa was kidnapped, he would find her captors and break each of their necks with his bare hands. He cracked his knuckles as if to underline the point.

"Why do you do that?" I asked.

Khalid answered by taking my left hand and pulling on each finger until the knuckle cracked.

"Ow," I protested. He ignored me and reached for my other

hand. Pull, *crack*, pull, *crack*. My scab cracked open a bit and pus oozed out. I instinctively reached to touch the scab on my shoulder. I could still feel the toilet paper used to staunch the blood. I craned my neck to look at the wound. It had turned black and was about the size of a golf ball.

"You like?" Khalid asked after he had cracked all ten of my knuckles.

I shrugged, and he pointed at my feet.

"No," I said, shaking my head to underline *my* point. I hadn't taken off my socks since I was dropped in the hole—though I had finally taken off my shoes—and I had no intention of finding out what condition my feet were in. My white socks were now a light shade of brown. It had been three, four days without a shower and I knew I was really starting to smell. Especially after having to wear the filthy clothes they gave me on the first day. My stomach began to turn at the memory of the smell. I lit a cigarette and puffed away, blowing the smoke into a stream toward the entrance.

"You smoke too much," Khalid told me. "It is bad. You shouldn't smoke so much."

"You're the one who's giving them to me, and what else is there to do in here?"

"You writing. Give me the book." He reached for my notebook. I handed it over, certain he wouldn't be able to read much of what I'd written. He flipped through the pages, stopping at my notes from the stories I'd done in the previous weeks.

"What is this?" He pointed at a name and a number. It was Isabelle, my contact at the Canadian embassy in Kabul. I told him it was a friend and watched as he copied the number onto his palm. I hoped to God he wouldn't call it. I couldn't imagine poor Isabelle, who was probably already worried sick about me after I didn't show up at the embassy for Thanksgiving dinner, having to answer a call from Khalid or his father. He flipped through a few more pages, pointing and asking what things were. His finger fell on the name of the last refugee I had interviewed at the camp.

"What is this?"

"Some man at the refugee camp. He has nothing to do with anything, just a poor man from Helmand province who had to move his family to Kabul to escape the fighting."

I had spent my last few minutes at the camp with him and his family. He had eight children, three daughters who were about the age of the little girl in the pink scarf, four sons who were older, and a baby boy who might have been about a year old. They had left Helmand after a rocket destroyed their home. The man said he had a business there, but he was afraid it had been taken over by the Taliban. They lived in two small mud houses in the camp, lots of room compared to other refugees there but hardly enough for such a big family. The children were laughing and chasing each other outside, and I had taken lots of pictures of the family, with the intention of writing a story on them for the network's website.

Just before we left, the man, like the cobbler we'd met earlier, insisted on making us tea, a traditional Afghan symbol of hospitality, even in a refugee camp where people have nothing. I was loath to drink his tea, since the family could barely afford to feed itself, but he insisted, pushing a glass of the hot, sweet liquid into my hands. He had a cell phone, which astonished me. We exchanged numbers, and Shokoor and I made our way back to the car.

I didn't think of it until then, but suddenly it dawned on me that perhaps this man was connected to my kidnappers. Maybe he called Khalid and told him where I was. Maybe he was a Taliban sympathizer. Maybe he was the one who had given me away.

"Do you know this man?" I asked my captor. "Khalid, you know him, don't you?"

The tall Afghan turned to me and stared directly into my eyes. He stroked his goatee and shook his head. "I do not know."

"You're lying," I said in a stroke of anger. "This man told you I was at the refugee camp. He called you and then you drove in to take me. That's the truth, isn't it?"

Khalid shook his head emphatically. "It is not, Mellissa."

"Then how did you know I was there? Why did you take me? Someone told you I was at the camp, didn't they?"

Khalid sighed and shook his head again. He and his friends knew that the camp was a place where foreigners often visited, he told me. This was not a surprise to me. There were always UN staff going in and out, just like the group we had encountered when we first arrived there. The gang of kidnappers was out looking for someone to take. The men didn't know who would be there, just that it was a good place to kidnap a foreigner, because the refugees are powerless to help and there are few police nearby. It was also on the outskirts of Kabul, making a getaway much easier.

"We see you. We think first you Hazara. But then we think police coming. So we take you."

The Hazaras are an ethnic minority in Afghanistan, and it wasn't the first time someone mistook me for one. Their origins aren't clear, but it's generally believed that they are related to the Mongolians. Their features are Eurasian, and they look almost like the Tibetans or Uighurs of central and western China. The Hazaras suffered extreme oppression under the Taliban and, in fact, were targeted for ethnic cleansing. Their position improved greatly after the Taliban were forced from power. I'd seen Hazaras working on the base in Kandahar and, because of my own small stature, some of the soldiers with whom I'd gone out on missions used to joke that they were taking along their "little Hazara."

I'd actually believed, perhaps naively, that it would help me blend in with my surroundings and maybe protect me a bit from threats like Khalid and his gang of kidnappers. How wrong could I have been?

"You really thought I was Hazara?" I wanted to know.

Khalid nodded.

"So why did you take me anyway? You know a Hazara probably couldn't afford to pay you."

"Yes, but we had to be fast. Police coming. So we take you."

"And aren't you lucky that I'm not a Hazara." My sarcasm was lost on him.

"First, we think you China," he said, shaking his head. "Bad. They no money." I looked at him quizzically, and he explained that there were Chinese workers not far away, building a road. Another group had kidnapped a couple of them, but no one would pay a ransom for their release, so after several months in captivity, they were killed. "They cut their head," he said, with a knowing smile.

It suddenly dawned on me—the randomness of what had happened—and I felt guilty for suspecting the innocent Afghan with the cell phone at the camp and felt angry at Khalid. I grabbed my notebook out of his hands and flipped it open. I meant to continue my letter to Paul but was distracted by the names and numbers Khalid had been asking me about. How I wished I could turn back the clock. If I hadn't spoken to that family in the camp, maybe I would have been long gone by the time my kidnappers arrived. They would have simply kidnapped someone else. But how could I possibly wish this on anyone else? Was I that selfish that I would rather save myself and let some other poor, unsuspecting person suffer through this ordeal? It was a tough one, but I rationalized it by telling myself that it wasn't me who would be saved but my family and friends—it was they who should be spared whatever hell they might be going through right now.

I tried to imagine what my girlfriends in Toronto were doing. Jen, Kas, Maureen, and Angela. And my girlfriends in Regina—Stef, Coreen, and Shelley. The CBC would surely be telling them everything it could, trying to offer reassurance. I hoped they weren't worrying about me too much. *I hope they are all self-medicating with good red wine and a top-shelf vodka,* I said to myself tongue-in-cheek; I felt a pang in my chest, I missed them so much. But it gave me great comfort to know that they had each other, and I would have given anything at that moment to be clinking wineglasses with them.

It wasn't fair. But then, life isn't fair, a little voice in the back of my mind reminded me.

I felt the hot rush of tears and quickly turned to face the wall so that Khalid would not see me. I did not want my kidnappers to see me cry. But it was too late. His hand was on my back.

"No cry, please, Mellissa," he said gently.

I wiped my eyes and told him I was okay.

He took my hands and looked at me intently. "This will finish. You go to Kabul."

"When? *When?*" I asked.

"Soon, inshallah, soon."

"How soon? A few days? A week? Tell me when." I was almost pleading, but I didn't care anymore.

"I will call my father and tell him to fix the money."

"You mean you haven't yet? You told me you were going to do that on the first day! You lied to me, Khalid. Why should I believe you?"

The young Afghan shook his head. "I call, but this thing take time."

I didn't like the sound of that. I didn't want to spend another day, another second, in this hole. I stood up and hit my head on one of the beams. Then my hair got caught in a hook there.

"Fuck!"

"Shh! No talk too loud!" It sounded like an order.

I was just about to argue that no one would be able to hear me when I heard footsteps above. Khalid froze. He put his finger to his lips. A woman's voice yelled at someone. I didn't understand what she was saying, but Khalid did. He smiled.

"What is she saying?" I asked. The woman yelled again, louder this time.

"She angry from her son. She say his father will be angry from him too."

We listened quietly from our little hole in the ground. Undoubtedly, the woman had no idea she was practically standing on top of me.

"You mean she's angry *with* him," I corrected. More yelling, and then a child's voice. A dog barked.

"She say his father will . . . hit him." Khalid raised his arm as if he was about to whack someone across the face. Soon the yelling and barking and footsteps began to fade. I pictured a woman in a burka, or perhaps a big headscarf, maybe with a cane, chasing after her young son and threatening punishment at the hands of his father. How many times does this scene replay itself in a day throughout the world?

Khalid was smiling. "My mother—she say that all the time!"

"I think everyone's mother does." I smiled too. I'm pretty sure my mother probably said the same thing when my sister and I were little. *Wait until your father gets home. Then you'll see what kind of trouble you're in!*

"You are not afraid from your father?" Khalid asked.

I corrected his grammar again. "No, I'm not afraid *of* my father. Maybe I was when I was younger, but not anymore. I'm older now."

"How old are you?" he asked.

"I'm thirty-five," I said.

"You not," he responded.

I nodded, yes, but he didn't believe me, so I took my passport out of my pants pocket and opened it to show him my date of birth. He stared at me for a long time, then shook his head. "You older than my brothers."

I nodded again. I felt old. Old and tired. I leaned against the wall and lit another cigarette. I was going through the pack very quickly, and Khalid took it from me, putting it back into the breast pocket of his black kameez. He reached out his hand and made a V with his fingers, indicating he wanted to take my smoke.

It wasn't tasting so good to me, so I passed it to him and he took a long drag, blowing smoke out his big flat nostrils. He handed it back to me, and soon I was putting out the butt on the wall, then flicking it out into the tunnel.

"You must eat," he said, opening another package of sandwich cookies. I shook my head and told him I wasn't hungry, but he took three cookies out and pressed them into my hand.

"Eat," he ordered before poking a straw through a pouch of pomegranate juice and handing it to me.

I didn't realize how thirsty I was until I took a sip. The package was gone in under a minute. Khalid took out another one. "You must eat. I bring you—what you want?"

I laughed. I wasn't hungry, but if I could eat one thing in the world, I wanted a big, juicy cheeseburger with fries—not exactly a readily available dish in Afghanistan. It was all I'd been eating on the base in Kandahar. We all joked about how bad the food is there, but I rather liked the burgers and fries served at the DFAC's—the dining facility's—grill station. There was also a good salad bar, and

I'd often give up on the so-so entrees in favour of a salad and a burger and maybe a few fries.

"You like rice?" Khalid was asking. "Chips?"

I liked both, but I told him not to bother. I wasn't hungry, and besides, maybe fasting for a few days would be good for me, given the number of burgers I'd had over the past few weeks. I was only half serious, of course.

"I bring for you," he told me. "I will bring for you."

"It's okay, Khalid. I am okay eating cookies."

He held up the box of chocolate cookies and the package of fruit creme cookies. "You like this or this?"

I pointed to the chocolate one.

"I bring more," he promised.

"Khalid, don't bring me anything more. I don't need anything. The only thing I need is for you to bring me back to Kabul. Please. I don't need any of this stuff. I just need to go home."

I felt a sudden longing for home and tears threatened to fall again. I blinked hard and bit my lip until I could almost taste blood. "I just want to go home."

Khalid was studying me carefully, so I turned around and faced the wall again. He said nothing and opened a package of cookies. I could hear him crunching away and brushing off the crumbs. I lay down on my side and closed my eyes. I fished my rosary from my pocket and started to pray again.

Hail Mary, full of grace, the Lord is with thee.

I think it was after the second Hail Mary that I heard Khalid's voice. It was quiet and soft and sounded like an echo.

"Inshallah, soon, Mellissa, soon. Inshallah."

Dearest M,

It's just after 7 a.m. on Thursday, October 16, and it's now been almost five full days since you've been gone. I slept well, which is amazing considering I spend my days and nights in turmoil. So many fantasies and fears racing through my head, and wondering, always wondering, what you're going though. Sleeping in your clothes, if you're able to wash, what time they get you up in the morning, what they're feeding you. And most of all, if they've been moving you about, and just what awful coldness and discomfort you've been going through. Can you brush your teeth? What about your contact lenses?

I'm sitting in the garden and it's chilly until the sun comes up over the next door roofs. I have a pot of tea and I like the solitude because I can completely be with you, trying to get inside your head. This was the day we were supposed to do the Terry Fox Run, and that was one of the first things I thought of when I woke up. We'd be halfway around by now. Those are the good thoughts that I try to keep at the front of my mind, in the hope of keeping the demons away.

xx

Tick, tick, tick, tick, tick, tick, BOOM! Tick, tick, tick, tick, *BOOM!*

I sat up with a start. I looked over at Shafirgullah, snoring loudly next to me. He had come down to trade places with Khalid a few hours before.

Tick, tick, tick, tick, tick, BOOM!

Automatic gunfire. Mortars, maybe. I looked at the clock—it was just after midnight. It was loud, as if the fighting was going on just above our heads. I looked over at Shafirgullah, but he was a snoring lump, oblivious to the noise. And then I heard it. The unmistakable sound of a helicopter. Maybe two. That had to mean that the Americans or British were close.

I wondered again where we were in relation to Kabul. I thought we might have been west of the city, but I couldn't tell where we had driven from the refugee camp. The noises grew louder and, for a while, it sounded like the helicopter was hovering right above the hole.

Maybe someone had found out where I was. Maybe this was help, a rescue mission perhaps, spearheaded by the Special Forces. I imagined what might happen if someone actually found me. They'd come through the top of the hole—and then what? Would they kill Shafirgullah with a gunshot? What if he had a knife? Would he try to kill me first? He didn't have a gun, so I wasn't worried that he would shoot me before my rescuers made it down, but he might try to strangle me. I was confident I could take him under normal circumstances—but I knew I wouldn't have any strength to sustain a long fight. My wounds were still tender, and a steady diet of cookies and juice wasn't exactly a great source of energy and protein.

I imagined myself struggling with Shafirgullah. I could see his hands around my neck. I'd kick him in the groin and then go for the back of his neck with my fists once he doubled over in pain. Then the rush of soldiers would come through the tunnel and pull me to safety. Shafirgullah would be captured alive and taken to the prison at Bagram. Or they would shoot him dead right there. I hoped they wouldn't kill him. I didn't want to see him killed right in front of me.

Dearest M,

We're worried the Afghans will try to mount a rescue mission, and you'll be caught in a crossfire. My heart jumps at the thought. The people at the embassy say they've been assured by the Afghans that will not happen, and a rescue would only be tried with the consent of the Canadian government. I sure as hell hope so . . .

xx

The young Afghan snorted loudly in his sleep, startling me back to reality. The helicopter noise now sounded more distant, and the *rat-tat-tat* of gunfire had also faded.

The firefight was over. Both sides had moved on.

Except I was now wide awake. *Thank you very much, boys.* The last thing I needed was to be woken up when it was so hard to get to sleep in the first place.

I picked up the package of cigarettes and lit one. I could hardly believe I was smoking so much again. I had quit years ago, having only the odd drag of a friend's cigarette if I was drinking—and it had been a while since I had even done that.

But when soldiers sat down with me and offered me a smoke, it just felt rude to say no. Besides, there's nothing like sharing a cigarette to break down barriers between people. The summer before, I had made a lot of friends sitting out there in the heat, smoking cigarette after cigarette. And by the time we left to go on our first operation, I felt like I was part of the company.

The soldiers were really quite an amazing species. They were fighting a war that had become increasingly unpopular at home, yet they did it because they believed they were making a difference for people half a world away. I have never met a soldier who didn't truly believe he or she was in Afghanistan because it was the right thing to do.

"It's a broken country," I had said to Major Dave Quick, who was in charge of India Company, of the 2nd Battalion, Royal

Canadian Regiment—the battle group unit that my cameraman, Sat Nandlall, and I were attached to for more than a week.

"It doesn't mean it can't be fixed," he replied.

I blew out the last of the cigarette and threw the glowing butt into the trash-can toilet by the entrance of the hole. It seemed to me, sitting in this small, dank cave, that Dave Quick had been wrong. This was a lawless place where corruption runs through the country's political blood, where governors can be bribed and deals are cut to release insurgents from prison. Which I hoped wasn't being done in my case. Khalid had told me they were asking for money, and for his friend who was in prison at Bagram Air Base to be released, in exchange for my freedom. My heart sank when he told me about the friend because I knew such arrangements could take a long time, and President Karzai would have to get involved, and to be honest, I hated the thought that some kidnapper or suicide bomber was going to be released to wreak more havoc on the Afghan people because of me. I had told Khalid not to ask for the friend, that it would never happen. Khalid had responded by telling me he had promised his friend he would secure his freedom one day with one of his hostages.

The conditions at Bagram were terrible for prisoners, he told me. The Americans beat them up, and tortured them to try to get as much information as they could. I'd told Khalid I understood—I knew someone who had recently been released from Bagram after being held for almost a year, without a single charge ever being laid. That person was Jojo, Paul's and CTV's fixer in Kandahar. He was arrested for no apparent reason the year before when he was visiting a journalist, our friend Steve Chao, who was on the base for the network at the time. The military suspected him of having close connections to the Taliban.

And then suddenly one day he was released, and given a new set of clothes and new shoes. When we met him at the bus station in Kandahar, he told us stories of being left out in the snow for hours without a coat, about how the prison guards allowed other prisoners to beat him, about how they wouldn't let him sleep. He cried as we drove into Kandahar City.

In those eleven months, Jojo had changed. He had gone from being an eager, enthusiastic young man to being a bitter, angry one. He vowed that what happened to him should never happen to anyone again. He estimated that half of the prisoners at Bagram were innocent Afghans like him, beaten and made to suffer just on suspicion.

I had no doubt that Khalid's friend was guilty of something, so I didn't try to draw the comparison of innocence, but Khalid's interest was piqued by the fact I knew someone who had spent time in Bagram.

"When you leave here, you must tell Jojo to call me," he'd said. "I must talk to him."

I was sure that Jojo was probably making phone calls to try to figure out who had taken me, and he'd probably really like to talk to Khalid right about now. I'd laughed and told him I would tell Jojo to call him for sure. And he probably would.

I noticed the spot of light on the wall behind Shafirgullah's head. The sun had come up. Another morning, another sleepless night.

If I could sleep half as much as my captors, this would be a lot easier, I thought yet again. The clock said seven and I realized I was nearly losing track of the days—something I never do. It was Friday. I had been in the hole for almost a week.

Shafirgullah was still sound asleep. I didn't expect him to be awake for a while longer, so I stood up and stretched my legs. They were stiff. I sat back down, settling in for another day of mostly solitude. I already knew the drill. Shafirgullah would wake up, do his ablutions, eat two packages of cookies, and quiz me on all the Afghan words he had taught me. Door, blanket, finger, head, everything we could point to in the confines of the cave.

Then we'd have a smoke, and then he might let me play the snake game on his phone for a few minutes. And I'd wait for the minutes and hours to pass. I got the sense he was starting to get bored as well. He'd come into the hole last night to replace Khalid, smiling—no, laughing—holding up two fingers and saying, "You, Kabul. Two day." Which I'd mistakenly understood as "today"—but I knew that couldn't be true. "Two day," he repeated. Two days actually made sense. Maybe Khalid's father had made contact with Paul, or someone from the CBC; maybe they had worked out some kind of deal for my release. It was possible. Anything was possible, but I had to keep reminding myself not to get my hopes up. Still, it was hard not to. Maybe I'd be out by Sunday. There was a flight to Kandahar on Monday. I'd be back in time to pack up my stuff and get the flight to Dubai on Wednesday, back on schedule—the day my tour was supposed to end.

Shafirgullah spent a lot of time on the phone that day. I got to play Snake Xenzia only once on his phone—for about ten minutes—and then he wanted to put his SIM card back in and make phone calls.

"Who are you talking to?" I kept asking. "Is it Khalid? Am I going to Kabul on Sunday?"

He just laughed. "Khalid, Kabul, he come tonight."

"I want to go to Kabul," I told him.

"You go Kabul, I go Kabul," he laughed. "Two day."

This conversation went on all day, and by the end I had it all planned out. I was sure the Afghan authorities were going to want to talk to me. I'd do that once I got back to the city and returned to the Serena Hotel to collect my belongings.

Damn, I hoped my belongings were okay. I was supposed to have checked out on Tuesday, and I wondered if the hotel had sent someone to collect everything and empty the room, or was I still paying for it? I had a substantial amount of American cash from the CBC in the hotel's safe to pay Shokoor and Sameem's salary for the month. I wondered if it was still there and what had happened to the rest of my stuff, including my laptop. Thank goodness I wasn't carrying that with me or my kidnappers would surely have taken it. They had already taken my Marantz—the digital audio recorder I had carried with me to the camp that morning, and the microphone that went with it, even though I warned them they would have no use for it. They had asked me to show them how to use it, but the batteries had run out so I hadn't even been able to do that. Besides, I'd said, it would be useless to them without the editing equipment that was on my laptop. They didn't care and took it anyway, as if to make a point. I imagined they were going to take it apart and use the guts inside to make IEDs—improvised explosive devices. The thought made me feel sick to my stomach.

Khalid didn't come until later in the evening—well past the usual time of around six or six-thirty. The now-familiar sound of digging and the shower of dust that followed came at closer to eight o'clock that night. Shafirgullah scrambled out of the hole and his tall friend crawled in carrying three white plastic bags. Khalid smiled at me.

"I bring you chips," he said proudly, untying one of the bags and pulling out a large package wrapped in newspapers. "Look at!"

I unwrapped the newspaper to reveal a mound of freshly fried potatoes—french fries—and a few pieces of ripped Afghan bread.

"Shogufa make," he said, taking a fry and putting it in his mouth. "Eat!"

I took one of the fries and gingerly put it in my mouth. It was lukewarm, but I welcomed the taste of salt. A few days of nothing but cookies and juice was beginning to wear on my palate, which normally craves salt over sugar.

"You like?" he asked eagerly. I took a few more and nodded, stuffing them in my mouth.

"Eat some bread," he said, ripping off a chunk and holding it out to me. I took it and chewed and nodded.

"French fries," I said. "Shogufa made herself?"

"Yes, she is good. She know I like. She make. Eat. You must eat more!"

I took a few more and sat back. I wasn't hungry, which was odd given my limited diet over the past few days, never mind that french fries are one of my favourite foods in the world.

"Why you no eat?" Khalid seemed upset.

I told him I was full and that I'd eaten enough. But the truth was that the fries made me extremely homesick. I'd eaten them almost every day before I came to Kabul. Paul and Al and Bob Weber, the Canadian press reporter, all teased me that I was going to start looking like a french fry because I ate so many. I'd exercised self-restraint for a few days, but Al always had chips on his plate and I would end up stealing half of them.

This was also a running joke with my girlfriends. Jen and I had gone to a sports bar in Toronto just a few nights before I left for Afghanistan—and ordered everything that was bad for us—beer, chicken wings, hamburger sliders, nachos. And then after we filled our bellies, we decided to order a side of fries for dessert.

So it didn't seem right that I was being fed french fries while being kept a prisoner in a dark hole. Fries, in my mind, were to be enjoyed with levity and laughter and friends. I couldn't eat them at that moment, no matter how much I liked fries, because it made me so lonely for my real life.

Khalid seemed upset that I wasn't eating, but he couldn't force me. He ate the remaining fries himself, which were cold by then, and most of the bread. "I keep hot next time," he promised, almost apologetic in his tone. "They too cold now."

I told him not to worry and to tell Shogufa that I was grateful for her gesture.

Khalid reached into one of the bags and pulled out a newspaper. "You are important person," he said, giving me a knowing look. I wasn't sure what he meant, so I shook my head no.

"Yes," he insisted, and handed me an English-language Afghan newspaper—*The Afghan Times.* "Look."

On the front page, an article about Marina Sung, a twenty-seven-year-old Canadian reporter who had been kidnapped from a refugee camp on the outskirts of Kabul. Obviously, they got some facts wrong, but it was clearly about me. It quoted the police chief in Kandahar as saying that the police were doing everything they could to find me. It also quoted someone from the refugee camp. It was badly written—the English was poor. The article was short, but my heart sank as I read it. It was one of my worst fears—that my captors would now think that I was more important than I am and increase their demands for my release. Maybe they would ask for more money, more prisoners to be let out of jail. But then it might also work the other way: maybe knowing that the police were on the case and looking for me would pressure them into releasing me, into "finishing my case," as Khalid liked to refer to it.

"You are important person," Khalid kept saying.

I'm not, I insisted. I tried to explain to him that as a reporter, I might be known by some people in Canada, but for the most part, it wasn't a very important job, and I wasn't at all an important person. He refused to believe me, but I kept insisting. I told him reporters in Canada don't make a lot of money. But my parents must have money if they could send me to school so I could be a reporter? I told him no, my parents didn't work, and our family grew up with very little money. "Your company have money," he argued. I shook my head. I told him no, I worked for a public television station that had very little money (at least in the news division).

He wouldn't believe me. We argued back and forth for a while and then I gave up. There was no way of dissuading him from what he believed. Tired of arguing, I picked up the newspaper again. There was an article on Sarah Palin—the US elections were coming up and she was on the campaign trail, speaking in Texas.

Khalid pointed at the picture of her. "She very *shayesta*. Very pretty. I like her."

"She is friend of George Bush," I told him. "You no like her."

"Friend of George Bush? You lying!" He shook his head in disbelief. I told him I wasn't, that she was the vice-presidential candidate for George Bush's party in the elections that were about to take place. Again he refused to believe me. She can't be a friend of George Bush, he argued. Afghanistan hates Bush, and he was the reason for everything bad that had happened to his country. He told me about friends who were imprisoned and tortured and killed by George Bush's army, and that if he were to ever see Bush, he would kill him by beheading.

He ran his index finger over the picture of Sarah Palin. "She very pretty," he kept repeating. "She cannot be George Bush friend."

"She is," I goaded him a little. "So what would you do if you see her? Would you cut off her head too?"

"If I see her, I will . . . I will . . . touch her," he said, staring intently at her picture. This came as a surprise to me. Sex was such a forbidden subject in this culture, and the subject had never come up in conversation before. But now that he had started, he wasn't about to stop. "I hungry for her. I would—touch her," he said, spitting out the words as if they were thoughts that he had been trying to suppress but that suddenly didn't need to be silenced.

"I touch her," he continued, "and then I will cut her head off." He smiled to himself at the thought and nodded. "I cut her neck. I cut her head off."

"That's not very nice," I told him. "Not a very nice thing to do to someone if you like them."

"I no like George Bush friend," he said, "I hungry for her. I touch, then I kill her. I cut her head off." He continued for a while on this train of thought, talking more to himself than to me. I was starting to feel uncomfortable, so I lit a cigarette and let the smoke and silence fill the room instead.

I scanned the rest of the newspaper. There was an article about President Karzai and the election that was set to take place in a year. And an article about Barack Obama's campaign. Who had won the election back home in Canada? I wondered. It had taken place on Tuesday, the day after Thanksgiving. Elections were a big deal at the CBC, and I knew the entire network would be busy preparing for it. I'd filed a story the week before about soldiers voting at the base in Kandahar in the advance polls; I'd spoken to them about their thoughts on democracy and the voting process.

The US election was happening in a few weeks. November 4. It was going to be historic, and I said a silent prayer that I would be able to watch the results come in.

Khalid interrupted my thoughts. "Do you know who is Obama?"

"He's hopefully going to be the next president of the United States," I replied.

"He is good? You like?"

I nodded and put it in the simplest terms I could, explaining that he had voted against the US invasion of Iraq, that he was the opposite of George Bush, and that maybe things would improve if he won the election.

"You think he win?"

"I hope so."

"Why you no like George Bush?" I could tell he was extremely curious about this. Like many Afghans, Khalid had difficulty understanding that people in the West have a choice when it comes to political leadership. So I tried to explain that not all Americans had voted for Bush, and that not everyone thought we should be involved in Afghanistan or Iraq. This intrigued him greatly, and he wanted to know more. It was a lesson in Western democracy, and I had an interested student.

"George Bush bad," he concluded after a long discussion. "Taliban good."

No, I argued, how could the Taliban be good when so much of the population was repressed during their time in power? Women had to stay at home, girls weren't allowed to go to school; there was no freedom to speak of for most people.

"But there is no war with Taliban," Khalid replied. "Karzai bad. Afghan people no like Karzai." This was hard to argue. Shokoor and I were to do a story on voter registration, and he had told me that many Afghans had come to see Hamid Karzai as no more than a puppet of George Bush. They were also tired of the rampant corruption in his government. His half-brother, Ahmed Wali Karzai—the most powerful politician in Kandahar province—had been accused of being a prominent dealer in Afghanistan's lucrative drug trade, controlling much of the opium that was being produced in the south of the country. It was an allegation he had vehemently denied at a press conference I'd attended a little more than a week before I went to Kabul. But whether it was true or not, his reputation, and that of his brother, had taken a big hit in recent years and re-election was not guaranteed.

I asked Khalid if he was going to vote next year. He shook his head and motioned with his hands as if he were holding a Kalashnikov.

"I not vote. I kill people who go vote."

"What good would that do?" I challenged. "People should be able to go out and vote without fear of being killed." Khalid was echoing the Taliban's strategy the last time around. They'd threatened to blow up polling stations and intimidated hundreds of thousands of Afghans into staying away. I was pretty sure Khalid and his gang weren't card-carrying Taliban, but it didn't surprise me that they would subscribe to the same militant philosophies.

I studied the young Afghan closely. "Have you ever killed anyone?"

He took a cigarette out of the package and licked the end of it before lighting it. He took a few long drags, then turned to look me in the eye.

I repeated the question. "Have you ever killed anyone?"

"Yes, Mellissa. I kill some people. You think I am bad person?"

"Who did you kill?"

"Some people. I shoot," he said, pointing his index finger like it was the barrel of a gun.

"Where they Afghans? Americans?"

"Americans. They shoot us."

"Were they soldiers?"

"They not dress like soldiers, but they are."

"How many of them were there?" I wasn't sure if I believed him. I thought he was telling the truth about having killed before, but I didn't believe he'd ever been in a gunfight with NATO soldiers. I imagined he might have killed someone in the process of a robbery, or something like that, rather than in a firefight with foreign troops.

"Many. They shoot us. They kill my friend and take my other friend to Bagram. I shoot with my gun . . . and two fall. I shoot again. They are . . ." He made a motion with his hand to show they were lying flat on the ground. "They fall down. I shoot. Then my friend fall and I am go away."

"You ran away and left your friend?"

"I had to. Or they shoot me. Or take me to Bagram. With my friend."

"Is this the friend you promised to get freed? The friend you want them to release for me?"

He nodded. "He my good friend."

"But you know, Khalid, that if you ask for him to be released, it will take a long time to finish my case. And we all want my case to finish as soon as possible. I have to go home. My parents are worried about me. They will get sick. It's not fair to them. They will release your friend sometime soon, I'm sure. They released my friend Jojo, remember?" I was trying my best to reassure him that he could still get what he wanted by releasing me sooner rather than later, but even I wasn't convinced that was true.

Khalid stroked his goatee with his hand and then spoke slowly.

"Mellissa, I want to finish your case soon. But my father! He will finish your case. You understand? A little, little?"

I nodded but told him it was very important to tell his father to finish it soon because I had to get home.

"Do you understand, Khalid?"

"Yes. I tell my father."

Khalid took my right hand in his big dirty hands. I winced when he squeezed it because of the scab.

"It hurt?" he asked apologetically.

I nodded yes.

"Shafirgullah—he sorry," he said.

"It will heal over and be okay. I'm not worried about it. It just hurts a lot right now, and I can't feel my middle and index fingers. But I'm sure it will be fine once the scab comes off."

Khalid stroked the back of my hand.

"Mellissa, I sorry you hurt. I tell my father. I tell him you sick. I tell him to finish." He paused for a second.

We both lit cigarettes so we wouldn't have to go down the same path again. How long does it take? Weeks. Months. What happened the last time? They released in two weeks. What if you're asking for too much money? Not too much money. Your parents can afford. No, they can't; I'm poor; my parents are poor.

It was a conversation we'd had a few times already, and it had barely been a week since we started on the hike from the mountain outside Kabul.

I took another cigarette and held out my hand for Khalid's lighter. He reprimanded me for smoking too much but handed it over and took a smoke out of the package for himself. We both took long deliberate drags, and then he sat back.

"Sleep coming to me," he said, pulling the blanket over his shoulders. "You must sleep, Mellissa."

"Sleep is not coming to me," I replied. "Good night."

"Good night, Mellissa."

I blew out the lamp and let the darkness swallow me up once more.

"Mellissa! Mellissa!"

I woke up with a start. Someone was calling me. I thought it was a dream at first. But I heard the voice again.

"Mellissa!"

It was coming from above.

"Mellissa! Shafirgullah!" And then some words in Pashto.

I sat up and shook Shafirgullah's leg to wake him. He'd been sound asleep since he came down to replace Khalid the evening before. "Shafirgullah!" I whispered, pointing up to the ceiling. The Afghan rubbed his eyes. Voices were coming in through one of the pipes, yelled in Pashto.

Shafirgullah stood up and spoke into the pipe. Then he turned to me. "Abdulrahman," he said.

"Mellissa," the voice said again. I could tell now that it was the fat Afghan. I hoped he wasn't coming back down to the cave. But my heart was racing. It was Sunday. A full week had passed. Maybe this was it. Maybe he and Khalid were coming to dig me out of the hole and take me back to Kabul.

"Yes?" I answered.

"Where are you from?" Abdulrahman asked.

"I'm from Vancouver," I answered. I thought we had had this conversation before.

He asked me another question, but I couldn't understand it.

"What? I can't hear you," I said loudly into the pipe, tiptoeing to get as close to it as I could.

"What elementary school you go?" he repeated.

Elementary school? I was confused for a second. Why did he want to know what elementary school I had gone to?

And then it dawned on me. Proof of life. These were the proof-of-life questions the negotiators needed the answers to as proof to everyone back home—and here in Afghanistan—that I was alive.

"Captain Cook," I said.

"What?"

"*Cap-tin Cook,*" I tried to enunciate. I normally do enunciate my words, a habit developed from reading scripts every day, but in this case, I was afraid that the language barrier might confuse the answers, and I didn't want that to happen.

"What? Cap-tin *Cup?*" Abdulrahman repeated.

"CAP-TIN COOK!"

"Spell for me."

"C-A-P-T-A-I . . ." I started.

"C-A-E-P," he said back to me.

"C-A-P! P like *Paul!*" I yelled.

"C-A-P . . ." he repeated.

"Yes, C-A-P-T-A-I-N."

"C-A-P-E—"

"*No!* Listen to me, Abdulrahman!"

It took at least another ten minutes before I was satisfied with his spelling of "Captain Cook."

"Okay, Mellissa," he yelled down the pipe. "Now—what is your father name?"

"Kellog," I answered.

"What?" He clearly didn't hear or understand.

I know my dad's name is unusual—I used to tell people it was "Kellogg, like the cereal, but with only one 'g.'" It was a made-up English translation of his Chinese name, which is pronounced *Kay-luk*. But it wasn't like Abdulrahman knew of the cereal, so that translation would be lost on him.

"Spell for me," he called down.

"K-E-L-L-O-G," I yelled.

"K-I-L-U-J," he repeated.

"No, no, K-E. Eeeee!"

"E," came the answer.

It took another ten minutes before I thought he had it right.

"Okay, thank you," he yelled. "We go now."

"Wait, wait! Abdulrahman, what is happening? Has the money been fixed?" I had so many questions. "Who are you talking to? Who is asking these questions?"

There was scuffling around. "We go now. Goodbye!" He said something to Shafirgullah, and then I could hear the pounding of footsteps loud over my head, before they faded into the distance.

Shafirgullah looked at me and shrugged.

"What was that about?" I asked him. "I'm going to Kabul, yes?"

He nodded. "Yes. Kabul. You." He pointed at me. "I go Kabul. You Kabul."

My mind started to race. They would relay the answers later this morning, if they weren't already on the phone right now. The negotiators would be satisfied of my well-being. Then I would be released. *Maybe as soon as this afternoon. Or tonight.* I wondered how they would hand me over. Would it be the same way we came to this spot? I imagined myself riding on Khalid's motorcycle, holding onto the sides, through the winding roads of the village, before getting onto a main road. Then his friend with the car would meet us, and we'd get in the back. It would be dark, and the lights would flash by occasionally as we made our way into the city.

They would be waiting for me at the refugee camp. Black SUVs, security people with guns. Maybe Paul would be in one of the vehicles. Or maybe they wouldn't let him come out. I wouldn't want him there anyway. It might be dangerous, some sort of stand-off. Both sides would have guns, waiting for the other to make the first, perhaps fatal, move, hedging their bets in a game of cat and mouse that could end with both parties getting what they came for, or leaving with less than they started with.

But I could see Paul as soon as tonight! This thought kept me going for a while. I was excited, looking forward to being reunited. I'd show him my scars, and tell him I was okay, and we'd go back to the Serena, where I could have a hot shower, and then we'd go to the Asian restaurant at the hotel and talk about everything over dinner.

"Mellissa. Kabul." Shafirgullah was almost taunting me.

He sat up, as though he had just realized he'd been awakened from his sleep, and motioned for me to turn around.

"Bathroom," he said.

I turned around and let him finish with his ablutions. The routine was the same every day: He washed with some of the water from the watering can, then brushed his teeth with the stick-and-string contraption. Then he opened a package of chocolate sandwich cookies, washing them down with two pouches of juice. My juice package was still half full. I'd been trying not to eat or drink too much, to limit the number of times I needed to use the trash-can toilet. That was something I could never get used to: the lack of privacy in such a small space. It was suffocating. I've always guarded my privacy carefully, and as a woman, I was agonizingly aware that I was sharing the space with a man. How ironic, I thought, that in a Muslim country I'd be stuck in close quarters with a man monitoring my most private moments, and watching over my every move. It felt wrong and strange, like the world was upside down.

I took a sip of juice. It was still cool, and an indication that the temperature was dropping a little more every day. It was late October, and things cooled down considerably in the evenings. If I were back at the base, I would be putting on my Vancouver Canucks fleece sweater to walk from the work tent to the sleep tent at night. It wouldn't be long, I thought, before this hole would become a cooler, buried deep down somewhere in northern Afghanistan.

A chill ran through my body, even though it was still relatively warm in the hole. Abdulrahman must have kicked over one of the rocks that covered the opening to the pipe outside because a big beam of daylight was streaming into the cave, hitting the wall above Shafirgullah's pillow. I held my hand up to the light and made hand shadows—a duck's head, a bat—like my sister and I used to do when we were little, in the light that came into our bedroom from the hallway, when the grown-ups were still up but it was past our bedtime.

Shafirgullah laughed at my hand shadows and held his hand in front of the light as well. He turned his thumb and index finger into the shape of a handgun, which was pointed at the shadow my head made on the wall. He laughed again.

"That is not funny, Shafirgullah," I said, shaking my head at him. He threw his head back and laughed some more. I turned my back to him and closed my eyes, trying to drown out his laugh by reciting the rosary in my head.

Then I heard a chanting. Shafirgullah's eyes were closed and he was kneeling, his head bowed. He was praying again, reciting passages from the Koran. I was starting to feel assaulted by the prayers. Every morning before dawn, I could hear the call to prayer somewhere in the distance. And then again around noon and again in the evening. This must be what non-Christians feel in North America, I thought, when they hear church bells ringing. Still, I heeded the imam's calls, praying instead in my own way, eyes closed, head down, to my own God, hoping that He would hear me.

Shafirgullah's chanting was getting louder, though, and I was starting to get annoyed that I couldn't even pray in peace. So I started singing my Hail Marys out loud.

Hail Mary, fu-ll of graaace. The Looord is with yoooou. Blessed are you among wo-men, and blessed is the fruit of your womb, Jeee-eee-sus.

Shafirgullah looked up at me. He smiled, and waved for me to continue.

Holy Mar-ee, mother of God, pray for us si-i-in-ners, now and at the hour of death. A-men.

He clapped and smiled. "Very nice."

I motioned for him to keep chanting. He did, and although I didn't understand a word, I thought he carried a note quite well, and I started to get lulled into the rhythm of the prayer. I thought I could hear the words "Afghanistan" and "Allah," but I wasn't entirely sure.

He stopped and nodded his head my way. "You."

I shrugged and said I wasn't sure what to sing now, even though I knew he couldn't understand what I was saying.

"You," he insisted.

I wasn't sure what to sing, so I reverted back to the hymns from church, the ones that had been drummed into my head as a girl in Catholic school.

You who dwell in the shelter of the Lord,
Who abide in His shadow for life,
Say to the Lord, "My Refuge, my Rock in Whom I trust."

And He will raise you up on eagle's wings,
Bear you on the breath of dawn,

Make you to shine like the sun,
And hold you in the palm of His Hand.

The snare of the fowler will never capture you,
And famine will bring you no fear;
Under His wings your refuge,
His faithfulness your shield.

And He will raise you up on eagle's wings,
Bear you on the breath of dawn,
Make you to shine like the sun,
And hold you in the palm of His Hand.

You need not fear the terror of the night,
Nor the arrow that flies by day,
Though thousands fall about you,
Near you it shall not come.

And He will raise you up on eagle's wings,
Bear you on the breath of dawn,
Make you to shine like the sun,
And hold you in the palm of His Hand.

Shafirgullah seemed to like that and clapped loudly after I finished.

"You," I said to him, but he really didn't need much prompting, launching into another passage of the Koran. His voice was soft and lyrical and almost sweet, and for a moment I forgot where I was. I imagined I was at a mosque back in Canada, where I'd attended several prayers with the imam who was helping me with a story on fundamentalism and how it can take root in young people.

I'd always thought the Koran sounded best when its passages were sung—unlike those of the Bible. My sister and I used to have a hard time stifling our giggles whenever our parish priest sang a prayer during Mass. Father O'Brien was the nicest man, but he could not carry a tune to save his soul, or anyone else's.

On the other hand, I'd never heard someone sing the Koran out of tune—or at least, it never sounded out of tune to me. Maybe it was just the way it was written, and was more conducive to being put to music than the Bible. Or maybe Muslims were just better singers.

Shafirgullah was a pretty good singer, and he continued on for another half hour. Now, not many Catholics, no matter how devout, know the Bible well enough to quote directly from it at any length. One might have a favourite passage or two, but that was nothing compared with the way Muslims could quote the Koran. I wondered why that was. Maybe the Koran was written in a way that made it easier to memorize, and chant.

As for me, there were only a couple of passages from the Bible I knew by heart, and I knew them because they were the ones I had loved as a child, the ones I would say to myself over and over whenever I needed divine intervention. The one I knew best was a passage from the Gospel according to Mark, in which Jesus spoke to the people who had turned his house of prayer into a market:

> *Put your trust in God. I solemnly assure you, whoever says to this mountain, "Be lifted up and thrown into the sea," and has no inner doubts but believes that what he says will happen, shall have it done for him. I give you my word, if you are ready to believe you will receive whatever you ask for in prayer, it shall be done for you.*

This passage for me always summons up an image of a mountain literally being lifted up and thrown into the sea, even though I know it is meant metaphorically—it speaks to one's need to believe in the power of prayer. *This hole I am in is a mountain,* I thought, and I had said those lines to myself many times over the last week.

Now, as I sat listening to my captor recite the Koran, I began to wonder if it was actually true. Was it possible that we were both praying to the same God? I began to wonder if God was hearing me, or listening to me at all.

What if I called you Allah instead of God? I asked silently. *Do you respond better to "Allah"? Because you can't possibly be listening to him and me at the same time. Maybe if I called you Allah, you'd help me out of this horrible place and let me go home to the people I love. Why are you answering his prayers and not mine?*

"You!" Shafirgullah's voice interrupted my argument with God in the same way the sound of a glass breaking interrupts conversation at a cocktail party.

"Me what?" Then I realized he wanted me to sing. It was my turn, and I was running out of hymns I knew by heart.

> *You shall cross the barren desert, but you shall not die of thirst.*
> *You shall wander far in safety though you do not know the way.*
> *You shall speak your words in foreign lands and all will understand.*
> *You shall see the face of God and live.*
>
> *Be not afraid.*
> *I go before you always.*
> *Come follow me,*
> *and I will give you rest.*
>
> *If you pass through raging waters in the sea, you shall not drown.*
> *If you walk amid the burning flames, you shall not be harmed.*
> *If you stand before the pow'r of hell and death is at your side,*

Know that I am with you through it all.
Be not afraid.
I go before you always.
Come follow me,
and I will give you rest.

Shafirgullah laughed and clapped when I had finished. I wasn't sure what he would have done if he actually knew I was singing a Christian hymn. After all, he hadn't given up trying to convince me that I needed to convert to Islam. We had the same argument each night he came back to the hole.

"Why you no Muslim? You must be Muslim."

"I am Christian, but we believe in the same God," I would argue back. "It's the same God. I just pray differently from you."

His English wasn't good enough to sustain a full argument, so the conversation basically ended there, with him reiterating that I "must" be Muslim.

We went back and forth almost all afternoon, chanting and singing, until the point of light behind his head faded and night started to cast its shadow. I waited for the sound of digging; this was going to be my hour of freedom. They had the proof of life they needed, and now they were going to come and take me back to Kabul in exchange for some sum of money. I knew they would not come to take me out during the day—such activities needed the cloak of darkness, in case someone was watching. And my kidnappers were paranoid of airplanes and drones, of being spotted by Americans or the Afghan police.

Minutes passed into hours and there was no sound. Not even footsteps. Soon, it was after nine o'clock.

"Where Khalid?" I asked. Shafirgullah was again working the makeshift toothbrush around his mouth. He shrugged.

"They're not coming tonight?"

"I don't know," the young Afghan said, looking at his cell phone. He punched a few numbers in it and I could hear an automated operator's voice. Shafirgullah hung up and stood up, dialing again and holding his phone to the ceiling to try to get better reception. Unable to get through, he tried a different number.

"As-Salaam Alaikum," he said. A brief phone conversation ensued before he hung up and turned back to me. "Khalid Kabul."

My heart sank. If Khalid was in Kabul, there was no way I was getting out that night.

"Why Khalid in Kabul?" I asked.

Shafirgullah shrugged. He reached for the last box of juice, unwrapped the straw, and plunged it into the hole at the top.

"They no come tonight," he told me.

I knew there was no point in asking why not, because he wouldn't know, and even if he did, he wouldn't be able to tell me in English.

"Cigarette?" he asked instead, waving a fresh box of smokes in my face. I nodded, and he handed me the package. I took the box of matches and tried to light one, but they were damp. Shafirgullah also tried, and we went through about a dozen matches until we were able to finally get one going. We smoked three cigarettes in a row, using the embers from one to light another, knowing that there were only a few dry matches left. And then we sat there in a nicotine-induced haze. My head was beginning to hurt, and I didn't even notice the lamp was dimming until he pointed at it.

"*Tsiragh,*" he said, the Pashto word for lamp. Khalid had brought a battery-operated hand-held lamp a couple of days before, replacing the kerosene lamp that had been polluting the air and our lungs for the last few days. I handed it over and watched as Shafirgullah took the batteries out one by one, pitching us into complete darkness. He put the batteries back in and shook the lamp. The light was still very dim, but I didn't mind, since my headache was beginning to worsen. I wondered if it was from the nicotine or the smoke or the dust.

"*Tsiragh*. Bad." Shafirgullah put the lamp back down.

"Battery," I said.

"Yes, battery," he repeated. The word sounded the same in both languages for once.

"Tomorrow," he said.

"And matches," I said, shaking the almost empty matchbox.

My head was now pounding, and I lay down and closed my eyes, praying that sleep would come more easily that night. The refrain from the last hymn I had sung echoed in my head.

> *Be not afraid, I go before you always.*
> *Come follow me, and I will give you rest.*

———————

Mercifully, I had fallen soundly asleep—the alarm clock now said six o'clock. It had to be morning. I'd missed the pre-dawn call to prayer. It was the longest I'd slept in a week. I went to the bathroom in the trash can—as I'd been doing most mornings, taking advantage of the fact that my captor was still snoring—and washed my hands with water from the watering can. Then I stood up and stretched and did kicks with my legs, just to keep them active. A routine, of sorts, although I didn't want to admit even to myself that I was falling into one. It would mean that I was getting used to being a prisoner, and I wasn't about to let myself go there.

Shafirgullah was still snoring when I heard the sound of footsteps above us. Could they be coming to release me? It made sense.

Khalid had said it would either be after dark or before daylight. I heard someone calling out in Pashto, so I shook Shafirgullah's leg. He sat up and rubbed his eyes. Whoever was outside kept speaking. Shafirgullah stood up and leaned toward the opening of one of the pipes.

"Salaam," he said. A brief conversation followed, and then the sound of something sliding in through the pipes. A box of cigarettes, followed by matches, a lighter. Then batteries and several boxes of juice—and two sleeves of cookies. Supplies, since no one had come the night before.

"Abdullah," Shafirgullah told me, pointing up to the ceiling. I nodded, and put the juice and cookies into one of the white plastic bags, after taking an apple juice. I was thirsty and hadn't had anything to drink since the previous afternoon. The juice was cold and tasted good.

"You, biscuit?" Shafirgullah was holding out half a box of chocolate sandwich cookies. I shook my head. He shrugged and stuffed the remaining cookies down his mouth, one at a time. It amazed me how much he ate. At least three packages of cookies a day, and several boxes of juice. I felt sick just thinking about it. I was really only eating to pass time, and to make sure I at least had a few calories to burn in case I ever needed to walk—or run—out of here. I could feel already that my hiking pants were a little loose. I'd been wanting to lose a few pounds, but this was not the weight-loss program I'd had in mind.

I stood up and stretched again, pointing my toe to the opening of the pipe overhead, and almost falling over. I steadied myself by putting a hand on the dirt wall.

Shafirgullah looked at me quizzically. I tried to explain that I was trying to get a little exercise, but that wasn't a concept he understood at all. He pulled out his cell phone and played Snake Xenzia for the next half an hour or so, while I continued to do my stretches for the second time that morning.

Shafirgullah was on and off the phone almost all day, and I assumed he was talking to his brother or Khalid, until I heard what sounded like a woman's voice coming through the receiver.

"Who was that?" I asked, curious. "Your mother?"

"Girlfriend," he said with a grin, flashing his teeth at me.

"You have girlfriend?" I replied.

He laughed and nodded. "Like Khalid," he said. Again, the language barrier stopped me from finding out anything more about her, so I left it at that and instead asked whether Khalid was coming back that night.

"No Khalid."

I despaired at the thought of spending another twenty-four hours in this place with Shafirgullah. He wasn't disgusting like Abdulrahman, but it was very difficult having nothing to say to each other, and a language barrier that prevented any semblance of a normal conversation.

More than anything, that's what I was missing. A normal conversation. As a journalist, I spend my entire days in conversations with people, whether it's my editors and producers, or the people I'm interviewing for a story, or the cameraperson, with whom I might spend hours and hours driving from one location to another. Or I'd be chatting with my friends on our BlackBerrys, which had become an essential in our lives. We were all single, and it was a way of keeping tabs on each other—to bitch and gossip or organize a drink and dinner on the way home from work. I spend my life talking to people and to have that suddenly taken away made me feel completely lost.

I missed the voices of my friends, those quick electronic notes with updates and questions, and plans to meet up. I missed the connections. I pulled out my notebook and flipped it to an empty page. I could see there weren't many more blank pages left, and I said a silent prayer to God that I would see freedom before the back cover of the notebook.

Hey dude,

I know you're probably really worried about me back home and I'm just writing to tell you that I'm okay. My kidnappers are not hurting me, and they're treating me well. Please tell everyone not to worry. I miss you guys a lot. I would give an arm and a leg to be having a beer with you right now, at Gretzky's, watching a hockey game, and eating sliders until our guts are spilling over our jeans. How are the Canucks doing? I know it's early in the season, but I'm not hopeful that it's going to be so great. They'll make the playoffs, but they're definitely not a Presidents' Trophy or Stanley Cup contender this year.

I don't know if you'll ever get this note, and I sure hope that if you do, I'm the one who gives it to you when this is all over, but I just wanted to say I miss you a lot.

I've been thinking a lot about our vacation this summer and what a great time we had in Italy, and how lucky we were to have that time together. I wish I could turn back the calendar and relive those two weeks.

I'm not trying to sound fatalistic or anything, but I'm just doing a lot of thinking since there's nothing else to do in here. Except smoke. Yes, I'm off the wagon. Or back on, or however you choose to look at it. Like a chimney, so the next time we go running, I'll be the one huffing and puffing behind you.

And we're going running again. There's not a doubt in my mind I'm getting out of here and we'll get back to our lives.

Love you lots, dude, and I hope to see you soon. Tell everyone I said hi. I'll write to them too. Have lots of drinks for me, because I haven't had anything in weeks.

"Give me," Shafirgullah interrupted, obviously curious about what I'd been scribbling in my notepad. I handed it over, knowing he would not be able to understand any of my letters. He scanned the pages several times, then ripped the letter to Jen out, folded it, and stuffed it in his pocket.

"Hey!" I said angrily. "Give that back. It's not meant for you."

Shafirgullah cackled.

"Give it back to me. It's not yours, and you don't understand a word, you fuckhead!" I knew he wouldn't understand, so I kept swearing. "*Diu nay ma,* you fucker," I spat out in Chinese—the worst Chinese swear words you could say to someone. I'd heard my dad say it a few times when he was really angry. When my mother first translated the phrase, I was at first horrified, then delighted. It was a phrase I could use and which most people wouldn't understand. Translation: *Go fuck your mother.*

Shafirgullah kept cackling. And he shook his head repeatedly. The letter was his now, and in case I'd forgotten my position, he was my captor and I was his prisoner. I had no privacy, no right to anything, no freedom to even write a letter.

I told him several times again to fuck his mother, but it didn't change a thing.

It didn't matter, I told myself. I was not getting Jen's letter back. But I'd soon be able to say all that I wrote to her in person. At least that was my hope.

I could hear the pitter-patter of what sounded like big rain-drops hitting the ground outside. Rain at the end of October was not unusual in Afghanistan. It had rained several weeks before in Kandahar, and we had been worried about our sleep tents flooding. The rain turned everything to sloppy, brown mud and made a mess everywhere around Kandahar Airfield.

Rain never bothered me. Growing up in Vancouver, in the Pacific Northwest, you couldn't hate rain because then you'd hate the weather half of the year. As a kid, I used to love playing in puddles, jumping in with galoshes and stirring the mud with my boots. When I got older, I got used to running in the rain. I didn't mind—as long as I was dressed properly. The rain just made me run faster. I would pretend that I was running from the storm, between the drops, which had the added benefit of washing all the sweat off my face.

Rain was Mother Nature's way of washing away everything that was dirty, of giving us a clean slate to start over with. So I took the rain outside as a sign that maybe my time in the hole was coming to an end.

Crack! There was a loud noise over our heads, and then another, and a rumble that sounded a little farther away. I assumed it was a mortar, or a rocket-propelled grenade, and listened for the crackle of gunfire that was sure to follow. Nothing. But then another *crack!*

And that's when I realized it was thunder. Shafirgullah pointed above and nodded. It was the sky.

I love thunderstorms. Well, let's put it this way: I love the idea of watching them from the comfort of a cozy couch, tucked under a blanket with a cup of tea and a good book. When I was posted to the Prairies as a correspondent, I drove through a series of thunderstorms with my cameraman, Mike, as we made our way from Regina to Grasslands National Park in southwestern Saskatchewan. The rain came down in buckets, and our windshield wipers were futile. Lightning flashed in broken, jagged streaks across the dark, endless sky in front of us, almost daring us to continue on.

The payoff was the most beautiful rainbow I'd ever seen in my life: a perfect arch, with all the colours at their most vivid, perfect enough to make you believe there really could be a pot of gold at the end.

So I took the thunder outside as a good omen too—that perhaps my pot of gold, my freedom, was just around the corner.

I had been in the hole for ten days now, not counting the day I was kidnapped. I knew it was the middle of the week, but I was again starting to get the dates mixed up. So I opened my notebook and drew up a little calendar. I felt like a prisoner who scratches off the days on the cell wall.

October

S	M	T	W	T	F	S
12	13	14	15	16	17	18
19	20	21	22	23	24	25
26	27	28	29	30	31	

November

S	M	T	W	T	F	S
						1
2	3	4	5	6	7	8
9	10	11	12	13	14	15
16	17	18	19	20	21	22
23	24	25	26	27	28	29
30						

December

S	M	T	W	T	F	S
	1	2	3	4	5	6
7	8	9	10	11	12	13
14	15	16	17	18	19	20
21	22	23	24	25		

I stopped at December 25—the thought of being there past Christmas was unbearable. It was now October 22, the day we were supposed to leave Kandahar. Paul and Al and I should have been on the plane to Dubai at that very moment, looking forward to sipping cocktails at the swim-up bar in our hotel, followed by dinner in a real restaurant. We always stopped for a night on the way in and out of Afghanistan and a couple of nights on the way out, a reward of sorts after a few weeks of sleeping on a lumpy cot in a dusty tent on a base where there was no booze—but regular rocket attacks in the middle of the night. My heart sank thinking of what Paul and Al were doing right then. Especially Paul. I knew he probably wouldn't leave Afghanistan until this mess was over. A rumbling wave of guilt washed over me just thinking about what he might be going through.

It was all in front of me now, my life, on this piece of paper. I had been kidnapped on the twelfth of October. Thanksgiving was the thirteenth. The Canadian election was on the fourteenth. (I was still wondering who had won.) The Terry Fox Run was on the fifteenth. Paul and Al and I had been registered for it, and we'd been ready. The US Army ten-miler a few weeks before had been a warm-up. We had all finished it in an hour and twenty minutes, leaving us in great shape for the shorter Terry Fox Run. I wondered if they had run it without me. Somehow, I didn't think so.

I looked at the calendar again. My grandmother would have turned ninety-two that week, on October 20. I never forgot her birthday, and every year on that day I said a prayer that she and my grandfather were doing okay in heaven. This year, I asked her to intercede on my behalf, to use her connections up there to help me get out of the hole I was in. And for the first time since she passed away eight years ago, I was glad she wasn't alive. I know how much she would have worried and suffered. It was bad enough to imagine what my parents and my sister were feeling.

The calendar fuelled a sense of urgency I'd been trying to quash. The dates were calling out to me, reminders of things I had to do, plans that had already been made, events that were happening. November 4, the US election, and I'd been planning on having friends over to watch what was going to be a historic vote. November 27 was American Thanksgiving, and I'd been planning to visit my sister in Los Angeles. And on top of all that, I was supposed to move from Regina back to Toronto for a new job at the network as a national radio/TV reporter. I still had to find a place to live, and the move had to be done before Christmas so that I could start work in the new year.

I suddenly felt like I was running out of time, that everything was happening too fast, but my freedom wasn't coming fast enough.

"Shafirgullah," I called out to my captor. "Where Khalid? Khalid coming tonight?"

He shrugged. "No Khalid. Khalid Kabul." He reached over me to grab the plastic bag that was behind my pillow. The night before, Shafirgullah had brought down a bowl of warm rice pilau in a metal dish with a metal covering. I had eaten several spoonfuls, savouring the saltiness of the rice, a welcome relief from all the sugar I'd been ingesting with the cookies and juice. Now the rice was cold, and Shafirgullah was shoving it down his throat by the spoonful. I'd never seen anyone eat that fast before. Within seconds, the entire bowl of rice was gone.

I tucked myself under the dirty blue duvet. My feet were cold and clammy, and I couldn't warm them up, no matter how hard I rubbed them. A shock of cold air was blowing into the hole from the openings at the pipes. It was almost November, and the weather was definitely changing. I'd been told that there was no such thing as an Afghan autumn. The weather went from being very hot in August and September to rainy in October and cold by November.

It sounded like the rain was coming down in sheets, like one of those great Prairie storms back home. I closed my eyes and imagined I was outside, letting the rain wash all the dirt, dust, and smells off my body and my clothes. I must have dozed because I jumped when I heard the clomping of footsteps overhead. Shafirgullah heard them too, and put his finger over his lips, indicating for me to stay quiet. It must have been someone outside the gang. *Clomp, clomp, clomp, clomp, clomp.* Then voices. Shafirgullah sat up, his finger still over his lips. I didn't move. The footsteps faded after a while, and when he was sure they were gone, Shafirgullah put the

SIM card into his cell phone and dialed. I thought I heard Khalid's voice coming over the receiver, but I couldn't be sure. The men spoke in urgent tones, and then Shafirgullah hung up.

"What was that?" I asked, pointing to the ceiling. "Who was there?"

Shafirgullah looked a little worried. He dialed another number and spoke quickly in Pashto.

"Taliban," he answered after hanging up the phone.

"Taliban?" I repeated. "I thought you were Taliban." I pointed at him. "You. Taliban."

"All Taliban!" he replied.

I thought this was all very strange. Perhaps they wanted to find out where my kidnappers were holding me. My mind started to run away from me again. I knew that hostages were often taken by one group and then traded to another, and then another. Gangs of kidnappers would sell their prizes to other gangs, and, eventually, the poor unsuspecting hostage would end up in the hands of some senior Al Qaeda person. I prayed that this wasn't going to happen to me. It would mean that all the negotiating that had been done thus far would have to be started all over again with another group. More money, further demands, and it could be months before I was freed.

The rain had stopped, and the storm had passed, but my state of mind was frantic. Whose footsteps were those that had so worried my kidnappers? Could they really belong to the Taliban? Maybe it was the police. Maybe they had come looking for me. This was a possibility I could allow myself to consider further.

Maybe someone in the village had seen my kidnappers bring me here, as hard as they had worked to hide me. Maybe the farmer we had passed along the way noticed me on the back of the motor-cycle. Perhaps it was one of those women wearing a burka who we had passed riding through town. Maybe she called the police after suspecting something was wrong. Maybe someone had seen them move me to the abandoned house that afternoon.

The next time there were unknown footsteps, maybe I should yell. There would be nothing Shafirgullah could do. The police would hear me, and then they would dig me out of the hole. They'd arrest him, or Khalid, or whoever was with me. It might be my best option for getting out. My mind was racing.

And then, like a voice on my other shoulder, the thought came to me—*what if it* was *the Taliban?* They would kill Shafirgullah or Khalid, and I'd be moved somewhere new, and the whole process would have to begin again.

There was no way to know. I was either going to have to take a chance or play it safe and let whatever was already in progress run its course.

The next time I heard footsteps was later that same evening. This time, voices called down to Shafirgullah before they started to dig. We wrapped ourselves in our blankets and waited for the shower of dust to settle. As soon as the covering to the shaft was removed, Shafirgullah moved the wooden door to the side, put on his shoes, and scrambled up the tunnel. I took the opportunity to go to the bathroom and light a cigarette. The air coming into the hole was cold, and I shivered as I covered myself with the duvet.

Thump. A figure was crawling toward me. I assumed it was Khalid, but when he appeared in the entrance, I realized it wasn't.

"Hello, Mellissa!" It was Abdullah, Shafirgullah's brother.

"Hello, Abdullah." I tried a smile.

He was all smiles.

"I stay tonight. Okay, Mellissa?"

"Okay, Abdullah." I didn't have much of a choice, and at least it wasn't Shafirgullah for another night.

The digging started above, and soon the hole was sealed again, leaving me with yet another young Afghan. At least they had kept their promise of not sending Abdulrahman back.

Abdullah's English was better than his brother's, and because he hadn't spent much time down in the cave, he seemed eager to talk.

"How are you, Mellissa?"

"I am fine, Abdullah. I want to go back to Kabul."

"Yes, you go. You go. Maybe in two days." Two days? I couldn't believe that he would be privy to the negotiations between Khalid's father and whoever was negotiating for me. But I did wonder whether he might have picked something up from his brother, who seemed to be constantly on the phone to Khalid and Zahir in Pakistan. I didn't want to get my hopes up, but he was adamant.

"Yes, yes," he insisted. "You go. Maybe two days."

"We'll see, Abdullah," I replied. "I don't believe you, but I hope you are right. I hope what you say is true."

"I am right!" He picked up the Farsi–English phrase book and started reading the English parts, stopping to ask me how to pronounce certain words.

"It is a beee-yoo-ti-ful day," he read, smiling as I nodded when he said the word correctly.

We worked through half of the phrase book—going through all the sections for greetings, how to order food, what to buy at the market—and were on the section about going to work when I think we both got bored of reading.

I lit a cigarette, as I was doing with alarming regularity, and took a long drag, blowing out the smoke in a straight stream toward the wooden door. Abdullah watched me and lit one for himself with a lighter he had in the breast pocket of his kameez. From the same pocket he then pulled out a little plastic bag containing a small block of something black.

"You like?" He held it up to me.

"What is it?" I asked, thinking it was probably tobacco of some sort, or maybe even hashish.

"Niswar," he answered. "You know niswar?"

I shook my head.

"What does it do?" I asked.

Abdullah laughed. "Niswar—it make you feel good. *Good*. But it is bad!" He laughed some more. "Do not tell my brother I am take niswar!"

He ripped a bit off the black square and popped it in his mouth, sucking on it slowly. "Mmm. Niswar." Holding the piece out to me, he insisted, "You try."

I shook my head no, and as much as I thought that drugs might not be a bad idea if I was going to be stuck in the hole for much longer, there was no way I was about to try something I'd never had before while I was trapped in a small space with a strange man.

Abdullah closed his eyes and kept sucking. I lit another cigarette and watched him. The drug, whatever it was, had an almost immediate effect. He was mellowed out, leaning back and resting his head against the wall, eyes closed and mouth still working on the piece of niswar. Soon, Abdullah was in an almost trance-like state, in his own world, oblivious to me and anything else. He sang softly to himself, and it wasn't long before I heard the sound of snoring.

So much for scintillating conversation, I thought. I opened my notebook again and found a precious blank page.

Dear Stef,

How are you? I'm still here, still in this dark hole, and still okay. My scabs are almost at the point where they're falling off, and I'm taking that as a sign that this ordeal might be over soon. The scabs are from the stab wounds the first day, when the kidnappers were pushing me into the car. I hit one of them and he didn't like it, so he stuck a knife into my shoulder. Nice, huh? We can both think of people we'd like to do that to, but we'd never actually do it!

I'm sure you and everyone else are really worried about me—and I'm writing to tell you that I'm fine. Please try not to worry. I know that's easier said than done, but you know me, and you know I'll hang in there.

It rained today. There was thunder and lightning and everything, and it reminded me of being in the Prairies. I couldn't see outside, but I'm sure there was a rainbow like we see after almost every Prairie storm. It's a good sign that I'll be home soon—so don't worry. Give Jack and Simon and Luke a scratch from Auntie M and say hi to everyone else for me. Gerry and Shelley and Mal and Coreen and little Henry.

I know everyone is praying for me, and I'm thankful for the prayers. Keep them up, and I promise I'll be back soon.

Love you.

Stefani Langenegger was my best friend in Saskatchewan. We worked together a lot. She filed for national radio news, while I did the same job for television. We travelled all over the province and were at each other's house at least three times a week after work, not including weekends, drinking wine, and rum and coke, and eating our way through the Prairie winters. I had been exiled to Regina by the network—to do penance in a remote bureau for a few years. The guy in charge of network news in Toronto wasn't a big fan of my work. I didn't mind being far away from him either, but I wouldn't necessarily have chosen to move to the bald, cold Canadian Prairie. If I hadn't met Langenegger, I don't know what I would have done. She rescued me from becoming a hermit and hiding out in my apartment. She introduced me to her circle of wonderful friends and, best of all, she was a fellow Canucks fan. She would sit on the other end of the couch as we both yelled profanities at the referees.

I felt a pang of guilt thinking that I was putting her through another bout of hell. Earlier in the year, she had driven me to the emergency ward at the hospital in Regina. I had woken up one morning in severe pain, unable to get out of bed. After a battery of tests, the young emergency room physician diagnosed me with stage 4 ovarian cancer. It was shocking news, and I was sent to a bigger hospital, where an oncologist would be waiting for me.

Stef left work immediately after I called her for a ride, and on the way I told her what the doctor said. The car came to a screeching halt. "What? That's crazy, Fungy. They can't just know that from a CT scan! Did they do a biopsy? No, so how can they tell you that?"

She was angry and worried, and when I had surgery the next day, she was there. Fortunately it turned about to be a benign tumour—though it was the size of a small melon!—and I was sent home to recuperate, minus an ovary and with a four-inch trophy scar down the centre of my abdomen. Stef and Shelley and Coreen spent the next few weeks bringing me food and keeping me company as I got my strength back. Even before I was thrown into that nightmare, I knew I was extremely fortunate to have the most amazing friends anyone could have. You can't overestimate the power of girlfriends. I knew that they were out there, thinking good thoughts and saying prayers, and that made it impossible not to believe that *this* nightmare would end well, and that I would soon be going home.

My thoughts were disturbed by Abdullah's loud snores, which reminded me that home was still very far away. It was past midnight, and the lamp was fading again. New batteries came every few days, but they were made in China and prone to a short life span. I decided to save whatever juice was left in them and turned the light off. I was starting to get used to the darkness, which was sometimes preferable to the artificial fluorescent lamp. But as usual,

I had trouble sleeping. I closed my eyes and tossed and turned until the clock's little hand hit three. And then I must have dozed off.

———————————

Abdullah woke early. The effects of the niswar appeared to have worn off, and he was cheery and talkative while he did his morning ablutions. He had the same routine as his brother, right down to using the toothbrush contraption. The only thing he didn't do was comb his hair several times with a fine comb, looking at himself in a pocket mirror. Instead, he put his skullcap neatly on his head and seemed ready to face the day.

He asked if I could read him some of the stories in the old schoolbook—the one Khalid had brought the first week. I read a few stories about Ali and Hamid going to the store and to school, and Abdullah nodded, apparently understanding what was being read to him. Then he reached for the Farsi–English phrase book and flipped through it.

"I am angry at you!"

I looked over at him, unsure if he was reading from the book. He was pointing to a phrase in the book. It did say, "I am angry at you."

"I am angry at you! Mellissa, I am angry at you!"

"Why you angry, Abdullah?" I asked.

"You not Muslim!" was the reply.

Not this again. I'd had this conversation with every one of my captors, and there was no reason to think I could escape it with this one, but I was tired of it, and didn't want to engage anymore.

"I am Christian," I answered.

"Why you not Muslim? You must be Muslim. Muslim the best. Koran the best. You must be Muslim."

"I don't know enough about Islam to be Muslim. I don't know the Koran. How can I be Muslim?"

"You must read Koran!" Abdullah's eyes were flashing now, and he moved in closer to me so that his face was just inches from mine. He was almost spitting in my eyes. I backed away.

"I promise, Abdullah, that when I get home to Canada I will read the Koran and learn more about Islam," I said.

"You must be Muslim!" he repeated.

"I need to know more about it before I can become Muslim," I argued. "I can't just stop being Christian because you're telling me to."

"Muslim. You. Then you are my friend," he told me.

I nodded. I promised myself I would try to learn more about Islam when I got out of this place. And it wasn't just because I was trying to appease my captor—I was genuinely curious. I wanted to know where it said in the Koran that it was okay to kidnap someone and force them to convert. Although, I reminded myself, Christians did much worse during the Crusades.

Abdullah seemed satisfied that he had persuaded me to study the teachings of Muhammad and rewarded himself with another piece of niswar. He spent the rest of the day in a haze, which was fine by me. He didn't even bat an eye when I stood up to do my exercises.

And he didn't notice the sound of footsteps overhead late in the afternoon.

I sat up but didn't say anything. Abdullah's eyes were closed, and he wasn't moving. He was fast asleep. *Clomp, clomp, clomp, clomp, clomp.*

I stood up and put my ear to a pipe hole, but I couldn't hear any voices. After several minutes, the footsteps faded. Now I was really curious. If it had been one of the gang, they would have called down a pipe to Abdullah. So perhaps it was a villager wandering around the area, like the woman we heard calling to her son earlier. The only other options were the police, or another gang, trying to find out where my captors were hiding me.

Later that night when Khalid came to replace Abdullah, I told him I had heard footsteps again. He seemed perturbed.

"Who are they?" I asked, picking up a cold french fry from the grease-stained newspaper wrapper. It was the second time he'd brought me fries and bread. Khalid shook his head and looked at me closely.

"Is it the police?" I pressed.

"It is Taliban. Taliban—are all around this place," he said solemnly. "They know we have you."

"But you're all Taliban. You're all the same," I argued. "What do they want?"

"Do you know . . . two people"—I assumed he meant two other groups aside from this particular gang of kidnappers—"they know we have you. They give us they money. Then they will take you."

"You wouldn't do that, Khalid," I said. "My friends will give you the money. You talked to them. They'll give you the money you want. I'll give you the money if I could."

My friends and family didn't love me, Khalid told me, and weren't going to pay the ransom. Anyway, he continued, "Taliban . . . they give me, how to say, more money. Why do I not take more money?" This was precisely what I didn't want to happen. To be sold from one band of kidnappers to another, or worse, to the real Taliban.

"Khalid, you can't just take money from anyone. You took me, you're responsible for me." I was pleading again. He said nothing but looked to be deep in thought, which heightened my sense of unease. I wasn't sure what to do, but I felt like I had to keep talking.

"Besides," I blurted out, "I'm not feeling well, and you can't sell a sick hostage to the Taliban. They will be angry, and then they will hunt you down and kill you."

"You are sick?" he asked. I nodded and rubbed my stomach. It wasn't exactly a lie. My tummy had been off for the last few days, and I was running out of Cipro, breaking it into little pieces to conserve what I had.

"My stomach hurts," I told him. "It's been hurting for days. It will only get worse, and I will need to see a doctor soon."

He stared at me for a while. "You must eat. You not eating."

"I ate a little. You see—I had some chips. But I am not hungry. You cannot eat if you are not hungry," I told him.

He broke off a piece of bread and handed it to me. I shook my head no. He took my hand and shoved it into my palm. "Eat a little, little," he said. "Please."

I took a small bite. It was cold and chewy and hard, and I shook my head again. "I cannot eat. My stomach is not good."

"You have pain?"

"Yes. Pain. How to say it in Pashto?"

"*Dard*," he told me.

"I have *dard*," I repeated. "You must help me get out of this place soon, Khalid. My pain will get worse, and I will need to see a doctor." He looked at me like he wasn't sure what to say and whether he believed me. So I told him about my operation earlier in the year. And then I lifted up my shirt to show him the scar on my stomach. His eyes widened.

"What is that?" he asked.

"It's where they operated on me. A few months ago. I had a big tumour." I was pretty sure he wouldn't know what the word meant, so I made a ball with my hands.

"A tumour, in my stomach." I pointed at my belly. "That is why I have *dard* here now. I will need to see a doctor if my pain does not go away.

Khalid sighed and put his head in his hands.

"Why you no tell me?" he asked. I could tell that he didn't like the idea of having a sick hostage on his hands. I hoped it would help expedite the process, lend a new and different sense of urgency to "finishing my case" and getting me off his hands.

"When was I going to tell you? Would it have made a difference? You already took me," I argued. "You didn't know I was sick."

"Eat," he told me. It was all he could think of to say. "Maybe we find doctor."

"A doctor? Here? They wouldn't know how to treat me. I need special medicines and only the doctors back home in Canada know what to do. It's a special case. I had a major operation."

I knew it wouldn't be possible for them to get a doctor to see me. I was a hostage, and they would be afraid of any doctor giving them up. But I knew from the look on Khalid's face that this was something he hadn't counted on, and he was at a loss as to what to do about me, especially if I got worse.

"Shogufa," he said, "is a little little *dard*."

"Shogufa is sick?" I asked. "What is wrong with her?"

"She have *nas*—stomach—pain. *Dard*. Like you."

"Has she seen a doctor? She should see a doctor or she will end up like me, with a tumour that needs to be taken out." I wasn't just saying that to scare him. After my tumour scare, I'd been warning all my friends to make sure they see a doctor if they felt even the least bit of abnormal pain. I had ignored the pain in my belly for months, and it had cost me an ovary.

"You must tell her to see a doctor, Khalid. You don't want her to have what I had." He nodded yes, he would make her see someone.

"Do it soon, Khalid," I insisted. "Do you love her?"

He nodded again. "Yes. I love her. We get married."

"Well, if you really love her, you'll make sure she sees a doctor."

He took his cell phone out of his pocket and put the SIM card back in. It kept sliding out, and he reached back into his pocket and pulled out a piece of a toothpick, which he then tucked into the back of the phone to hold the SIM card in place. He punched in some numbers, and I could hear the phone ringing on the other end. A woman's voice answered.

"Salaam," Khalid said. His voice was deep and serious, but the conversation, which lasted several minutes, was punctuated by a few laughs.

He hung up and turned to me. "I tell her. Doctor. Okay?"

"You just called her to tell her that?" I asked.

"I tell her what you say."

It was quite amazing, I thought, that my kidnapper, in the midst of dealing with his hostage, would call his girlfriend to tell her to see a doctor for the pain in her stomach. There was something about it that was endearing, and it made me believe that deep down, beneath the bravado of being at best a bandit and at worst a Taliban sympathizer, this was a young man who could be human and thoughtful and kind. The same one who would think to bring me french fries that he asked his girlfriend to make. The same one who took my hand on that first day and told me not to be afraid.

"Good, I'm glad," I told him. "It's important. You don't want her to be sick, like me."

"No, sick bad," he said. I rubbed my stomach again and reached for the package of cigarettes.

"You no smoke," Khalid objected. "You smoke too much."

"It doesn't make me sick. It's okay." I held out my hand for his lighter, but he took the pack of smokes out of my hand.

"Khalid! Let me have one. Please."

He looked at me carefully, as if studying me, and then took a cigarette out of the package, licked the ends, lit it, and handed it to me.

"Why do you lick the ends?" I asked, making a licking motion in case he didn't know the word.

"So this . . . how do I say . . ." He pointed at the end of my cigarette.

"The ash?" I asked.

"Yes. So it not go everywhere." It was true. The wetness at the end of the cigarette held the ash together in one long cylinder, which I was able to flick into the trash can. We smoked another cigarette after that, and continued smoking until the package was empty and my head was heavy with smoke.

"No more," Khalid said. "Sleep come to me." He lay back and stretched his legs out. "Sleep no come to you? You must sleep," he told me, his eyes already closed. "You sick. You must sleep, Mellissa."

"I will try, Khalid. Good night."

I heard his breathing deepen after a few minutes. I wished that sleep could come to me as easily, but I was not the least bit tired, so I decided to keep the lamp on for a while longer and flipped open my notebook. There were only a few pages left, and I remembered the prayer I had said the other day. *Please God, please don't let me run out of pages before I am freed. Please help me out of this hole before I have no more space to write.* I wrote those exact words on one of the few precious pages I had left. And then I continued.

Please, God, please help me. Please help me out of here. Please help my family and my friends back home. Let them know, if you can, that I'm okay. They are suffering more than me, and it's not fair to them. Please help them get through this. They're suffering a lot, I know, and they need you. More than I do. Please, give them some comfort and tell them I will be all right.

Please, please, please. Help me, God. Help me.

I put the pen down and noticed that one of the "p"s of "please" had smudged. A teardrop had fallen out of my eye and onto the page. I wiped my eyes with my dirt-stained hands. I had refused to allow myself to break down, but in the simple act of writing a desperate prayer to God, I had let down all of my defences.

I put the notebook down, turned off the lamp, and allowed the sobs to rock me to sleep.

Dearest M,

It's just after noon and I'm trying to picture where you are and what you're doing. And I just can't. Have you been able to wash your hair, do you even have a brush, are you looking after yourself, what are you wearing? Do you remember that we were supposed to be heading for Dubai this afternoon? We'll get there, M.

xx

Khalid was agitated. He had woken early and turned on his cell phone, which rang almost immediately. Two quick conversations followed, the second one more urgent sounding than the first. I didn't understand any of it, but he seemed to be asking lots of questions. After the calls, he was silent for a while, then sighed deeply several times.

He got up and went to relieve himself in the plastic bottle. When he sat back down, he buried his face in his hands. I asked him what was wrong, but he wouldn't tell me. The phone rang again. He answered, listened to the speaker on the other end, and then hung up. I picked up the cigarettes and lit one, blowing smoke in a little stream.

"No smoke!" he hushed me, putting his fingers to his lips and grabbing the cigarette out of my mouth.

"What's wrong with you?" I asked, annoyed.

"No talking," he ordered.

I glared at him for a second, then turned my back to him, flipping open my notebook. I reread the prayer I had written the night before. *Amen*, I thought. *Please help me get out of this godforsaken place.* He was on the phone again, speaking in staccato tones. Questions were asked and presumably answered. He dialed another number. Maybe the negotiations were bearing fruit, and freedom was imminent. It had been four days since Abdulrahman asked the proof-of-life questions and surely by now the AKE people had the answers and were satisfied that I was indeed alive.

It actually wasn't until that moment that it occurred to me that my friends and family feared I might be dead. Because I was alive and living every second of this nightmare, I assumed that everyone else knew that as well. My friends almost always knew where I was and what I was doing. Now, the only thing they knew for certain was that I had been taken by some Afghans, and the worst-case scenario for them would certainly be that my kidnappers had killed me.

But now they had proof of life. Answers to several questions only I would know. I hoped that would set their minds at ease for a little while. *I'm alive!* I wanted to yell. *I'm okay, don't worry about me, I'll be home soon!* I just wished there was some way I could tell everyone I was okay. I wondered if Khalid's father had sent the phone video that Abdulrahman had taken on my second day in captivity. On the one hand, I hoped they had, so that everyone at home could see that I was alive. But on the other, I worried that it would scare them even more to see a grainy image of me at some undisclosed location, kind of like the way we're used to seeing videos of hostages on TV, flanked by masked men and reading a prepared statement they hadn't written. I was running out of pages in my notebook, but I defiantly flipped to an empty page and began to write.

Dear P,

Another day, and another day of hoping and praying that I'll see you soon. Every day, my kidnappers tell me that it will only be two or three more days, and then the day passes and nothing happens. I hope you know that I'm okay, darling.

The most frustrating thing is that I can't tell you. I know you're probably sick with worry, as is everyone else back home, and that upsets me more than anything.

I know we were supposed to be in Dubai now, but I promise you we'll get there. I'm not sure where you are, maybe at KAF or maybe you're up here in Kabul. Please just wait for me. I'm coming back, and I can't wait to see you.

I think something is going on, and maybe you know more than I do, because

Khalid seems agitated this morning and he's been on the phone non-stop. It makes me wonder if the negotiations are nearing an end. I know you're in contact with them, because he told me that they keep calling your number. By now, I'm sure the AKE people have made you surrender your phone. It's better off, P. I wouldn't want you to have to deal with the stress of talking to these losers.

I hope you're okay. And wherever you are this morning, please know that I'm thinking about you and wishing that we'd just come back from running the flight line to a cappuccino at the Green Bean. I miss you so much. Soon, P, soon.

xox

I had mastered the art of balancing the hand-held lamp on my knees, with the bulb turned down toward my notepad, so that I could see what I was writing.

"Off the light," Khalid suddenly ordered.

"Why?" I asked. "I'm still writing. And I like having the light on." Even though it was artificial light, I needed to have it on during the day; in some way, it helped me to deal with the slow passage of time in this place.

"Off the light."

"Tell me why and I'll turn it off." I held the lamp between my legs, and the fluorescent beam bounced off the wall behind his head.

"Off it. I tell you."

I sighed and turned it off. "Okay," I said in the darkness. "What is happening?"

"Taliban are all around" came the answer out of the darkness.

"What do you mean?"

"Taliban. They looking for us." I wasn't sure whether to believe him or not—part of me thought that their saying the Taliban wanted to "buy" me was a ploy to keep me from calling out whenever I heard people overhead.

"They know we have you."

I decided to play devil's advocate. "So why don't you just take their money and give me to them?" No answer. I pressed him. The darkness somehow made it easier to challenge him. "It's the same money, so why don't you just take it and give me to them? Then you don't have to wait."

"It is my father. He talk to them," he replied. Khalid's phone rang and he jumped. I could see the silhouette of his bearded chin against the bright light of the phone.

"As-Salaam Alaikum," he said softly. The conversation didn't last long. He was back to me in a matter of seconds.

"*Tsiragh,*" he said. I handed him the lamp. He turned it on and promptly lit a cigarette. I surmised that if there were Taliban looking for us, they were gone. Shafirgullah or someone else must have called to let him know. They were probably watching the area from afar. I reached for a cigarette as well.

"What if it's not the Taliban?" I asked. "What if it's the police?"

"No police," Khalid replied. I was pretty sure he was right. There was no way the police would be able to find me. And the Afghan National Police were a sorry lot. I had done a story about them the summer before, when I was out at the forward operating base (FOB) at Ma'sum Ghar and attached to Major Dave Quick's battle group unit. It was a Sunday afternoon and the unit had received a call. My cameraman, Sat, and I were in the media tent, chain-smoking, waiting for something to happen, when Quick came in and told us to be ready in five minutes.

"What's happening?" we asked.

"ANP extraction." The Afghan National Police had been caught in a shootout with Taliban insurgents. Three of their officers were dead, and they needed the Canadians to help them extract the bodies from the scene. Initial reports from the ANP indicated there were about three hundred Taliban in the area. Sat and I hopped into an RG-31 Nyala, a more heavily protected armoured vehicle, with a crew of five. There were about ten vehicles in our convoy as we drove out from the base—a few RGs, some LAVs (light armoured vehicles), and a Bison, an eight-wheeled armoured vehicle.

We moved slowly down the dirt road. Children played in a wadi just a few metres from the base. They barely looked up, so familiar were they with these big foreign convoys rumbling through their living space. Nearby, women were hanging laundry outside their mud homes. Life seemed strangely normal in rural Afghanistan as I watched it from an armoured personnel carrier. We made a pit stop at FOB Wilson, where we picked up a few ANP officers, whose job would be to guide us into the checkpoint where their colleagues had been killed.

About a kilometre from the checkpoint, everyone got out of the vehicles, and we continued the trek on foot. The air felt thick and hot; the temperature was near fifty degrees Celsius. The soldiers were tiring under the weight of their backpacks and weapons. Several went down from heat exhaustion. Sat stopped to offer one his CamelBak, which was filled with cool water. Suddenly, rapid gunfire shattered the stillness. The ANP were trying to scare off the Taliban so we could make our way through the trenches, the wadis, and the marijuana fields that made up the landscape of Zhari district.

Once we got to the checkpoint, the Canadians secured the perimeter, assessed the situation, and called for air cover. The ANP officers gathered up the bodies of their fallen colleagues, put them in the body bags the Canadians had provided, and drove off in their rundown version of a police cruiser, a beat-up pickup truck, leaving India Company stranded at the checkpoint, since there was no one checking the road out to make sure it hadn't been lined with fresh bombs during the time the Canadians were helping the ANP with the dead.

Quick consulted with headquarters before deciding that we would head back to Ma'sum Ghar, rather than staying overnight. It was just getting dark, and the soldiers were tired, hungry, and hot. A few of them gave me cold bottled water from the vehicles that had driven into the checkpoint, along with a ration they fixed for me of hot macaroni and cheese, made by pouring water into the bag that contained the freeze-dried noodles and powdered cheese.

Once we got going, the convoy had barely made it out of the checkpoint when it came to a complete stop. The road had given way and one of the vehicles had nearly flipped over. Everyone had to dismount, and the soldiers took up defensive positions. It was an extremely vulnerable position to be in—stuck at night in the middle of Taliban territory, and basically immobile. I sat down next to the gunner in our RG-31, who was keeping watch around us with his night-vision lenses. He pointed out two, three, four, at least five Taliban watching us from their vantage points atop the grape huts, the mud-brick buildings used for drying grapes. The soldiers were nervous and waited for the inevitable strike, but apart from sporadic gunfire, it never came.

Six hours later, after another vehicle got stuck in the mud, the convoy finally made it around the destroyed road and back to the forward operating base, and when I had a chance to talk to Major Quick the next morning, his frustration with the ANP came through.

"The biggest challenge," he told me, "was trying to figure out what happened before we left. We had conflicting reports that upward of 300 Taliban were in the area. Then it went to 150. It's extremely hard to determine what is the truth. And that was a good example of how difficult it is to work with the ANP."

I knew that Khalid was right. The ANP would never find me here. They had enough problems of their own, and investigative detective work was just not a skill they would learn overnight. But then maybe, just maybe, the Canadians were looking for me. I didn't like the thought of them diverting resources from the war to go on a wild goose chase for a kidnapped journalist, but it gave me some comfort to think that someone like Dave Quick might be on the case. In the little time I'd spent with our troops, my respect for the work they did and their motives for going to Afghanistan had multiplied tenfold. Every soldier I met told me the same thing. They were there because they believed that they could make life better for ordinary Afghans, that they could contribute, even in a small way, to improving society there, and that they knew they were putting their own lives in danger to try to make a difference.

The debate back in Canada over whether our soldiers should be in Afghanistan had always bothered me. The fact was, they were here, risking their lives to take on an almost impossible task in one of the most inhospitable and dangerous places on earth. I believed that even if you didn't support the mission, you needed to support these young men and women. They were eager, smart, and resourceful.

"Police bad," Khalid said, interjecting himself into my train of thought.

I nodded. "Yes, police bad." I was thinking of the ANP. "Taliban bad too," I added. "So who is good?"

Khalid scratched his head. He didn't seem to have an answer to that. "Mullah Omar good. Bin Laden good." As expected. Shafirgullah had said the same thing the week before.

"Why are they good if they kill people?" I challenged.

"They Muslim. They kill people no Muslim. Good."

I've been in this hole too long, I thought. I was starting to have the same conversation over and over again with my captors—and myself, for that matter.

At least with Khalid there was a little more conversation, perhaps a little more trust—but after almost two weeks, even we were running out of things to talk about. There were only so many times I could ask him about his plans to get married, what Shogufa was like ("very pretty"), whether her parents approved of their relationship ("they like me"), and what their plans were for the future ("suicide bombing").

Khalid was still worried, though. He was unsure whose footsteps we'd heard earlier in the day, and I could see that on his face. He made several more phone calls in the afternoon, taking his SIM card in and out of the Nokia phone. Then I recognized some of the names on the display screen. *Paul, Shokoor, Toronto, Sameem.* It was *my* SIM card he was using to make the calls.

"Let me see," I said, holding out my hand. "That's *my* phone, Khalid." He handed it over, warning me not to try to dial. I scrolled through my phone and the SMS messages still contained in it. There was the one from Paul: *What can you tell me?* That was the message he had sent after Shokoor told him about my kidnapping. One from Shokoor: *We are late, sorry, Mellissa*—sent the morning he and his brother were coming to get me at the hotel in Kabul, to take me to the refugee camp. Then another from Paul: *Miss you, M, hurry back.*

I put the phone down as my eyes welled up. *I'm hurrying, P. I'm hurrying, and I miss you too. More than you know.*

Khalid took the phone back. "Do not cry, Mellissa," he said, taking my hand. "I no like you cry. I want you happy."

"How can I be happy when I'm stuck here? When you've taken me away from everything? How can I be happy here?"

My captor sighed. "I am sorry for you, Mellissa," he said. "I am sorry."

"If you are really sorry, you'll let me go, Khalid. You'll take me back to Kabul on your motorcycle and take me back to my hotel."

"It is not my choice," he said. "My father . . ."

"Your father will understand. Please, Khalid. I am sick, and I'm going to get sicker. I will be of no use to you if I die here. You must let me go home to Canada, where I can see a doctor." I knew he was worried about my health: he had been asking me practically every hour on the hour how I was feeling and if I had any *dard*. I did have pain, but it was in my head. I thought the weather must be changing outside because that's when I get the worst migraines. It's been that way since I was in high school. I could predict a thunderstorm by the strength of my headaches, and I was usually right. Doctors prescribed me every migraine drug they could, but unless I took it before the symptoms hit, I was reduced to lying in a dark room in a fetal position, waiting for it all to pass. I could feel a migraine coming on now, and I didn't have any Maxalt or Imitrex, but I did have Tylenol, which I never went anywhere without. I dug down deep in my knapsack and pulled out the bottle with the red cap, then popped three pills in my mouth, washing them down with a gulp of apple juice.

"What you eat?" Khalid asked. He had been watching me.

"It's my medication," I said, rattling the bottle. There were only a few left. "I'm running out. It's for my pain. That's why I need to go home, Khalid. I need to see my doctor." He took the bottle of Tylenol from me and opened it. He poured a few out into his big palm and studied them for a while before putting them back in the bottle.

"We find doctor," he told me.

"You can't. I need my doctor at home in Canada. She's the only one who knows because she knows about my operation, and she's the only one who can prescribe me my medication," I said earnestly.

"We find doctor here," he insisted.

"No, it won't work," I argued. "I could get sicker if I see the wrong doctor. It's dangerous." Khalid sighed and put his head in his hands again.

Sensing that he might perhaps consider what I was saying, I pressed on. "You have to call your father and tell him I am sick, and that he needs to finish my case soon. I won't be any good to you if I die in here, Khalid. You wouldn't want that."

I was interrupted by a loud bang. And then another one. Mortars. And then the sound of an aircraft flying overhead. Gunfire followed. The noise went on for a long time, maybe a couple hours. It had to be NATO forces engaging the insurgents in the area. Khalid leaned back on his pillow and cracked the knuckles on his hands, then on his feet. He seemed resigned to the fact that he was staying another night. There was no way the others would come and dig him out as long as there was this much activity above.

We both lit cigarettes and waited. The noises would crescendo and then fade. At times, it sounded like whoever was firing was right above the hole. I thought about calling out, but I figured there was too much noise for anyone outside to hear me to risk the wrath of Khalid. Instead, I imagined what might happen if I did cry out. It was the umpteenth time I'd gone over this in my mind: Was it my best chance of escape? A few nights earlier, when Abdullah left, the kidnappers had left me alone in the cave for quite some time—almost half an hour. I'd crawled up the tunnel and looked up the uncovered shaft. No one was there. I'd heard voices a little farther away from the entrance, and I'd stood up to see if I could see anything, but the ground was a good two feet above my head. I was just trying to get my footing on one of the sides when I heard voices and footsteps approaching the hole. I dropped down and dove headfirst into the tunnel, covering my kameez and pants with a thick layer of dirt.

But the possibility that I might get another chance to escape teased me almost every time my captors came to replace each other. I was growing desperate. It had been five days since the proof-of-life questions, and I'd heard nothing concrete about my release, and every time I asked Khalid what was going on, he told me my friends and my family didn't love me because they were not prepared to hand over any money. I knew that would be the official line—especially if the Canadian government was involved, because it is its policy not to pay ransoms or negotiate with terrorists. I wondered if my sister and my parents would try to find the money. I know I would pay if someone I cared about was being held hostage. It's a difficult situation because paying ransom encourages kidnappers to just keep on kidnapping. But when it comes down to it, you're talking about someone's life. And when someone you love is in danger or at risk, you do whatever you can to ensure their safety. If it were my sister, or Paul, in this hole, I knew I'd be trying to find money to secure her or his release.

We'd heard earlier in the year that Amanda Lindhout, a Canadian freelance reporter whom we'd met in Kandahar the year before, was kidnapped while in Somalia and that her family was trying desperately to raise the ransom money. I thought about where she might be now. I couldn't imagine being in captivity for as long as she was. It had been months since her capture, and I supposed her parents were still trying to come up with the money. At least my parents had the support of a television network. I hoped they were being updated regularly, and that they'd been told I had answered the proof-of-life questions on Sunday.

And so, what happened next? Were the proof-of-life questions enough? Or were they just the beginning, in terms of negotiating with these guys? Would the AKE people demand more proof? Would there be more questions? Would they need to see me or talk to me themselves?

I had so many questions and no answers. And as a journalist, that was excruciatingly frustrating. I couldn't do what I was accustomed to doing—picking up the phone and dialing a number and asking a question. There was no way to get credible information—my kidnappers were not ones to tell me the truth, and I had no way of double-sourcing or fact checking what they told me. I was in a black hole of communication and information—and there was nothing I could do about it.

I couldn't allow my thoughts to spiral me into despair—it was all too easy to sit here and feel sorry for myself, and I hated the idea of being a victim. So rather than let my thoughts continue to carry me away, I tried to distract myself the only way I could think of. I opened another package of cookies.

There was one box of cookies left—the chocolate ones I liked the best. On the box was a picture of a cartoon prince. I'd already studied the nutritional value of the cookies ad nauseam—but now for the first time I noticed there was a story in English about a prince. Prince cookies, they were called, and they made him big and strong so he could rule over his kingdom. Cute, I thought. Maybe he would come and rescue me.

Khalid sat up—he must have dozed off for a while—and reached for the cookies. "You like this one?" he asked.

I nodded and told him they tasted much better than the fruit creme kind.

"I bring more. What else I can bring you for? Chips? Bread?"

"Nothing, Khalid. Just bring me back to Kabul. Please."

"I bring you more chips," he said, smiling. "Shogufa make. You like. You must eat."

I was exhausted with this constant exchange. I just shook my head and rubbed my stomach again. *"Dard,"* I said weakly when he looked at me questioningly.

I wasn't sure if it was psychosomatic, but the more I told him I was in pain, the more pain I felt in my stomach. It was sharp and reminded me of the pain I'd felt right before my surgery. I reached for the Tylenol bottle in my knapsack and swallowed two pills with a sip of apple juice. Khalid watched intently, his brow furrowing as I put the Tylenol back.

"Mellissa, you are sick."

"I've been sick for a long time, Khalid. You didn't know this when you took me."

"We get doctor," he said. Unless the group had a trustworthy doctor they could bring to the hole, I knew this was not going to happen. It would be too much trouble to dig me out during the day and take me into the village to see someone. They would never take the risk that someone might notice or that I might try to escape.

I just shook my head. "No doctor."

Khalid considered the options for a while, and I could tell he was troubled because he tossed and turned and couldn't get comfortable, even after I had turned off the lamp to try to get some sleep.

"Sleep not coming to me," he told me after a while. "*Tsiragh.*" I turned on the lamp and shone it into his eyes.

"Sleep not come to you?" he asked.

I shook my head. We lit cigarettes, and Khalid asked me what my house looked like in Canada. I described for him my cozy one-bedroom condo in Regina. The more I talked about it, the more homesick I felt. I missed my bed, my couch, my television; my routine at home.

He told me about his family's house in Peshawar, where he would be going after my "case was finished." He was also hoping to bring Shogufa there to live, and when I asked whether she'd like it there, he told me that even though there were fifteen other people living in the house, they would have their own room. He assured me that she would be very happy living with his family.

Finally, sleep came to Khalid, and I was once again left alone with the sound of his snoring. I took out my rosary and started praying, asking God to please let me fall asleep. He must have been listening because the next thing I heard was tapping overhead. I sat up and reached for the lamp. The alarm clock told me it was just after six.

Tap. Tap. Tap. Tap. It sounded like someone was poking a stick on the ground, looking for the hole. *Tap. Tap. Tap.* Then footsteps. Whoever it was, he was walking all around the covering of the hole. *Tap. Tap. Tap. Tap.* I wondered who it could be. Dare I call out? Khalid was still sound asleep. I wasn't sure what to do.

Tap. Tap. Tap. Tap. It couldn't have been someone from my gang because no one called down to us. The tapping continued. After about half an hour, I could hear the footsteps fading into the distance.

When Khalid woke up, I told him what I'd heard. He took out his cell phone and made a few calls.

"Taliban," he told me. "They are all over this place." He made a gesture with his hands to emphasize the words "all over." But I didn't believe him. I thought it might be the police, acting on a tip and trying to find me. That's why my kidnappers were nervous. "Taliban want me to give you to them," Khalid repeated. "They give us the money."

"I don't believe you," I said stubbornly. "If they are giving you the money, then why don't you just give me to them?"

"We give your friends five days," he said. "Or we kill you."

"Five days is not a lot of time to get all that money together. They will need more time."

Khalid assured me they wouldn't kill me, that it was just a threat to get "my friends" to come up with the money sooner rather than later. But when I asked what might happen if five days passed and nothing happened, he didn't have an answer.

"Then you kill me?" I asked.

He shook his head. "I promise you. I no kill you. I tell you on the first day. I no kill you. You are my sister. I no kill my sister."

"You promise?" I insisted. It wasn't that I was afraid of being killed. My philosophy about life is that I try to live a good one, but if my time is up, it's up, and God has his reason for moving me out of this world. But I desperately wanted to get inside the head of my kidnapper, to try to get a few clues about what would happen next.

"I promise, Mellissa. I no kill you. But we may go from here," he said.

"What do you mean? You want to move me?" I asked.

Khalid nodded. "This place. Not safe."

Dearest M,

It's after eleven o'clock, darling, and I hate the thought of going to sleep. I think of you lying in the darkness somewhere, on a hard, filthy floor, and it scares the hell out of me. Are they abusing you? Are you alone? I try to be positive that it will end soon and you will come back safely, but there are moments when a deep sense of despair takes over, and I'm afraid I've lost you.

Love you, M.

Two days later, Khalid returned with a Kalashnikov. It hadn't really occurred to me that my kidnappers had been guarding me without a gun until then, and it was easy to understand why. It wouldn't have been hard for me to grab the gun and shoot Khalid or Shafirgullah while they slept, and then shoot whoever came into the hole next, and just keep shooting my way out. It was a risk, and not a risk they had wanted to take—until now. Obviously, something had changed.

"Take this," Khalid said, handing me the gun, and he crawled back up the tunnel to bring down other supplies.

I cradled the Kalashnikov in my hands, turning it over and around, studying the old Soviet assault rifle carefully. I put my hand around the pistol grip and my finger on the trigger. The magazine had been removed—I assumed that Khalid kept that close. I wondered how many people the gun had killed since it was made, and who had owned it before.

Khalid returned with several bulging white plastic bags and a can of water. He smiled at me. "You like gun?" he asked. I handed it back to him and told him big guns scared me, but I would learn how to use it if he taught me.

"Maybe I teach you," he said. "But see this first." He handed back the camera he had stolen out of my bag the first day, and I took the camera out of its case.

"Shogufa," he said. "You want to see Shogufa." He turned the camera on, and there, on the screen, was the image of a very pretty young girl.

"Yes, she is very *shayesta*, no?" he asked.

She *was* very *shayesta*. She had long black hair and big dark eyes, and even under her orange headscarf, I could tell she was beautiful. There was a series of photos: Shogufa in what appeared to be a garden, looking shyly at Khalid from a doorway. Shogufa with two other girls—her sisters, Khalid told me—and then with a little girl, another sister. There were dozens of photos of other women and children, at Shogufa's family's home, I assumed. Khalid pointed out Shogufa's mother (his aunt) and other relatives. They all looked happy, smiling, and normal. I wondered if they condoned what the men in their family did for a living. I imagined that their lives were cloistered, sheltered from the guns and the violence, the threats and the kidnappings. I scrolled through what felt like dozens of photos, and then I came to one of Khalid holding a gun to my head. That was the first day, when he discovered the camera and he and Shafir-gullah took turns taking pictures with their hostage.

I went back some more. All the pictures I had taken at the refugee camp. The family I'd planned on doing a photo essay about: the cobbler and his son in their mud hut. The woman who had lost her family when a bomb destroyed her home. All of these people whose stories and struggles I'd wanted so much for Canadians at home to hear, to see, so that they could understand that there was a painfully human cost to the war in Afghanistan. I now feared I would never get to tell their stories.

I kept scrolling. It was Eid at the PRT, and there was my little girl in the pink scarf, staring at me with her big eyes. Two little boys, sitting on the dirty ground with their burka-hidden mothers, hoping to get into the compound so they could receive the Eid gifts the soldiers were handing out. Inside, a little girl with short hair and a blue dress, likely no more than three or four years old, sitting in the back of a wagon while her father collected the gifts for their family. A Canadian soldier in his fatigues, handing out cooking oil to a young boy.

A picture of Paul, crouched down, smiling at a woman with a baby. I wondered where he might be at that moment. I scrolled back some more. A photo of my girlfriends in Toronto the night before I left for Afghanistan. I'd cooked dinner at my friend Kas's house, where a bunch of us had gathered. It was now rare that we were all in the same city together, but there they all were—Kas, Angela, Marie, and Jen, with plates of turkey meatballs and macaroni and cheese, and glasses of wine—a happy send-off before I went on assignment halfway around the world to a war zone.

Khalid was looking at the pictures too. He pointed at the wine on the table in the photo. I was pretty sure that his fundamental-ist interpretation of Islam frowned on women who drank alcohol. "You drink?" he asked, pointing to the big glass of wine that was in front of Kas. We tended to pour each other *big* glasses.

"That's my friend's," I told him. "I was having a martini." I knew he would never know what that meant, so I continued to try to push the envelope a little. "Martinis are stronger than wine."

"You drink?" he asked again. I nodded, and he shook his head disapprovingly. "It is bad," he said.

"No, it is good," I argued, smiling to myself. My friends and I joke that our lives revolve around booze. It might be an exaggera-tion, but not much of one. Beer and wine and vodka were staples at any gathering, and I took pride in the fact that, unlike most Asian people I knew, whose faces would turn beet red after just one drink, almost everyone in my family could hold their alcohol. Just think-ing about it made me thirsty. One drink, or twenty, could certainly help me pass the time in here. I'd been several weeks without drink already. We had smuggled a few bottles of illicit hooch—"lens cleaner" we journalists called it—into the dry Kandahar base, but it went quickly given the number of thirsty journalists there and the long hours we worked. It was probably good for me, I thought, to go without booze for a while longer, but I promised myself I would find a good martini as soon as I was free again.

Khalid took the camera back and pointed it in my direction. I put my head down, not wanting to be photographed in the cave—it felt somehow like I was accepting my place as a hostage, and I didn't want to resign myself to reality. He took a picture anyway, then put the camera into its case. It was just as well. I couldn't bring myself to go through any more memories.

Khalid had brought more french fries. "Chips, Mellissa, you must eat," he said, pulling out a newspaper-wrapped bundle. "Shafirgullah say you no eating."

It was true. My stomach had been bad the last few days and, during the time Shafirgullah was with me, I could barely get a cookie down without feeling as if I were going to throw up. I was down to my last two Cipro, and I'd been taking small bites out of the big bitter pills, hoping to make them last. Shafirgullah had noticed and must have told Khalid. They were obviously keeping a close eye on my health.

"I haven't been hungry," I told him as he unwrapped the fries. They had been packed with a few torn-off pieces of bread. I took one and put it in my mouth. It was cold and salty, and I couldn't eat any more.

Khalid was visibly upset. "You must eat. Shogufa made for you!"

"Please thank her for me. She is a good cook, and I know she went to a lot of trouble, but I'm not hungry, Khalid. My stomach is *dard*."

My captor responded by ripping off a piece of bread and putting it in my hand. "Eat this," he ordered. Then he reached into one of the plastic bags and pulled out a small box. White pills encased in plastic. I didn't know what they were. "I talk to doctor. He give me medicine," he told me.

"What doctor? What did you tell him?" I asked.

"I tell him you *dard*. He say this is good. Take one."

I studied the pills. There was no date on them, no name, no description. I wondered if he really got them from a doctor or maybe they were something Abdulrahman had—he had tried to give me pills for the pain in my shoulder from the stab wound.

"I can't take these pills, Khalid. I don't know what's in them. They might not go with the pills I've been taking already, and I could get sicker. That wouldn't be very good."

Khalid looked both frustrated and concerned. I felt bad for him. Perhaps he had indeed gone to the trouble of consulting a doctor and getting the medication and I wasn't grateful and eager to take it. But I wasn't about to ingest any drug I didn't know. I put the pills in my pocket, next to my passport, and thanked him, saying I would maybe take them later if I felt worse. That seemed to pacify Khalid a little. He pushed the bundle of french fries and bread in my direction.

"Eat. A little, little," he was almost begging me.

I obliged by taking a couple of cold fries and chewing slowly. "They are delicious," I told him. "Please tell Shogufa I like them very much."

He seemed happy about this. "Shogufa. She make for you. She no happy you here."

I'd been wondering what Shogufa thought, I told him. She couldn't be happy that her future husband was holding a woman hostage in a dark hole. Khalid said no, she wasn't; she wanted him to let me go. I thought about the pictures I had seen of her. Likely she was uneducated, living with her parents until she was married off—and then she'd spend the rest of her life under a burka: the fate of most women in this war-torn country.

Things had improved a little since the Taliban were overthrown, but women in Afghanistan generally aren't able to choose from a plethora of opportunities, as women in the West are. In my short time in Afghanistan, though, I'd met quite a few women who were determined to defy that fate, creating lives of their own. I thought about Shukria Barakzai, who I'd interviewed the summer before. A journalist-turned-politician, she invited me into her home, where she lived with her three daughters, and talked openly about why she chose—at great risk to herself and her family—to lead such a public life.

"I grew up with war in this country," she said in near-perfect English as she poured tea into short glasses for us. "Peace is still a dream for me."

She attended university in Kabul in the 1990s but was forced to leave school when the Taliban took power. After the US-led invasion in 2001, she went back and got her degree, and started a newspaper for women, which was the brave beginning of her campaign for women's rights. She was outspoken on subjects like violence against women, and maternal and infant mortality. Barakzai was a natural politician, eventually becoming a member of the Afghan parliament, where she continued to press for changes that would give women more opportunities and equal rights. An attractive woman with deep, dark eyes that sparkled as she talked, she was passionate about her country and believed she had an important contribution to make to her society and to women in Afghanistan.

But her determination came at a huge cost. Death threats were delivered to her door on a daily basis. A car bomb exploded outside the gates of her house. She was a target of the Taliban, who even after being overthrown were just as determined not to let women advance. But despite the threats and intimidation, Barakzai continued to go about her business, accepting fully the dangers that came with her position.

"At least you know you are dying for something," she told me. "I'm happy that I'm dying for my country, my goals, for my nation. No one can protect you from a suicide attack. God knows, one day, when, where, how, they will succeed. So I should try my best, and I have to use the time I have."

Barakzai's youngest daughter joined us after the camera had been turned off, climbing into her mother's lap. She was only three years old, a cute dark-haired innocent who didn't have any idea what her mother was trying to do. Barakzai pulled a comb out of her purse and started combing her daughter's hair. "I hope they are not fighting for the same thing I am fighting for today," she said, referring to her children. "I would love to give them some better future in society. But I believe it will take a long time. A generation, maybe. It's a long time, but I believe it can happen."

I couldn't imagine what it would be like to know that you were risking your life to go to work every day, that an assassin's bullet stalked you wherever you went. I couldn't help but look at her with admiration. Here was someone who was really trying to make a difference in her poor, besieged country. I felt small and insignificant just being in her presence. But it was important for me to at least be able to tell her story. It was people like Shukria Barakzai who gave the rest of us hope that the world truly could be a better place.

I took another bite of the bread Shogufa had made, chewing slowly. "Khalid, does Shogufa go to school? What does she want to do when she gets older?"

He scratched his head, unsure, perhaps, of how to answer.

"She no school. She be bomber, like me. We die together," he said after a few more french fries.

"She doesn't want to go to school? She doesn't want to have a job?" I asked.

"I don't know," he said. "She want to get married. She want to have child. I want five childs."

What if she doesn't want five children? I asked him. But it didn't matter. He had five siblings, and he wanted the same for his own family.

"You know," I began, "it's not fair for your children if you die in a suicide bombing. And if Shogufa dies in a suicide bombing! Who will look after them? You can't have children and then leave them to go and kill other people."

"My mother. She will have them," he answered.

I gave up. It was useless to try to reason with someone who refused to consider that there may be alternative beliefs to his. It was late anyway, and I could feel a cool breeze coming into the hole from the pipes. Khalid seemed to notice too, and he opened one of the bags. It was filled with cut-off shirt cuffs and sleeves, and scraps of cloth. He grabbed a handful and stuffed it into a pipe opening, then gave me the bag and pointed at the other pipe. I took some of the scraps and did the same, to block the cool air that was coming in. It was only going to get colder. And if, God forbid, I was there into the winter, we would surely need more blankets. I shuddered at the thought.

It was warmer in the hole with the pipes covered, but my feet were still clammy. I couldn't get them warm, even when I took off my socks and tucked them under the blanket.

Khalid fell asleep almost immediately after telling me to "off the light." I turned the light back on once I heard him snoring. It wasn't even midnight. I picked up my notebook and counted the number of empty pages left. I was losing hope that I'd be released before I ran out of pages, but I defiantly flipped to a fresh page and started writing.

Hi Mom and Dad,

I just want to start by saying that I'm so sorry for putting you through this. I know how worried you must be, and I can't imagine what you are going through. I'm so sorry. I know it's hard for you to understand why I wanted to come here, and you probably think that no story is worth my life. You need to know that I am okay. My kidnappers are treating me very well, and they have not hurt me. I'm being fed and kept in a small room, but I am fine. I just hope you are okay. I've been praying a lot—there's not much else to do—but it's been okay.

I didn't know what else to say. I'm not a parent, and probably will never be, so there was no way I could really comprehend what they were going through. I thought about all the parents I'd interviewed. Parents who'd lost their young children in tragic accidents; parents who didn't know where their children were (those were the among the hardest interviews); and parents of fallen soldiers. For me, those were the most heart-wrenching.

CBC used to do a special broadcast around Christmastime on the soldiers who'd been killed in Afghanistan the previous year. We interviewed families of the soldiers so that Canadians could get to know who these young men and women were who had died fighting the war in Afghanistan. I'd done several of those interviews the year before my first tour to Afghanistan, and they had helped me understand more deeply the sacrifice military families make.

I will never forget the father who broke down halfway through telling me how much his son loved his three young children. Or the mother who talked about her son's love of cars. Their children were all unique, but there was one thread of consistency: They all went to Afghanistan because they thought they should be there. They felt like they were making a difference for people who needed their help. The parents all understood the risks, and when their children were at war, they lived with the knowledge—and the fear—that there might come a knock at their door in the middle of the night. If you had a child who was in the military, that was a part of life.

My parents, however, were in a different category. They may not have liked that I wanted to cover the conflict in Afghanistan, but my job didn't come with the same dangerous risks that a soldier's did—my job wasn't on the front lines. So they didn't have to steel themselves for anything because the assumption was that I'd be safe. Now, they were faced with the uncertainty of where their daughter was and what might happen to her. I felt terribly guilty for putting them through what must surely be a version of hell.

I paused, tired of writing, then flipped through my notebook until I found a blank space on the back of a page that had already been written on. I started to write again—all the prayers I knew by heart, until the pen fell out of my hand, jolting me awake so I could "off the light."

Khalid woke up early the next morning and, after he went to the bathroom and washed his hands and face, told me he'd had a dream—"when you see in sleep"—he called it. It wasn't a good dream, and he seemed really bothered by it.

"What was it about?" I asked.

"Shogufa. Someone take Shogufa." His voice was flat and his face ashen.

"Someone kidnapped her?" I asked. He nodded. I paused for a second but decided to go ahead and say it anyway. "Now you know how it feels, how my parents and my friends and my sister must feel. It's not good, is it."

He shook his head no and conceded that it was a horrible, helpless feeling. He told me that in his dream he didn't know who had taken her, and he had run through the streets of the village in search of her, but no one could help him find her. She had disappeared.

He took his cell phone out of his pocket and put the SIM card in. He punched in a few numbers and I could hear the automated female voice on the other end saying in Pashto that the person he had phoned was unavailable. He ended the call and dialed again. And again. "She no answer," he said, looking at me.

"It's early," I assured him. "She's probably still sleeping."

Khalid wasn't convinced and dialled yet again. Finally, an hour later, Shogufa answered, and she and Khalid spoke for several minutes.

"See," I told him, "she was just sleeping. She's fine. Think about my family. They're not fine because they cannot call me." When he didn't respond, I reached for the cell phone he still held in his hand.

"Please, Khalid, let me make a phone call."

"I cannot, Mellissa. I sorry," he responded, taking out the SIM card and putting the phone back in his pocket.

"Please, just a short one, so I can tell Paul I am okay."

He shook his head. "My father . . . he will kill me."

"He doesn't have to know. Please. My family and friends are so worried about me. I just want to tell them I am okay and you are looking after me."

"I cannot, Mellissa. I sorry."

I knew there was no changing his mind, and I was tired of begging. I felt like I'd been begging since the day I was kidnapped. Begging them not to shoot me, begging them to let me make a phone call, begging to be released, begging God to hear my prayers, begging, begging, begging. And I'm not a beggar by any means. In fact, maybe this was my lesson for being too proud to ask for anything, especially help, from anyone. It drives my friends crazy sometimes, usually when I'm in the kitchen. I remember one time when I was cooking dinner for thirty at Kas's condo in Toronto, for an engagement party for Maureen and her fiancé Dr. Don Low. It happened to be the hottest day of the year, and the air conditioning wasn't working. And as usual, I had planned a menu that might have been a little too ambitious: herb-roasted salmon, chicken stuffed with sun-dried tomatoes and goat cheese, roasted potatoes, three salads—spinach, pasta, and Caesar—and chocolate cupcakes for dessert. And I wouldn't let anyone into the kitchen to help, even as I was sweating and rushing to get dinner on the table.

In Italy on our holiday the summer before, it was much the same. As the designated cook at our rented villa, I planned all the dinners and insisted on doing all the shopping. And I wouldn't let anyone into the kitchen to help me, protesting that it was a small kitchen (which it was). I might have relented one night and allowed Angela to chop some onions, but that was about it. The girls learned after a few days that it was much better to just lie around the pool and give me an hour in the kitchen before coming in for cocktails. It worked out okay for them too.

I suppose I was proud to be self-sufficient because I was raised that way. My mother had once warned me to "never rely on other people." Her warning must have stuck because now my parents often accuse me of being too self-sufficient—which I think they sometimes translate as being selfish. So it was getting harder and harder to hear myself begging my kidnappers for freedom, for something I had taken for granted my entire life.

Khalid noticed I had grown quiet, and he took his Kalashnikov from behind his pillow. He asked me to pass one of the scraps of cloth to him and I did. I watched in fascination as he took his gun apart piece by piece, cleaning each carefully with the fabric scraps. He handed me the barrel and a cloth and motioned for me to do the same. I did, and then he handed me the wooden hand guard. We continued in this way until every surface of the weapon had been rubbed clean. Then he put the gun back together.

"Here," he said, putting the rifle in my hand. "Hold like this." He took my hand and put my finger on the trigger. "This. You can kill someone now." The magazine was not attached, so I pulled the trigger. Even without bullets, it was a powerful feeling to hold a gun like that. Khalid pointed to his forehead. "You can shoot me," he laughed. I put the gun to his head, the same way he did to me on that first day, the same way Shafirgullah had pointed his gun to Shokoor's head when they were trying to shove me into the car.

I pretended I was pulling the trigger. Khalid laughed, knowing he was safe, the loaded magazine in his hand.

I closed my eyes and tried to imagine what it would be like if I was pulling the trigger for real, sending a bullet into my captor's brain and ending his life right then, right there, in the hole. I would probably be thrown back by the force of the shot, and then I'd watch a red mark grow on his head as his eyes rolled toward the back of his head and he slumped over. It was a cruel and horrific thought, and it excited me a little to think that I might be in a position to have that much power to decide whether someone lived or died.

But I knew it was not at all possible for me to take someone's life. I'd been through this already when I was thinking about strangling Shafirgullah in his sleep. And I certainly didn't think I could kill Khalid. He was the one person I felt I could maybe trust. After all, he'd called me his sister and promised he would never kill me.

He seemed to read my mind. "You no kill me."

I shook my head. "No, Khalid, I could not kill you. I don't want to kill you."

"You my sister. You no kill me. I no kill you."

It was my turn to laugh. "If I kill you, I could go back to Kabul tonight."

Khalid laughed and asked me what I'd do then when Shafir-gullah came down the hole. I said I'd shoot him too, and everyone else who tried to come in. Maybe it *was* my best chance of escape. I'd have plenty of ammunition to be able to shoot my way back to Kabul, should I be chased by Taliban or anyone else. But I would forever be haunted if I were to kill Khalid. The image of his head slumped over and dripping blood would stay with me for the rest of my life. After all, it wasn't exactly self-defence after he had prom-ised not to kill me.

My kidnapper was watching me carefully. He knew he was in no danger and wouldn't have been even if the gun had been loaded. Something bonded us together at that moment. An understanding, perhaps, that we held each other's lives in our hands. Me less so than him, perhaps, but he wasn't invincible in that space. If we were both going to survive, I had to trust that he was going to keep his promise not to kill me, and he had to trust that I wasn't going to kill him to try to escape. I stared straight into his eyes, as if daring him to shoot me, knowing that he wouldn't. He held my gaze. I didn't even realize that I was still holding the gun.

Khalid held out his hand and I gave it to him. He placed it back behind his pillow and put the magazine in his breast pocket. Then he reached for the package of cigarettes from his other pocket, took out a smoke, licked the ends, and lit it. He handed it to me and repeated the process with another cigarette. We both blew out streams of white smoke, which met in mid-air.

"You my sister, Mellissa. I no kill you. You no kill me."

Shafirgullah was snoring—he was deep into a four-hour afternoon nap when I heard footsteps outside. I never knew what to expect when I heard the sounds above our heads. This time there were several sets of shoes stomping. And then I heard a voice.

"Shafirgullah! Mellissa!"

It was Abdulrahman. So he hadn't yet gone to Pakistan as he told me he would, to join his wife and son. Was he waiting for my "case to finish" before crossing the border for the winter? Khalid had said his father expected him in Pakistan after my release, but he was hesitant because he didn't want to be far away from Shogufa. He even told me he was considering kidnapping someone else to delay his return to the family home.

"Mellissa!" This time I thought the voice sounded like Khalid's.

"Yes?" I called out, rousing Shafirgullah from his slumber. He sat up and looked at me. I pointed to the ceiling.

"Mellissa, it's Abdulrahman. I am with Khalid."

"Hello, Abdulrahman," I said. I was now standing and speaking directly into the pipe.

"Mellissa, you play piano?"

"Piano?" The question startled me. It had been years since I'd played the piano. I barely remembered the scales, it had been so long since I last placed my fingers on a keyboard. Why was Abdulrahman asking me?

"Yes, I play piano," I answered.

"What is name of your piano teacher?"

My piano teacher. My piano teacher. It felt like a trick question. Of course I knew her name, the answer was at the tip of my tongue, but why couldn't I spit it out? It was the incongruity of recalling a childhood memory of home while in a place that couldn't be farther away—it completely threw me.

I could picture her. Dark hair, very, very beautiful.

"What is her name?" Abdulrahman was getting impatient.

And then it came to me. "Suzanne!" I yelled. It took several minutes for him to get the spelling right—or, at least, until I was comfortable with his spelling.

"Where she from?" Abdulrahman asked.

"Vancouver," I said.

"Okay," Abdulrahman continued after a short pause. "What colour your school tie?"

"Maroon!" I yelled up the pipe.

After what felt like an eternity, we were both pretty sure he had all the answers spelled correctly. Abdulrahman thanked me and told me they were leaving.

"Wait, Abdulrahman! Where are you going? When will I get to go back to Kabul?"

"Soon, inshallah, soon," he told me. "Goodbye now. We come later." The men exchanged a few words in Pashto with Shafirgullah, and then their footsteps faded into the distance. I imagined they were going somewhere to call the negotiators and give them my answers.

I hoped it all meant that they were making progress. I wasn't really sure what to think. I looked up the pipe and saw a sliver of light through the rocks. Shafirgullah had sat back down and was stuffing cookies into his mouth. An early dinner, perhaps. I wasn't hungry so I sat back and lit a cigarette, and allowed my memories to take me away from where I was for a while. I flipped through my notebook and found my calendar. Today was October 28, day sixteen in the hole. It felt like an eternity had passed. Day sixteen. I wasn't even counting that first half day. I heard chanting. Shafirgullah was singing the Koran again. He had a good voice, and I closed my eyes and tried to let the music lift me from the place. It worked until he stopped.

"You!"

I opened my eyes and saw that he was staring at me, his eyes dark and beady. It was my turn, he was telling me, my turn to sing again.

You who dwell in the shelter of the Lord,
Who abide in His shadow for life,
Say to the Lord, "My Refuge, my Rock in Whom I trust."

And he will raise you up on eagle's wings,
Bear you on the breath of dawn,
Make you to shine like the sun,
And hold you in the palm of His Hand.

And back and forth, back and forth. I ran out of hymns, so I started singing other songs.

Oh, say, can you see, by the dawn's early light—
What so proudly we hailed at the twilight's last gleaming
Whose broad stripes and bright stars thru the perilous fight—
O'er the ramparts we watched, were so galantly streaming
And the rocket's red glare, the bombs bursting in air
Gave proof through the night that our flag was still there.
Oh, say does that star-spangled banner yet wave,
O'er the land of the free and the home of the brave?

My voice cracked a bit on the last *brave*, but I sang it loud and proud, like I was a New York Yankees fan belting it out at the first game of the World Series. Shafirgullah clearly had no idea what the song was because he clapped and smiled and laughed.

"You," I said, signalling that it was his turn.

He shook his head. "You, again."

Again I sang the American national anthem. Louder this time, just in case there was someone above the hole. We couldn't have been far from Bagram, where the Americans were based. Imagine if an American soldier from Bagram was in the area and heard the faint tones of his or her national anthem coming from somewhere underground. That would be a great way to get rescued. I raised my voice again—*And the rocket's red glare!* Shafirgullah looked completely entranced. I'd sung "O Canada" earlier, but it hadn't received this kind of reaction. I'm a proud Canadian, but I've always preferred the American anthem—I sing both at hockey games. "The Star Spangled Banner" seems to me to have more passion; of course it does—the poem from which its lyrics come was born out of a war. Shafirgullah was loving it. He clapped and clapped after I was done, before starting his Koran chanting again.

We took turns singing late into the night, until Shafirgullah was tired and fell asleep, to my great envy. I noticed that he had forgotten to put the Kalashnikov behind his pillow—it was lying between us, and I picked it up and turned it over and over in my hands. The magazine wasn't attached, so Shafirgullah was in no danger of being shot in the head while he slept, but again I imagined myself shooting my captor between the eyes. He wouldn't even feel anything. After all, he was the one who had plunged a knife into my shoulder and hand. I put the gun down and examined the scab on my hand. It was black and hard, and I gingerly picked at it. I could see pink beneath, a sign that the skin was healing. The wound no longer hurt, so I continued picking at the scab until it peeled off.

Then I tried to see the wound on my shoulder. As I had seen earlier, the pink toilet paper had become part of the scab. It was big and hard, and hurt when I picked gently at it. I decided to leave it alone for the time being. The last thing I wanted was for the wound to get infected, and my fingers weren't exactly clean. My fingernails hadn't been cut in more than two weeks, and a layer of dirt had formed under each nail. I reached for my backpack and took my nail clippers out of my makeup bag. One by one, I cut off my dirty nails, and that made me feel a little better. If only I could have a shower, I would feel a hundred times better. I couldn't stand how I smelled. I don't remember ever being so dirty in my life.

I took my hair out of its ponytail and shook out the dirt and dust. I tried to comb my hair out a bit with my fingers, but it was matted, and made my hands dirty, so I gave up, tied it up again, and rinsed my hands with water from the can.

My friends like to joke that I'm the messiest clean freak they know. Although my desk is typically covered in mountains of paper, I know where everything is. And despite the mess, the desk, and my computer and keyboard, is scrubbed and disinfected. And I always use hand sanitizer. In fact, I'd had a little bottle of it in my backpack. When I couldn't find it, I assumed it was one of the things Abdulrahman had filched after I arrived at the abandoned white house.

I felt disgusting. Khalid had come in the other night reeking of garlic so badly that I could hardly breathe. I knew Afghans ate a lot of raw garlic, but in a small space, the odour was almost unbearable. I had to chain-smoke to mask the smell. The smell of the trash-can toilet was no better. My captors may have been emptying it out every other night, but they were not cleaning it, and I was keeping it as far into the tunnel as I could, crawling up to bring it down when I had to go to the bathroom.

I opened my notebook again. There were maybe only three virgin pages left, but I scribbled on one anyway.

Dear P,

Do you think that if you had to, you could kill someone? I've been thinking about that a lot lately, and I've come to the conclusion that I can't—even if it was the only thing I could do to save my own life. Now, if you were the one in this hole, I would probably have no problem killing your captors, but for some reason, I can't bring myself to shoot these guys. I guess I'm not as tough and hard-core as I like to think I am. Don't tell anyone, okay? Fung's a wuss.

I'm just really tired today. They came and asked me a couple more proof-of-life questions, so I hope that my answers will make you feel a little better that I'm still alive and hanging in there. I can't imagine what you must be going through, and I'm really, really sorry. I'm trying hard to think positive, and I know these things take time, and I know everyone is trying really hard to get me home. I just hope it happens soon.

I'm with you, P. I'm coming back. I promise.

Love you,

xox

My blue pen was running out of ink, but I wasn't concerned— I had a few more in my knapsack. I had bought a bunch at the PX—the post exchange—in Kandahar before going to Kabul. I always travelled with lots of pens and pencils so that I could hand them out to Afghan children, which I had done at the refugee camp the day I was kidnapped. Soldiers and aid workers had told me time and time again that it was the best thing, maybe the only thing, I could do for the Afghan children I met while on assignment. Pens and paper were precious commodities in this war-ravaged country, and I still remembered the smiles on their faces upon receiving a simple pen from a stranger.

I took the rosary out of my pocket and stared at the cross. I traced it on my notepad underneath my last note to Paul and then made a pattern on it, colouring in the shapes I'd drawn. I was pleased with it—it looked like a Celtic cross. I drew a few more crosses with different designs, until my pen died. Then I turned off the lamp and prayed the rosary until I fell asleep.

Dearest M,

I'm worried that your kidnapping will bring a real change in your life, M, one of those events that will mark you forever. I long to hear your voice tonight, just a few words like, "I'm okay, really, I'm okay." That's all I need, and I can't imagine what your parents and Vanessa are going through.

Good night, dear M, and I dread to think of you sleeping in a dark, cold room, probably with your feet tied and perhaps even your hands. I know you will wake up a lot, and I know you will be praying a lot, and I suspect you've already forgiven the people who are doing this to you. Come back.

xx

No one came the next day, and Shafirgullah made several phone calls after dark to try to find out what was going on. He turned to me at one point and said, "You. Kabul. Sunday." This was not the first time he had told me my release was imminent. He had a bad habit of saying "two days" or "three days, inshallah" and nothing would happen, so I had learned not to believe him. He was a proven liar. But this was the first time he mentioned a specific day.

"Sunday," I said. "Today is Wednesday. So four more days."

"No, five days," he argued.

"No, today is Wednesday. So Thursday, Friday, Saturday, and Sunday."

He counted the days with his hands and then nodded. "Four day."

"I don't believe you," I told him. "I think you are lying. You always tell me I go soon, but it never happens."

"Sunday, Sunday!" he sang. "Sunday. You! Kabul!" It sounded more like a taunt than a promise, and I knew better than to get my hopes up, even though he was now pinpointing a day.

"Where is Khalid?" I asked. "I don't believe you. I want to talk to him."

"Khalid Kabul" came the pat answer.

"What is Khalid doing in Kabul?" I asked.

Shafirgullah shrugged and kept singing to himself. Sometimes I thought he was perhaps a little mentally disordered. In North

America, he would probably be diagnosed with a mild retardation. There was something off about him, but I couldn't put my finger on it. He wasn't manic or psychotic, but he was someone who would probably require therapy or some sort of treatment in any other, sane part of the world.

I was always disappointed when Khalid didn't show up because another twenty-four hours with Shafirgullah would be exhausting and monotonous, with little conversation to make time move along.

Suddenly, Shafirgullah stopped singing. I looked up and realized what had interrupted him. Footsteps. And then *thump, thump, thump.* Then the same sound we'd heard before: *tap, tap, tap,* as if someone was using a stick to poke the ground, looking for an opening. Shafirgullah put his finger to his lips, motioning for me not to speak. He grabbed his rifle and inserted the magazine. What did he think he could do with it? Shoot anyone who tried to come in? It would be a zero-sum game, and I would never survive a shootout here. Not one between my captors and the ANP or the Taliban, anyway.

Shafirgullah was worried. He held the rifle tightly and gave me a look indicating he didn't know who it was. The tapping went on for a while longer, and then several sets of footsteps faded into the distance.

Shafirgullah waited a while longer before taking his cell phone out and putting the SIM card in. He punched in a number and hit send. I could hear a male voice through the receiver. "As-Salaam Alaikum." It sounded like Khalid. The men spoke in hushed tones for several minutes.

"Taliban," Shafirgullah announced when he hung up the phone.

"Is that what Khalid said?" I asked.

"Yes. Khalid. Hezbollah."

"Hezbollah?" I asked.

"Khalid," he answered, nodding. "Hezbollah."

It figures, I thought, that Khalid wasn't his real name. Neither could Hezbollah be his name. Although it seemed kind of fitting that a would-be terrorist like Khalid would take the same name as the Lebanese militia organization. It's true what they say about one man's terrorist being another man's freedom fighter. Fortunately for me, my kidnappers were neither. They were a young band of crude criminals who used fundamentalist Islamist ideology as an excuse to commit petty crimes. Well, kidnapping may not be such a petty crime, but I might have had more respect for them if they were truly willing to die for their beliefs. However, it seemed that for them, religion was simply an excuse to indulge in thuggery.

Of course, I would be in serious trouble if they were truly Al Qaeda or Taliban because then I would be a political prisoner, and they'd not hesitate to behead me in front of a flag. And that I definitely didn't want. I thought about Daniel Pearl, the *Wall Street Journal* reporter who was kidnapped by Al Qaeda militants and then brutally beheaded—on tape—after several other videotapes were made of him denouncing the United States. Just the memory of what happened to him sent chills up and down my spine. I said a quiet thank you to God that my kidnappers were just a gang of petty thieves.

Shafirgullah seemed to have gotten over his earlier apprehension. With the footsteps now long gone, his appetite returned. He opened a box of chocolate cookies and ate every crumb, then half of another box. And then he picked at some dry bread a few days old. All washed down with two boxes of cherry juice.

I wondered if he was right, or telling the truth, that I would be released on Sunday. The thought had me excited, and as much as I didn't want to get my hopes up, I let my mind go crazy for a while. How would I be let go? I hoped they wouldn't just dump me off at the village, to find my own way back to Kabul. I had no cell phone—it was doubtful mine would be returned to me—no way to contact anyone, and God forbid I should be kidnapped again as I was trying to get back to the capital.

No, Khalid had told me before that they always dropped off their hostages at the place from where they were taken. So that would mean the refugee camp. I imagined riding back to Kabul on the back of the motorcycle, or even riding halfway back before the long-haired Afghan drove us the rest of the way in his beat-up blue car. We'd get to the camp and then what? Would they just leave me at the gates? Would someone be there looking for me? Would the ANP be lying in wait, ready to pounce on my kidnappers as soon as I was safe? I imagined Khalid resisting arrest, and being gunned down in a hail of bullets by Afghan officers trying to make a show of force. No, I thought, it was more likely he would let me walk back to the camp on my own, let me walk off into the night, making sure I was okay from the safe confines of the car.

I tried not to get too excited, but hope was all I had. Earlier, I had barely been able to imagine staying in the hole another day, but suddenly, four more days didn't seem so bad. I'd already been there for sixteen. What's another four? There would just be a little more dirt to scrub off at the end of it all. And boy, did I need a good scrub.

I flipped through the pages of my notebook to my calendar. Today was October 29. Sunday would be November 2, two days before the US election. Good, that meant I would be able to watch results somewhere. It was going to be such a historic night, and I didn't want to miss it. Barack Obama was most probably going to be elected the first black president in American history. I wanted to witness it, even from faraway Afghanistan, the place that would likely define his foreign policy for the next four years.

So this was good. I figured if I was released on Sunday night, Monday would be full of official obligations—after being reunited with Paul, I would likely have to speak with the Canadian ambassador, and meet with the Afghan police to debrief them. Then maybe Paul and I could get a military flight on Tuesday back to Kandahar, where I could collect my belongings, and we'd be on a flight back to Dubai on Wednesday, two weeks later than scheduled.

Methodically, I went through the dates. I probably wouldn't get back to Canada until the week of the tenth, and I'd go through Vancouver to see my parents and reassure them I was okay. I'd spend a week with them, before heading to Regina to start the moving process. That would put me into the last week of November. I then had to get to Toronto and find a place to live, but it was definitely doable.

Then it would be December. And Christmas was just around the corner. I had missed my friend Kas's Christmas party the year before, and I was thinking perhaps I could persuade her to have another one this year. A cocktail party, and I would do all the cooking. Yes, that would be the perfect way to celebrate my freedom—surrounded by my family and friends.

I started planning in my head, making a menu and drawing up the guest list. But I'd better let Kas know first. I flipped to the second-to-last empty page in my notebook and started writing.

Hey dude,

It's about eleven at night here in my little space, and I need to run something by you. First of all, I'm okay. I know you and the girls are probably really worried about me, but please try not to be. I hope you are having lots of drinks for me back home. I'm still moving to Toronto, inshallah, in time for Christmas—and I'm making some plans for us. You know your Christmas party last year? The one I missed? I'm hoping we can do it again—at your loft—and I'll cater it.

We'll do all your favourite things, turkey meatballs, but we'll do them as hors d'oeuvres, with toothpicks. Then we'll do a brie, wild mushroom, and caramelized onion pizza, cut into wedges. And then I'll make those little crab cakes I made at Moe's. Oh, and maybe those little spinach and feta pies. I can do those in advance with puff pastry and freeze them, and we'll bake them in your kitchen. And green onion cake, the ones I get in Chinatown, but I'll top them with a dill crème fraîche and smoked salmon. And mini chocolate cupcakes for dessert.

What do you think? We could invite everyone. It will be a big Christmas party—because you know the CBC doesn't have one anymore. Your place is big enough to hold, what, forty or fifty people? And we won't have to worry about the air conditioning this time!

I really miss you, dude—all of you guys, and I can't wait to get home and see you. We'll have our own private party—with just us girls—first. Okay?

Take care and say hi to everyone. I'll see you soon, I hope.

It was nearing midnight, and Toronto was nine and a half hours behind. I figured my friends were all probably at work, and Kas assigned a story for that night's newscast. I hoped she didn't have to report on me. That was one thing I really didn't want to think about, that I must be a story back home, and a big one—I couldn't remember any other Canadian being kidnapped in Afghanistan. I hoped other reporters were respecting my parents' and friends' privacy. I dreaded that my family was being constantly harassed by reporters who needed to file their stories. Journalists are sometimes asked to "get" someone: a grieving parent, an angry sibling, anyone who could lend emotion to a story. It's the part of the job I hate the most. I would make the phone call, but if the person didn't want to talk, I would leave my phone number and then leave them alone.

Sometimes things worked out. Years ago, while a local reporter covering the ongoing story of the missing women in Vancouver's Downtown Eastside, I was able to get close to several family members of the missing women. But I was always respectful of their wishes. If they didn't want to talk, I left them alone. If they needed someone to talk to, I would spend hours on the phone, just listening. In the end, I know that the families were satisfied with our coverage, and their participation in it, and I was proud of my colleagues for treating such a story—one with the potential to be so sensational—with restraint and respect.

But I know that not all reporters exercise the same restraint. Sometimes the thrill of getting the "get" overrides one's sense of what's right and how far to go. I said a silent prayer to God that my colleagues in the business would treat my family and friends with respect. I felt horribly guilty for exposing them to the glare of the spotlight, and I prayed that they would find the strength to deal with it.

Dearest M,

The news embargo has been holding, but we got a call that Reuters is agitating and wants to publish a story unless CBC gives them a good reason not to. Then we get a call from Valma in London saying that Turkish television in Kabul is offering clients the story of the missing Canadian journalist, including pictures from the camp and interviews with eyewitnesses. Margaret quickly got on the phone and persuaded the local bureau chief to call the story down. All of this was being done in the garden while we were having lunch. Surreal or what?

xx

Khalid brought me a brand new notebook with a shiny blue cover. It was not as thick as my notepad, but every page was a blank canvas, waiting for me to fill in the grey lines. He'd known for a while that I was running out of pages, and while I thanked him for his gift, I was secretly disappointed that my hope of being freed before running out of pages in my own notebook had been dashed.

"You must write," he told me. "Write, write." He would occasionally flip through my full notebook, reading—or trying to read—the letters to my friends and family. I didn't think he actually understood any of it, so I never hesitated to hand it over.

I flipped through the pages of the new book, then closed it, promising to write in it later. I wanted to ask Khalid about his nickname. "Hezbollah?"

He smiled. "I have many names."

"What other ones?"

"Many other names." He smiled a wide smile. Then asked me if I had email.

"Email?" I asked. "Of course I have email."

"What is your email?" Khalid asked me.

"Why do you want to know? Do you have email too?"

"I have email. Yes. When I go Pakistan. When you go to Canada, I will write you." He was staring intently at me. Was he serious? He wanted to stay in touch? This gave me hope, though, that I might be released soon.

"What is your email?" I asked him. He wrote it down for me. Hezb_ullah@yahoo.com.

"What is yours?" he asked.

I decided against giving him the address to my CBC account and gave him my Yahoo account instead. "You will write to me?" I asked.

"Yes, I write to you. You go to Canada, I write to you. You my sister! You will write to me?"

I nodded, knowing there was no way either of us would honour that agreement, but it was a compelling notion, the idea of hostage and kidnapper staying in touch, a continuation of a relationship formed out of captivity.

"Who do you email now?" I asked, half surprised but not astounded that this young Afghan in this remote area would have access to the Internet and email.

"My friends," he said with a smile. Then he changed the subject. "My sister husband—he in Kabul. He have work for me."

"What kind of work?"

"Important work. You will hear from it. When you go to Kabul, you will hear what is it I do for him. People will be dying from me."

I asked him who would be dying and why would he want to kill his own people, if it was just foreigners he hated. He tried to explain that the idea was just to create havoc. Afghans, he said, hated foreigners, which wasn't news to me. After thirty years of being invaded by them, the country had had enough, and most Afghans just wanted to be left alone to rebuild the country their way.

If there were no foreigners, I tried to argue, the Taliban would take over, and women and children would suffer again.

"Taliban good. Taliban are Afghanistan," he insisted. I knew there was no arguing this point, so I gave up.

I was, however, still hopeful that I might be released soon, given that he was talking about keeping in touch when I got back to Canada. Maybe Shafirgullah was right. Maybe Sunday would really be freedom day. Today was Thursday. The next day would be Halloween.

"Khalid," I asked, "Shafirgullah said my case will finish on Sunday. Is that true? Is that what your father said?"

"Inshallah, Mellissa. Soon. Inshallah."

"I'm tired of 'inshallah.' It's always 'inshallah.' 'Inshallah, inshallah.' Why can't you just say yes or no?"

"It must be inshallah. Without Allah, nothing happen."

"Well, Allah is taking too long," I said.

Khalid sighed and picked up the package of cigarettes. I shook my head. I had decided a few days before that I was smoking too much, and so was limiting myself to one cigarette an hour. I would have a few drags and then put it out, to relight later, or smoke half of it on the half-hour. But one cigarette an hour was already nearly a pack a day. I didn't even want to know how much damage I was doing to my lungs and how long it would take me to get back into running shape when I got out of there. Assuming that I was getting out of there. I wasn't sure what to think anymore. I was tired of getting my hopes up every time someone said "two days" or "three days." I was still hopeful about Sunday, but I had learned that with hope came the risk of crushing disappointment. Every time I heard digging, I'd wonder whether it would bring freedom, or just another night of detention with a new guard.

"I tell your friend three days," Khalid said, trying to explain.

"What do you mean?"

"I tell him . . . three days then I kill you." I took that to mean that he—or his father—had given the negotiators a deadline. Presumably for money. Or another prisoner. I thought of Khalid's friend at Bagram.

"What if they can't give it to you in three days?" I asked. "You're really going to kill me?"

Khalid laughed. "No, I no kill you."

"Will you let me go?" I asked.

He didn't answer. I wondered how long they would keep me before they decided I just wasn't worth the investment. They'd already invested almost three weeks in this hostage taking; maybe that was the point of no return. But if they were asking for a prisoner exchange, there was no telling how long it would take. I did not even want to hazard a guess. If only there was an opportunity for escape. Maybe if they were going to keep me longer, they would move me somewhere else and I'd have that chance.

I didn't know what to think anymore, and I was getting tired of thinking. "I just want to go home," I said out loud.

"Inshallah, you go soon," he said, a little exasperated. His phone rang, and a quick conversation in Pashto followed. After hanging up, he turned to me. "We need to make video."

"Video?" I asked. "I thought Abdulrahman did that on the first day! With his cell phone. And Zahir was supposed to take it to your father in Pakistan. Didn't he do that?"

Khalid shook his head. "I do not know. Your friends—they do not believe we have you."

What? How could they not believe they had me? I'd answered the second round of proof-of-life questions just a few days ago.

"They don't believe it is you," Khalid repeated.

This was not good news. The Sunday deadline looked less likely if they were demanding a video and the negotiators required further proof of life. "Well," I said, "if they need the video, let's do it tonight. Get Shafirgullah to bring a camera and then they can have the video tomorrow. That will work, won't it?"

"We need camera," he said.

"What do you mean, you need camera?" I asked. I was starting to lose my patience. "Don't you have a video camera?" Khalid shook his head. I couldn't believe it. My kidnappers were even less organized than I had first thought.

"What do you mean you don't have a video camera? What kind of kidnappers are you? You're wasting time. Your time and my time." My captor took off his skullcap and scratched his head. I was doing the calculations in my head. It was now Thursday. If the negotiators got the video by Friday, I could still be released by Sunday. But it was starting to seem like a long shot. I looked at Khalid. He seemed as annoyed and upset as me.

"I have an idea," I said. "I'll write a letter, and then they will know it's me." Khalid looked puzzled, so I tried to explain that I would write a letter that he—or his father or Zahir—could read to the negotiators. Then they would have proof that it was really me. Khalid liked this idea, and I ripped the last page out of my notebook and started writing in big letters with double spacing.

My name is Mellissa Fung, and I'm a reporter for CBC News.

I had to convey information to prove that it was me. I should talk about my family.

Tell everyone I'm sorry for all the trouble. My sister's name is Vanessa and she is a lawyer in Los Angeles. My parents are supposed to leave for Hong Kong next week, and I hope they will still go.

This was true. My parents were supposed to go to Hong Kong for a month to visit family and friends, and I had been worrying that my situation might screw up their vacation.

I am in some pain, from the surgery I had earlier this year, and I will need to see a doctor soon. Please help me.

The negotiators would be able to confirm that I'd had major surgery. I added only two words more, so there could be no doubt that it was me.

Go Canucks.

And then a message to Paul. I'd been writing to him all this time—letters he might never get.

xox

I handed the sheet of paper to Khalid. He read what I had written, then pointed to the second-to-last line. "What is this? Ca-nucks?"

"It's my hockey team," I said. "Do you know what is hockey?"

He shook his head, and I spent the next thirty minutes trying to explain our national game. He seemed intrigued, and so I continued to talk about my favourite sport. I can talk about hockey for hours. I explained that, similar to soccer, which was a game he knew, the goal was to get the puck into the net more times than your opponent. I had a little trouble getting him to understand the concept of skating on a sheet of ice. I then tried to explain the National Hockey League—with its teams in cities across North America—and how they played each other and the final prize was a big silver cup called the Stanley.

"Stanley?" he asked.

I nodded and explained that it was named after an important person whom the Queen had once appointed as her representative to Canada. This Khalid couldn't understand—and I wasn't surprised. Even if he had attended school, it was unlikely that he learned anything about the British Empire.

He folded my letter and put it in his pocket.

"Promise you will read that to them," I asked.

"I promise."

"Tomorrow. You must read this tomorrow. Then we won't need any video. They will know it's me. It will save time." He nodded and promised again to call the negotiators and read them my letter. I could only hope he wasn't going to throw out the letter as soon as he left the hole that night.

Khalid seemed relieved when the digging started that evening. His time was almost done. If I was being released on Sunday night, he would have only one more night down in the cave. Shafirgullah took over, and I could tell that he too was getting tired of having to come down every other night to watch over me. Besides, the place was a mess. The stench of the toilet bucket and body odour must have been unbearable. Even I wasn't completely desensitized. Shafirgullah started praying and chanting the Koran as soon as he came in, basically ignoring me and turning, as he always did, away from me and toward what I assumed was the direction of Mecca. It was a relief not to have to try to make conversation. I reached for my new blue notebook.

Dear P,

The first page of a new notepad. Khalid brought it for me because I was running out of space in my old one. I wonder how many more notepads I'll go through before I see you again. My kidnappers have been saying soon, soon, soon, but they've been saying that all the time. I'm not sure what to believe anymore. I guess I should just be thankful I can still talk to you.

I'm still okay, and the scab on my shoulder, I think, is almost ready to come off. Another good sign, maybe, that this nightmare is soon going to end.

I'm not sure where you are. Maybe you've left Afghanistan already, but I feel that you are close, and that makes me feel a little better. My kidnappers are starting to tire of coming in here every other night, and maybe that means the end is near.

I'm praying a lot, and trying to stay positive, but there are times when it's very hard and the darkness of this place threatens to swallow me completely.

I hope I'll see you soon. I miss you so much.

xox

I traced a few more crosses from my rosary on the page and coloured them in with the pen, admiring the patterns I drew. Shafirgullah had finished praying and was looking at my crosses. He frowned and reached for a new package of cookies, stuffing them one at a time into his mouth. I frowned at him in return, and he took two of the juice boxes out of the bag, guzzling one in seconds, then taking a few sips from the other. I looked in the bag. There were only three juice boxes left, and they would have to last us until the next evening. And then it would just be one more night until Sunday.

I dug around for an apple juice, stuck a straw in it, and took a sip. Shafirgullah was pulling out pieces of nan-i-Afghani from the bag. He ate it in chunks, chewing madly and washing it down with more juice. I suddenly found myself growing increasingly irritated by the way he ate—the noises he made while chewing, the way he wrinkled his nose, the way he chewed with his mouth open, with bits of bread flying out. I must have been glaring at him because he stared back at me. I got the feeling he was probably as sick of me as I was of him. We didn't speak for the rest of the night. He went to sleep very early, leaving me, thankfully, alone again with my thoughts and my prayers.

No one came the next night. Abdullah came by in the afternoon and dropped several packages of juice and cookies, and batteries and a pack of smokes, down the pipes. It was a signal that there would be no changing of the guard. Poor Shafirgullah would be stuck doing double-duty—but at least it would be the last time. A few days previously, Khalid had said, "No more girls," and I think he meant it. It was much easier for them to kidnap men, beat them up, and leave them alone for days than to have to keep constant watch over a woman.

Shafirgullah and I had struck a bit of a truce earlier in the day, singing songs again, and he even opened a package of cookies and offered them to me, before eating them all himself. *One more day*, I kept telling myself. *Twenty-four more hours. I can do it, I can do it.* I had developed a little routine to help the hours pass: at the top of the hour I would smoke half a cigarette, then pray the entire rosary— five decades, which is the equivalent of fifty Hail Marys, and all the prayers in between. Depending on whether I sung it, which I usually did, it would take me about twenty minutes. At the bottom of the hour I would finish the cigarette and then either write or try to nap (which never worked) until the top of the hour, when I'd do it all over again. Sometimes I would let my mind wander in the hope that it would take me somewhere far away, until my captor or something else reminded me that I was still in captivity.

It seemed a bit ironic to me that the faraway place so often in my thoughts these days was home. I'd spent my childhood dreaming of going to far-off places. The farther away, the better. There was a whole big world out there, and I wanted to see it all. My parents both worked in the travel industry, so as children my sister and I had the privilege of being able to travel quite a lot—and as a result, I'd developed serious wanderlust, which was one of the reasons why I was attracted to journalism. I would imagine myself reporting from places like Moscow, Berlin, Beirut—places that seemed so foreign to a young girl in Canada. Except that now, in Afghanistan, a place I couldn't even imagine as a child, I was dreaming of Canada.

I wondered where young women in Afghanistan dream about going when they get older. Did they even know there was a bigger world outside their country? Were they curious about the West? Did they want to explore farther?

I thought about some extraordinary young women I'd met the summer before. Shokoor and I were in Kabul shooting a few stories on Afghan women and children. It was a blazing hot day and we had arranged to meet Awista Ayub, an Afghan-American, at the Kaldup Askari military field in the middle of the city. We were parked in a lot adjacent to the field, and as soon as we stepped out of our van we heard the peal of laughter.

It was tournament day for the girls of Kabul, and some fifty young soccer players, divided among about eight teams, had traded their traditional headscarves for baseball caps—an amazing event in a country where women, just years before, were forbidden from even being spectators in that same arena.

The tournament was Awista's brainchild, part of the Afghan Youth Sports Exchange, an organization she started in order to teach leadership skills to young women in her home country. She herself had the opportunity to study and learn in the United States, and it was her dream to bring the same opportunities home to young women in Afghanistan who might otherwise not be able to play sports. It was about empowering girls in a country where girls grew up being told they were not equals. Sport, Awista told me, had the power to change all that.

She introduced me to one of the coaches, a man named Abdul Saboor Walizada. He was the coach of the Afghan national women's team, and he was there to offer advice, and scout. "More women," he told me, "are interested in playing, and there is a lot of talent among the girls you see here. We will have a strong national team."

In the few years since Awista had started the program, the number of girls participating had multiplied, from tens to hundreds. They had even played in Ghazi Stadium in Kabul, where the Taliban had routinely carried out public executions of women who were accused of violating the most minor of laws.

Awista was a remarkable person. She had studied at the University of Rochester, in New York, where she played goal for the women's hockey team. We talked a lot about how participating in team sports as young girls helped to shape our views and built our confidence as young women. It was what she was hoping to do for the young women of Afghanistan.

"I've seen these girls," she said. "They change. They come to the field in their school uniform and they have their long black jackets and their pants and their headscarves, and as soon as they put on their sports clothes, their personality changes, and these are girls you couldn't recognize as being the same girls who walked on the field."

She introduced me to some of the girls playing that day. Thirteen-year-old Maliha Mahmoodi told me through a translator that she'd been interested in soccer since she was very young but that there wasn't an opportunity to play, even just a few years ago. Now, here she was, and thrilled for the opportunity. "It means it shows progress in the country," she told me, her big brown eyes flashing with excitement. "When we play soccer, it's like serving the country, and it shows that girls in Afghanistan are equal."

Zainab Fakovi was sixteen, and she'd been watching boys and men play soccer since she was little but had just started playing herself a few years ago, with the Afghan Youth Sports Exchange. For her, the opportunity to play soccer meant more than just sport.

"It means I am a liberated girl, and it means girls can do anything we want. Men and women have equal rights." When I asked what she thought it meant for her future, and for Afghanistan's future, she didn't hesitate. "It means I can be whatever I want. It means our country can be the best in the world." When I asked her what she wanted to be, she looked straight at me and said, "A journalist. Like you."

Lesson learned already. Sports can empower. Awista's philosophy was playing out right in front of her eyes. But she credited the girls themselves. "I've seen some of these girls evolve in the last three years into being confident young women," she told me. "And I have no doubt that soccer has played a key role in giving them that confidence. And whether they choose to play soccer, or they choose to take that confidence into the classroom, I've definitely seen them being able to emerge as leaders and have an ability to make life decisions, and own those decisions and have the confidence to make those decisions. And I think that's a key lesson we can teach these young girls as they emerge as future leaders of this country."

It was one of the most uplifting and inspiring afternoons I think I've ever spent—in the company of these young women, laughing and running, and competing on the field, watched over by their older sister who had come back from America to help them see their own potential. No longer shackled to an old, oppressive culture, they were free to run and play and choose their future, with the full knowledge that they were participating in something that was forbidden to them just a few years before.

Remembering their determination buoyed my spirits. The next day was Sunday and soon I too would be free again.

Shafirgullah was bored. He played Snake Xenzia on his cell phone for about an hour, then handed the phone to me. I amused myself for a few minutes but handed it back to him after getting frustrated. Three weeks of trying to manoeuvre the snake around itself and I still couldn't master the stupid game.

I was sticking to my routine of praying the rosary every hour on the hour, trying hard to meditate as I recited the prayers and passed the beads through my fingers. I meditated on Jesus' birth, his travels, his teachings, his suffering, and ultimately, his crucifixion. I tried not to think about anything else. I wanted to focus on the prayers, not get distracted by other thoughts.

Halfway through, I was interrupted by the ringing of Shafir-gullah's cell phone.

"As-Salaam Alaikum," he said, and that was all I could under-stand. The conversation lasted a few minutes and then he hung up.

"Kabul," he said, looking at me. "You Kabul."

"*Saba?*" I asked, double-checking. As much as I didn't want to get my hopes up, I couldn't help myself. I had heard *saba*—the Pashto word for "tomorrow"—so many times from my kidnappers that I had stopped counting. "Tomorrow" never came.

"Inshallah, *saba*," Shafirgullah replied.

There was that word again. "Inshallah." God willing. I fingered my rosary again and pressed the crucifix into the back of my hand so hard that it made an indentation.

God, please. Please be willing. Please let tomorrow come soon and with it, let me go home to my family and friends. Please, let this be over and let me go back to my life. You are the only one who can help me. Please, please, please. I have never needed you so much. I know there must be a reason that I am going through this trial, and I trust in you to help me through it. But please, I need to go home soon. For my parents and my friends and for my own sanity. Please, God. Let this be over tomorrow.

Shafirgullah was also praying. He was on his knees, his head on the ground, facing the wall adjacent to the tunnel. He was chanting softly, murmuring almost, and his eyes were closed. I wondered what he was praying for. I was praying for freedom, and for my family, but I didn't know whether he was just reciting the Koran or asking for something. I sometimes feel a bit guilty—maybe it's the old Catholic guilt—that I never hesitate to kneel when I need help. *Please God, help me do well on this exam tomorrow. Please God, let me get this job. Please God, don't let my grandmother die. Please God, take her to heaven.*

I typically started my prayers by saying, *Thank you, God, for everything you've done for me today. And always.*

These days, it was a little hard to try to find something to thank him for, except for the fact that I was still alive. I needed help. Shafirgullah looked as if he were just praying for the sake of praying, but I wondered again if he was asking for anything. Forgiveness, maybe, for what he was doing? Help, perhaps, to avoid arrest?

After a while, I realized that his chanting had turned to snoring, and I turned out the lamp. The battery was dying anyway, and so I prayed in the dark until I fell asleep.

I woke early in anticipation. Sunday. Freedom day. They had been telling me, and I was almost convinced, that I would return to Kabul that night. I didn't know what to expect or when the digging would start, and my stomach was fluttering. I had to keep telling myself to remain calm, that it would happen at some point during the day and that I should just go about my routine like it was another average day in captivity.

So I stood up and did my exercises. I could feel that my muscles had started to atrophy after three weeks of sitting in pretty much one position. I wondered if I would remember how to walk when they took me out of the hole. Shafirgullah woke up around noon—it was a long sleep even by his standards, and he seemed groggy for it all day. He chugged down two boxes of juice and ate a box of chocolate cookies. His phone rang twice through the afternoon, and short conversations followed each time.

And then we waited. I prayed on the hour, thanking God for my coming freedom and asking him to forgive my captors for everything they had done. At noon, I figured there would be six more rosaries to pray. At one, five more, and I kept counting down all afternoon.

I started getting my belongings together. I put my notebooks in my backpack and my running shoes on. I ran my dirty fingers through my matted hair and washed my face with some of the water from the can.

Six o'clock came. No digging. I picked up my rosary again, resigned to praying one more decade. Seven o'clock. Still no digging. Fifty more Hail Marys.

Then, just after seven-thirty, I heard footsteps.

"Shafirgullah" came a voice from above. He answered, and the digging started.

My heart was pounding. It was happening. They were going to dig me out and take me back to Kabul. It was really going to happen. I would be back at my hotel in Kabul tonight. I would see Paul.

The digging stopped and a blast of cold air swept into the hole. I got up to crawl up the tunnel, but Shafirgullah stopped me.

"I go," he said. "You. Here."

I looked at him, sure that he was going ahead to help me out of the shaft at the end of the tunnel, but then I heard a loud thump. It was Khalid. Shafirgullah scrambled up the tunnel.

"Khalid," I said, "what is happening?"

"Shut up!" he yelled at me.

"What's wrong, Khalid? Why are you yelling at me?"

"Shut up!" he shouted.

"I thought I was going to Kabul tonight. You and Shafirgullah both said."

"You not go Kabul. You stay here!" He sounded like someone else, not the Khalid I knew. Not the same person I had spent the last three weeks with. Adrenaline seemed to be pumping through my entire body.

He took out a thick metal chain and started to wrap it around my ankles, locking it with a padlock. Then he wrapped one of the ends of the same chain around my right wrist.

"What are you doing?" I yelled.

"Shut up! We leave you here tonight."

"Why are you doing this, Khalid? You said I was your sister. This is how you treat your sister?"

"Shut up! We leave you. You do not know what happen." His voice was agitated, his eyes flashing.

"What's wrong, Khalid?" I said softly, tears in my eyes. "Tell me. Don't just do this to me without telling me anything. What is wrong?"

He stared at me for a while. "You don't know anything. I have bad thing happen. You no understand."

"Then tell me. Help me understand. What happened?"

He was getting impatient with me and then spat it out. "My mother die! Okay? My mother die!"

I didn't know what to say. I was so disappointed not to be leaving that night that I was at a loss for words at that moment. So I said the only thing I could think of under the circumstances. "I'm sorry, Khalid. I'm so sorry. What happened?"

He seemed taken aback, and told me again only that she had died.

"I didn't know she was sick, Khalid," I said, hoping to start a conversation again. If I was going to have to stay in the hole, I wanted the chain off my ankles. They were already starting to press into my flesh. He didn't respond for several seconds, just stared at the chain around my feet.

"We leave you here. If you call, we will hear you. You know the house—we are there, okay? We are there. If you call, I will come down and I will kill you."

"Khalid, please! Take the chain off. It hurts. I'm not going anywhere. Where can I go anyway? Please, don't make me wear them. Please."

"Shut up," he said. "I will kill you if you call out." And then he crawled out of the hole.

"Khalid, don't leave me here!" I shouted, but my voice was already muffled by the noise of digging. Dust filled the air, but I was too upset to move into my usual position under the duvet. Besides, I was chained to myself and my mobility was limited. It hurt to even try to move. The heavy chain was digging into my ankles and my wrist. So instead I sat there in a daze, my back against the wall, and let the dirt settle on my hair and on my notebook, and seep into my lungs.

The digging stopped after a few minutes. I heard the sound of footsteps fading into the distance. I was, for the first time in three weeks, truly alone.

Dearest M,

I'm going to climb into bed now, M, feeling guilty about sleeping in sheets under a warm duvet and you more than likely sprawled on a dirty mattress on the floor, with only a couple of blankets to keep you warm. I would trade places with you any time and I only wish it had been me who had been kidnapped, instead of you. My phone is on and I'm still hoping you will call in the middle of the night and say, "I'm free! Come and get me." If only it were that simple.

xx

I remained immobilized for a while, unable to move, in shock about what had just happened. How could I go from being almost certain that I was about to be released to being shackled and left alone with more questions than answers, all in the space of a few minutes?

I didn't know what to do. I wanted to cry, but I couldn't muster the tears. I wanted to shout, but I couldn't find my voice. I wanted to laugh at the absurdity of it, but I couldn't find the humour in it. I wanted to pray, but I was too angry at God. I threw the rosary down on the blanket and cursed it. I was on a prayer strike. No more praying.

So I smoked. I chain-smoked as many cigarettes as I could stomach until I felt like I was going to throw up smoke. About an hour later, I heard footsteps overhead. *Clomp, clomp, clomp, clomp.* And then a voice. "Mellissa!" It was Abdulrahman.

"Yes?" I called out.

"Do not talk too loudly," he called down.

"What is going on?" I ignored his order.

"Shh! There are people. They watching us. You no talk loudly."

"Who is watching us? And why have you left me here like this? What is happening?"

"Something . . . something happen. It is very bad. Khalid mother—she die."

I felt bad for Khalid. I couldn't imagine what it would be like to lose your mother suddenly. But at the same time, I felt a sense of despair. This was surely a setback for my release. I could be here for a lot longer than I was ready for.

"What is going to happen now?" I asked Abdulrahman. "Does Khalid have to go to Pakistan for the funeral? Are you going to Pakistan for the funeral?"

I seemed to remember that in Muslim culture, the body has to be buried as soon as possible after death. If Khalid's family was in Peshawar, he would have to leave that night, if she hadn't already been buried.

"No, we not go to Pakistan," Abdulrahman said. "Maybe Khalid go. We come back, four, five days."

"You're leaving me here for four or five days?" I asked, incredulous. I knew there wasn't enough juice, or cookies, to last me that long down there by myself.

"Maybe. We come back," he assured me.

Then I heard another voice. "Mellissa." It was Khalid.

"Khalid. Why are you doing this to me? You don't have to put me in a chain. I can't go anywhere. I can't open the door to up there anyway." I was pleading to have him come and unshackle me, but he wasn't listening. "Khalid. I am very sorry for you. I know you say you loved your mother very much. I can't imagine how hard this is. But I promise, I will not go anywhere."

"Okay," he replied. "We go now. But we come back."

"Wait! Don't go!" I called out. "I need more juice. I need more cookies. I will starve and I am already sick."

"We come back," he called down again. "Do not speak. If you hear someone, do not speak."

Abdulrahman chimed in. "Your name is Khalid. No speaking if someone say 'Mellissa'! We call you Khalid; then you speak. You understand?"

"My name is Khalid?" I asked. It took me a while to realize that they didn't want me to answer if someone outside the gang called down. I was to respond only when they addressed me as "Khalid."

"Yes, we go now," Abdulrahman said. "Goodbye."

"Wait! Khalid!" I called.

"Yes?"

"I'm really sorry about your mother. I am. I am sorry for you and your family." I meant it. I felt terrible for him. And his mother could not have been that old, given Khalid's and Zahir's ages.

"Thank you," the reply came from above. "Goodbye."

I heard their footsteps fade and soon silence filled the hole once again. I wasn't sure what to do next. I didn't want to smoke anymore, at least not that night. I looked at the alarm clock. It was just after nine. Now what? Khalid and his family would be spending the next few days dealing with their loss. I hoped they wouldn't forget they had a hostage whose "case" needed to be finished. But I was resigned to the fact that I may be in the hole a lot longer than I had been prepared to be.

I tried to loosen the chain around my wrist. I wriggled it around to try to free my hand, but it was too tight, as was the end around my ankles. I stood up and realized I couldn't really move my right arm without straining the chain around my feet. If I so much as lift my hand, the chain around my feet pulled, rubbing the metal right into my flesh. I'd have to try to avoid sudden movements. It was bad enough to be held hostage in a hole, but it felt a hundred times worse to be chained up. If I'd been lonely before, with no one to talk to but one of my Afghan guards, it was that much more desolate now, without even another presence in the hole to distract me from the reality of where I was.

I'd told Khalid once—I think it was on one of the first days of my captivity—that I'd rather be alone, but after just a few hours in the hole by myself, I realized it was better to have someone else around. Because with someone else there, I knew that the kidnappers were going to come back. There was a strange and steady comfort in knowing they weren't just going to leave me in the hole to rot.

Now, alone, I wondered if something had happened. The voices inside my head were out of control. What if the negotiations weren't going well? What if the whole notion that someone was even negotiating was just a figment of my imagination and no one was trying to secure my release on the outside? Maybe my kidnappers were sick of how long it was taking and were going to leave me there to die. What if they didn't come back? What if the real Taliban found me? What then?

I realized my heart rate was starting to speed up again and I forced myself to take a few deep breaths to calm down. *Don't worry,* I told myself out loud. *It will be okay. They're looking for you, and the Afghans will come back for you. Don't worry. You will be home soon.*

Khalid had left enough slack on the heavy chain to allow my hand to reach out a little. I grabbed my new notebook and removed the pen from the spine.

Dear P,

I don't know what is happening, but my kidnappers have left me alone in this hole for the first time since they took me.

I'm scared, darling. I don't know what they're planning, but my fear is that no one will come back here. I'm afraid—for the first time—that I might not survive this ordeal. You know that I am not afraid of death.

What worries me more is what will happen to my family if I never come home. I'm afraid it will permanently damage them. I know that life goes on after someone dies, but I still worry.

I worry less about you. You will move on, I know you will. You must. For me. I will be okay, hopefully up there in heaven. You have to know that. Death is something I'm ready to accept, if it's really my time. It will just be really unfair if we don't have more time together.

I am so sorry for everything I've put you through. I promise I will make it up to you if I get out of here. I hope you can forgive me.

I love you, P. I know you're not religious, but please try to find a prayer for me tonight. I'm scared.

xox

The tears finally flowed, freely and openly, and I was sobbing as I closed the notebook. I hadn't really cried hard since I was taken. Now, it was as if I was finally releasing everything—fear, hope, anger, sadness—all in one fell swoop. My body shook with it, and shook for a while. It was a real deluge, and I let the sobs overwhelm me and take over.

Okay, enough, I finally told myself, wiping the tears from my face, *stop it. Stop crying. Stop being a frigging wuss. What good is it going to do you to feel sorry for yourself? Stop crying and try to think of what you can do to get yourself out of here.*

Dearest M,

I'm afraid you're going to be a prisoner for a while longer, as much as that overwhelms me with fear and anxiety. And that's why I woke up at four in the morning and couldn't get back to sleep. And of course, I always turn out the light dreading a "bad news" call in the middle of the night, and then breathe a sigh every morning when the sun comes up.

I'm sure you're hearing and seeing the storm that's moving through, and I think of you being cold and wet and utterly miserable. I know you don't have any warm clothing, and I hope they brought something for you. This is the most depressing thing that could happen this afternoon. It marks the arrival of winter and will only get colder in the days to come. Oh, M, what a mess we're in.

I struggled again with the chain, trying to free my wrist, but it was on too tight. I stood up and tried to walk, but there was very little slack in the chain, so I could barely take baby steps. Still, I got on my knees and, holding the lamp in my left hand, crawled—slowly—up the tunnel on my belly, moving my knees forward together one step at a time, past the stinking toilet can and the urine-filled water bottle the captors were using. I held my breath so I wouldn't have to smell the stench. When I reached the end, I stood up in the shaft and pointed the light upward.

The covering of the hole. It looked like a piece of wood, but I couldn't be sure. I would have to climb the sides to get to the top, and the shaft was about eight feet deep. There was no way I could climb with my ankles chained together and then chained to my wrist.

I thought I heard rustling outside, a fair distance away. Maybe it was a villager.

"Salaam!" I called up. "As-Salaam Alaikum!"

Silence greeted my words. Dead silence. I tried again. Louder. Nothing.

I couldn't think of anything else I could do. If only I had something—a pole or a stick or something—I could try to move the hole covering. Then I could call out, despite Khalid's warning.

But there was nothing in the hole itself I could use. I knelt down and made my way back inside the cave. The chain was again digging into my ankles, and when I got back to my blue duvet I could see that my right ankle was red and raw. My captors had obviously known that I would try to get away. Of course they had known. What normal human being wouldn't try to escape? I wondered if other hostages had escaped. Surely, everyone who is ever captured would think about it, and maybe attempt it, at some point. I wondered if I could have escaped on that first day when they were marching me through the mountains. Maybe I should have run. I was in pretty good shape then and might have been able to outrun them and their bullets. Yes, that was probably the best chance I had of getting away. Why hadn't I taken it? Instead, I had let myself become their prisoner, let them keep me hostage in a hole for three weeks. Why hadn't I tried harder on that first day to get away from them?

But there was no point in asking. I hadn't run for obvious reasons. I had been stabbed and was bleeding. I didn't know where I was going; the kidnappers had guns.

I sat back down and crawled onto my blanket, trying to rest my ankles so the chain would stop digging into my skin. Bending my legs sideways seemed to work the best—but then I couldn't get my right arm in a comfortable position. If sleeping in the hole had been uncomfortable before, this was a whole new level of discomfort. I wished I had sleeping pills to put myself out for the night.

My prayer strike was short-lived. With my free hand, I reached into my pocket for the rosary. There was nothing else to do but pray, and it was usually how I got to sleep. So I started with the Hail Marys again. I focused on Mary herself. I imagined that God was too busy dealing with other, much more important things, like the war I had come to Afghanistan to cover, global warming, and AIDS in Africa. Things that needed his time and attention much more than little me in a hole. Mary would be my intercessor. She was the mother figure, the one who could make things happen.

I had never prayed so much or so hard in my life. I wasn't overly religious, but I knew my mother was, and she'd probably have her entire parish in Vancouver praying for me. I wondered if God could really ignore the prayers of all those people. I was sure he couldn't. The more people prayed, the more he'd have to do something to answer their prayers. He'd have to listen, if an entire congregation was praying, no?

In any case, I kept praying to Mary. I imagined she was telling me it was going to be okay, and that everything would work out, that I was not to worry. I imagined she was stroking my matted hair while I kept praying and praying and hoping that I would fall asleep.

Hail Mary, full of grace, the Lord is with thee.
Blessed art thou amongst women,
And blessed is the fruit of thy womb, Jesus.
Holy Mary, mother of God, pray for us sinners,
Now and at the hour of our death, Amen.
Please, Mary, please, please, please help me. Please let me get out of here okay. Please don't let me die in here. But if I do, please help me into heaven. Please, Mary, only you can help me. Please.

Sleep would not come, so I kept praying.

Please, Mary, tell my family that I am okay. Please don't let anything happen to them. Please take care of my friends. Please give them all some comfort from the constant worrying about me. Please tell them I will be home soon, and it will all be okay. Please, please, please.

Soon, the alarm clock told me it was six o'clock. It was morning, and I hadn't slept at all. The lamp was dimming and I was concerned that the bulb might not last much longer. I looked around and saw that Khalid had left a new bag, which I hadn't noticed the night before in all the mayhem. I opened it and looked inside. Four spare batteries, a few juice boxes, and three packages of cookies—the cheap fruit creme kind. A package of cigarettes. He had also left his lighter, which had a small flashlight on one end. I decided not to change the lamp batteries right away, to conserve as much power as I could, since I didn't know how long it would be until new supplies came. Maybe they'd come and slide stuff down the pipe, as they'd done before.

I opened a package of mango creme cookies and ate a couple, taking the top off first and trying not to chew too hard. I'd felt a bit of a toothache in my back teeth a few days ago—probably all the sugar I was consuming was eating into the enamel of my teeth. I wasn't even hungry, but I stuffed a couple more cookies down my mouth. I was only eating to kill time, and to make sure that I had a little energy. I dug through the juice boxes looking for apple, but there was only mango, which was my least favourite because it was thicker and coated the roof of my mouth in a sugary syrup. Still, my body needed fluids, and I wasn't about to drink the water in the can, which had been there for a few days now.

I played with the lighter for a while. I took the English school-book that my kidnappers had been trying to read and tore off a page. I held the flame under the bottom right-hand corner of the page and watched the paper catch on fire. The dampness in the room made it harder to burn, and the fire stopped halfway up the page, just below a drawing of a young boy, one of the characters in the story. The smell of burnt paper was a welcome relief to the stench in the hole, and I burned the rest of the page. Maybe the smoke would signal that there was someone here. Maybe if ISAF—International Security Assist-ance Force—troops were in the neighbourhood, they would follow the smell of smoke to the hole, and then I could call out and guide them to come and rescue me. I tore out a few more pages and burned them close to the pipe hole, the smoke carrying my hopes up to the surface. I closed my eyes and breathed in the smell of the smoke—it was something different for a change, and I imagined I was building a fire.

I've always associated fire with the comfort of home. My father's charcoal barbecues of my childhood, where he cooked amazing meals for our family—steaks and chicken and oysters—either at home or at the beach during a family picnic. The fireplace at Kelly's house on the beach in Tofino was the last place I had held a flame to paper to try to get a fire going. It had been a cold and grey West Coast summer day—I'd just come in from a few hours on the surf, ripped off my wetsuit, and was about to head to the shower, but I wanted to get a fire going first. It took a while, and Kelly and I were laughing at our inability to light it. The wood was damp, which was always my excuse. But eventually, we had a roaring fire, and we sat around reading and sipping Scotch, cozy on the couch under a fluffy blanket.

I suddenly remembered that I'd put Kelly's name down on my list of emergency contacts before I left for Afghanistan, and that her last message to me was that she had lost her cell phone. Or that it had broken. I couldn't recall now which. But I'd put Kelly down as a contact because she is the most organized and responsible person I know. She is meticulous and thoughtful and smart—which is why she is such a good journalist. She had left the CBC years before to become an independent producer, and in recent years had been travelling the world doing stories for National Geographic and Discovery Channel. I knew that if anything happened to me, she would be able to pick up the pieces and work through whatever complications might arise in my absence.

Kelly—or "Mooey," as I had nicknamed her because the two of us are known as "the cows"—had been nominated for a television award for one of her Discovery series and was supposed to be in Toronto the week before. I felt a pang of guilt for whatever I was putting her through, and for having to deal with the CBC and whatever authorities were handling my kidnapping back in Canada. As if she didn't already have enough on her plate. I'd put her down as an emergency contact without thinking that anyone would ever have to call my emergency contacts. I reached for my notepad.

Dear Mooey,

I am so sorry that you are probably having to deal with my disappearance back home. Or maybe you're not. Maybe your phone is dead and no one was able to get hold of you and you're blissfully unaware of what's going on.

Okay, so maybe that's wishful thinking on my part so I wouldn't have to feel so guilty about whatever it is I'm putting you through right now. Because I know it can't be good. You're dealing with the CBC, my parents, and probably the RCMP or CSIS. I think I owe you a lifetime's supply of Lagavulin, just for that.

I'm doing okay. My kidnappers have left me alone, and I have some juice and cookies to last me for a while. Hopefully, it won't be much longer before they realize they're not going to get a lot of money for me and let me go.

I'm not sure if you made it to Toronto, but if you did, I hope you won the Gemini and we can celebrate when I get home. I've been thinking a lot about Tofino, and the idea of getting back on a surfboard is inspiration enough to get me through the bad days. I hope we can hang out for a bit out there when I get out of here.

And lastly, I just wanted to say thank you—for everything you're no doubt doing while I'm away. You're the best friend anyone could ever ask for and I'm grateful to have you in my life. I know we joked about what we should do if one of us meets an untimely end, and I just wanted to remind you that I want half of my ashes scattered in the Pacific in Tofino and the other half dropped off the Empire State Building in New York. I've also left you some insurance money to do that.

There is a running joke among my small group of friends. Kelly had an amazing couch in her westside Vancouver flat, a couch I'd slept on, eaten on, drunk Scotch on for years. It was a luxurious green sectional, and she'd told us before leaving on a round-the-world assignment aboard a tall ship that she'd left it to me in her will. So we'd started referring to it as my couch—to the chagrin of our friends Sudha and Alan, who both thought it should be passed on to them.

I would give anything to be sitting on my green couch with you right now. I'm really sorry for everything I'm putting you through. I promise, if I make it home in one piece, I'll make it up to you.

I realized I was starting to sound a little fatalistic, but I couldn't help it. It was possible that my kidnappers might not come back for whatever reason. Maybe they would be killed in a coalition air strike on their way to Pakistan. Maybe they would have to flee the country. Maybe they would be arrested and refuse to give up my location. Anything could happen, and I had to be prepared for the possibility.

I did have a will back in Canada, even though I didn't have too many worldly possessions. What little money I did have in bonds and funds I'd left to my sister. The life insurance money was to be split between Vanessa and my parents, with a bit of it going to Kelly to pay for the scattering of my ashes—if there were any—on both ends of the continent. But I wished I'd left something to Paul. I flipped to an empty page and started scrawling again. I wanted to make sure a few things were not left in any doubt. Just in case.

Amendments to my last will and testament
*   To Paul Workman—my King James Bible.*

Paul wasn't religious, but he would appreciate that I had left him something that was important to me. I tried to think of what else needed to be left to others, and not just put in a box and given to the Salvation Army.

To Stefani Langenegger—my stuffed dog, Rover.

Rover is important to me. Years ago, when my parents moved my maternal grandmother into an elderly care home, I was racked with guilt. I had lived at home for a long time to look after her, after my grandfather passed away, but she had deteriorated to the point that not even with home-care nurses could the family meet her growing needs.

I had visited her every night after I got off work. On weekends I would take her lunch and a big bouquet of flowers, spending the afternoon with her and her roommates. She shared a room with three other women, all bedridden, and I started visiting with them and bringing them flowers too.

It was always hard to leave my grandmother there, by herself without family, and I wished I could leave her something, especially when I was away travelling, something I did quite a bit then. I was a political reporter and would be away for days at a time during an election campaign. On one campaign I was travelling with the premier of British Columbia. He made a stop at a care home not unlike the one my grandma was in. After the event, as we were all walking back to the campaign bus, we passed the gift shop. In the window was the cutest stuffed white puppy dog, staring out at me, almost begging me to adopt him. I stopped, holding up the bus and the premier's campaign, while the woman minding the store searched for the key to the display window.

My grandma loved Rover. He went everywhere with her, tucked

beside her under the blanket that covered her skinny legs as she sat in her wheelchair. Then one day, not long before she passed away, she tugged my sleeve, and said, "I don't think I can take care of Rover. He's very naughty and has been biting the nurses' ankles. Maybe he should stay with you. You can bring him when you come to see me."

And so I took him home, but he lived in my bag so that my grandma would be able to see him whenever I went to visit. Weeks later, when she was hospitalized with pneumonia, I brought him to the hospital and tucked him in with her while she was sleeping. He was with her when they moved her back to the care home and when she died the next day.

So Rover became my "dog." Because it's so hard for me to have a real dog, given my job, the little white stuffed toy was a surrogate. He moved to Toronto with me and, later to Regina, where my friends embraced him as if he were a real puppy. He was especially popular with Henry, my friends Mal and Coreen's two-year-old. And that's where he was now, with Henry's godmother, Stefani.

I thought about what else I had that was of any value. Abdul-rahman had made off with my grandmother's wedding ring. My other ring was the silver one from my sister. I hadn't taken it off since Vanessa gave it to me, and it wasn't something I thought I could give back to her.

To Kelly McClughan—my silver ring.

But I had to give my sister something. I would have given her grandma's ring, but I no longer had it. But I did have something else of my grandmother's that was, to me, even more special: her original Good Housekeeping cookbook, published in 1966. It was tattered and the spine was tearing, but I loved it because it was full of her writings, little notes on the sides, with recipes she'd culled from other sources and scribbled in the margins.

My grandma was an amazing woman. She had grown up without very much, the hated stepdaughter of her father's second wife. Working hard her entire life, she and my grandfather raised an only child—Joyce, my mother—and eventually moved with our family when we immigrated to Canada. With both of our parents working, she focused on her grandchildren, and our lives were the richer for it. She helped us with our homework, reading the classics again when we did at school, working through long algebra equations with us, walking us to and from school and to all those after-school lessons we were signed up for. But best of all, she baked.

She taught herself by following recipes, until she eventually started creating her own beautiful cakes and tortes. The best apple pie in the world, with homemade ice cream, which she cranked out from an old-fashioned salt and ice–powered ice cream maker. Cinnamon buns, with big fat raisins peeking out from a cream cheese glaze. Cookies and meringues and buttercream. My favourite was a maple walnut torte she made with layers of walnut meringue and chiffon cake, with a perfect maple buttercream. Her Black Forest cake, which I've tried to replicate but just can't make taste quite the way hers did. A chocolate–Grand Marnier torte, with layers of rich and moist dark chocolate cake with orange liqueur mousse, topped with chocolate ganache and ribbons of shaved chocolate.

I watched and learned, and she would let me help. My job was measuring ingredients and holding the electric mixer—and, of course, tasting the finished product. Then she'd make notes in her little blue cookbook.

Years later, I saved it from the garbage bin when my parents were renovating the house.

To my sister, Vanessa——Grandma's blue cookbook.

I didn't really have anything else of value. My friends were already looking after my possessions, as I'd been away from home for months before going to Afghanistan. My KitchenAid stand mixer, probably my favourite kitchen appliance, was at Coreen's house in Regina, where I knew she was putting it to good use.

To Coreen Larson——my KitchenAid stand mixer (please make the yummy Guinness chocolate cake with it).

I'd already left all my good Scotch and wine with my friends Gerry and Shelley Thue in Regina. I kept several single malts in my liquor drawer, and because another reporter would be staying in my apartment while I was gone, I moved the liquor to the Thues. Gerry was a single malt aficionado.

To the Thues——please drink the Scotch. Yes, Gerry, even the Lagavulin.

My prized Canucks jersey was my going-away present from the Vancouver newsroom when I left to take a job as a national reporter in Toronto. It had been signed by the entire hockey team, and I barely ever took it out of the clear resealable bag it had come in. I didn't even wear it to games, afraid that I'd slop mustard or ketchup or spill beer on it. There was only one person who would appreciate it and look after it the way I did.

To Jen Barr——my signed Canucks jersey.

That was pretty much it. All my worldly possessions. Not

much to show for thirty-six years on this earth. I flipped to the earlier note I had written to Paul and added to it.

I know I just asked you to pray for me, but in the event that those prayers don't work, and you find yourself reading this notebook at some point without me, I left you something that might help with praying in the future. I wish I could have given you so much more—but I need you to be okay if I don't come home.

Promise me, okay?

xox

I must have passed out sometime in the early evening. I woke up to the sound of footsteps above. I froze. Was it one of my kidnappers or someone looking for me?

"Mellissa!" It sounded like Abdulrahman.

"Yes!" I called up, struggling to stand. I shuffled over in my chain to the opening of the pipe and with my left hand took the fabric pieces out of it so that I could call up.

"You are Khalid! Not Mellissa!" Oh, right. I had forgotten that I'd been instructed not to answer to my own name.

"Mellissa!" he called down again. I didn't answer.

"Khalid!" was the next call.

"Yes?" I responded.

"Good. It is Abdulrahman. Do you need anything?"

"Yes, more batteries for the *tsiragh.* And more cigarettes."

"Battery and cigarettes," he repeated. He pronounced "cigarette" without the "a" so it sounded like "cigrette."

"Yes. When do I go to Kabul, Abdulrahman? What is going on? How is Khalid?"

"Inshallah, in a few days," he answered. "We will take you. Goodbye!"

His footsteps faded away, I was alone again. As much as I

despised Abdulrahman, his short visit made me feel a little better. At least my kidnappers hadn't forgotten about me. But of course they wouldn't. I was worth more to them alive than dead, and they had invested enough time in my kidnapping.

One way or another, I was getting out of here, and I would get out alive. I sat back down and opened my notebook.

Don't worry, P. I'm coming home. It will all be okay. We'll see each other soon. But keep praying, if you can. I need all the help I can get. Love you. xox

Dearest M,

I got a note from Kas last night who says she and the girls are drinking a lot to ease their fear and frustration (but what else is new!). She also says Jen Barr won a Gemini this week and dedicated it to you. Erin Boudreau in London also won and sent this note:

"But I must say, the golden hue of a Gemini doesn't feel right under these circumstances. I think about Mellissa all the time—when I eat breakfast, when I brush my teeth, when I try to concentrate at work. I hope you are hanging in there . . ."

I am just sorry, darling, that you will have to spend more nights in your hell. I know you have tremendous faith, and prayer will help you get through the worst of it, but still I worry. I've taken out that photograph of us from the harbour in Hong Kong and put it on the desk. I look at it and just know that we will go back there together.

Good night, M. I'm with you.

xx

I'd spent about forty-eight hours alone in the hole with my thoughts, my rosary, and my notebook, and was just lighting a cigarette when I heard footsteps again. But no one called down to me, and I wasn't sure what to do. Was I being released? Could it be the police? Maybe it was someone else.

Then I heard digging. I wasn't sure I was hearing right at first. But the sound became unmistakable. It had been a few days since I'd heard it.

"Khalid!" A voice from above. My heart slowed. It was my kidnappers after all. I ducked under the duvet to shield myself from the dust shower and waited. I heard the cover being taken off the opening of the hole, and then a thump. It was the real Khalid, and I watched as he crawled down the tunnel toward me.

"Khalid, what's going on?" I asked.

"We go now!" he replied, looking a little flustered. He started unlocking the padlocks on the chain that held my ankles together. I felt like a huge weight had been lifted. He was struggling with the lock on my wrist, twice trying all three keys, but none of them fit.

"Quick, we go," he told me. "Your shoes." He reached for my runners and I scrambled to put them on, without even untying the laces.

"Quick!"

"Wait," I said. "I need to bring my things. My notebook. My backpack." If I was being released, I wanted to be able to bring my possessions with me.

Khalid gave me an empty white plastic bag. "Put here," he ordered.

I emptied the contents of my backpack into the plastic: my wallet, my makeup bag, and both notebooks.

"Quick! Go!" He gave me a push into the tunnel and I crawled up. I still had the chain on my wrist, and it was dragging behind me. I got to the end of the tunnel and stood up.

"Mellissa!" It was Abdulrahman from above. Khalid had come up the tunnel and was now standing behind me. He wrapped his hands around my legs and lifted me up. "Lift your arms!" I heard Abdulrahman bark. I lifted my arms and felt two sets of hands on either side lifting me onto solid ground. I breathed the fresh air deeply. It was dark and I could barely make out the abandoned house to the left.

"Do not look!" Khalid shouted from the shaft as he scrambled to the top with my plastic bag. "Sit down!"

I obeyed. He took my black scarf and wrapped it around my eyes, so crudely that the scarf was restricting my ability to breathe.

"Ow!" I yelled. "Not so tight!" He loosened it and asked if I could see. I said no and was ordered to stand up.

"Walk."

"Walk where?" I asked. "I cannot see."

"Up!" Someone shoved the barrel of a gun into my back. I felt a cold rush of fear. Was I about to be executed? Where were we going? Khalid—at least, I thought it was Khalid—shoved the handles of the bag into my hand. We started walking, Khalid leading me by the elbow. Shafirgullah walked on my other side, and Abdulrahman was behind us. They led me through the village, and I stumbled several times over steps and the uneven ground.

"Where are we going?" I asked.

"Do not speak," Khalid said. My heart was pounding and my

skin was clammy. That must be the feeling of raw fear. I'd never felt anything like it before.

"We going away from here," Abdulrahman told me.

"Why? Where are we going? Why are we going now?" No answer from anyone. We just kept walking. Around walls, over bumps on the road, through alleys between houses.

"Sit down!" Khalid pushed my left shoulder down, and I dropped to the ground. So did my captors. We sat for a while, and they spoke in hushed tones in Pashto. They must have seen someone walking in the vicinity.

"Get up!" I felt Khalid's hand on my elbow, pushing it up, so I stood up. "Go!" And we continued rushing through the village—I assumed—with me blindfolded, unable to make out even the brightest of lights from under my scarf. I tripped several times and stubbed my toe. They seemed impatient, hauling me up again, all the while talking among themselves in rapid Pashto. We finally stumbled into an open area. The ground felt a bit sandy and I sensed there were no buildings around us.

"Do not stop," Khalid said quietly, still leading me by the elbow. We kept walking, and I kept stumbling over my feet, even on the sand. I felt awkward walking. It had been so long since I'd been able to, and now I was being forced to do it blindfolded. It felt like we were climbing a hill. The sand was slippery under my running shoes and it was difficult to go very fast.

"Sit down now." I did as I was told, and sensed my kidnappers sitting down next to me. "I am taking your scarf." I felt hands reach behind my head and the scarf came off. I blinked and looked around. We were in a sandy open area, and there was a small hill about thirty metres away. I could make out mountains farther ahead and to the left. I turned to look at where we had come from.

"Do not look!" Khalid turned my head around to face forward. It was just him and Shafirgullah with me. Abdulrahman must have left us somewhere along the way. Shafirgullah was carrying a big sack on a stick, like a hobo sack. Khalid also had a big pack with him, which he unpacked, looking for something. I saw that his pack held several plastic bags, which looked like they contained about a dozen juice boxes, a few packages of cigarettes, fruit creme cookies, and Afghan bread. Shafirgullah's pack was bigger but lighter. He sat down on it while Khalid fished out a package of cigarettes and put them in the pocket of his jacket.

"Khalid, where are we going?" I asked.

He lit a smoke and didn't answer right away, instead saying something to Shafirgullah in Pashto. "Where are we going? What is going on?" I insisted. I was running on adrenaline. My heart was still pounding, as it had been since they'd dug me out of the hole, about an hour before.

"We go away—to a better place," Khalid told me.

"Why?" I asked. "What was wrong with where we were before?"

"It is not safe," he said.

"Where are we going?" I kept repeating. "Where?"

"Walk! Go!" Khalid ordered. He yanked the chain that was still tethered to my right wrist, and the metal dug into my skin.

"Ow!" I cried. "Don't do that!"

I couldn't believe he was treating me like this. Even though he was the one who had chained me to myself two days before, I still found it difficult to accept that the one person out of the gang of kidnappers, the one I had come to rely on, had turned on me the way he had. I'd spent the last three weeks trying to build a relationship and gain his trust, and I thought he actually cared a little about my well-being. He'd called me "sister," promised not to kill me, talked to me about his wedding plans. I'd listened to him, told him about my family, gave him the little mirror in my makeup bag as a gift for Shogufa.

And in the last two days, we had reverted back to the relationship we started with on day one. Kidnapper and hostage. Gunman and captive. Fundamentalist and foreigner. I felt betrayed, but I realized I had been betrayed only by my own naïveté, if anything.

He yanked the chain again, not as hard this time, and led us toward the small hill. We trudged through the sand and up the hill. It wasn't very high, and over the edge I could see bushes, and mountains in the distance. I turned around and looked at the village we'd just left. It was bigger than I had thought, definitely not a village, but a town. There weren't many lights, and it was sprawling and flat, checkered with mud walls and mud houses.

"Do not look back," Khalid ordered, so I turned back around and looked ahead. He had been holding the end of my chain but dropped it to pick up his pack. I caught up to the end and picked it up. The chain was maybe twelve feet long, and it was heavy. Khalid led the way and Shafirgullah walked behind me, carrying his hobo sack, his gun pointed at my back. We veered left along what looked like a dried-up creek bed, and I could feel small branches rub against my raw ankles.

"Khalid, please tell me, what is going on?" I called out to him. "Did your father tell us to leave? Are we going to Kabul?"

He ignored me, but I was dogged, like the legislative reporter I once was, grilling a minister who was trying to avoid answering a question. Finally, he had had enough. He stopped walking and turned back to face me. "It is not my father!" he shouted. "I have no father!"

"What?" I was completely confused.

"It is not my father!" he repeated, a little louder this time.

"What are you saying? Then who have you been talking to all

this time? You told me it was your father." I still wasn't sure what he was telling me.

"I lie to you. The one in Pakistan. He is not my father." He started walking again.

I followed, running a little to catch up to him. "You lied? If he's not your father, who is he? And where is your father?"

"I have no father!"

"Did you lie about your mother too? She's not dead, is she." Khalid's only response was to walk faster. I was almost running to keep up.

"Khalid, if that person in Pakistan is not your father, who is he? And what about your mother?"

"My father is dead! I have no father!" He was yelling again.

I yelled back. "Then who is the person in Pakistan you are talking to?"

"It is my friend! My friend, okay?"

I was confused, but it was clear he wasn't going to give me any more information, so we continued walking. Soon we were in front of what looked like the base of a small mountain beyond some trees and bushes. I was getting tired. Three weeks of sitting in a hole had no doubt weakened my muscle strength considerably, and I was carrying around a chain that probably weighed close to seven kilograms. I was huffing and puffing when we finally stopped behind the trees.

"Sit," Khalid ordered. We all sat for a while, and my captors lit cigarettes. They offered me one and I took it, lighting it only after I had caught my breath. We sat for a while, and the two Afghans spoke to each other in Pashto, pointing at the mountains in front of us. I wished I could understand what they were saying. After a few minutes, Khalid stood up. "We go!"

I struggled to stand up. My legs felt like jelly. I didn't know how much farther we were going to go, but I knew I couldn't walk any faster. My kidnappers didn't seem to care. We started walking up another hill toward the mountain. The ground was rocky, the stones like shale, brittle and angular. The mountain was getting closer and closer, and I wondered if we were going to go around it, through it, or under it. I tripped several times as the hill got steeper, the rocks crumbling under our feet. I tried to step in the same places Khalid had stepped, but his legs were longer than mine and I couldn't match his strides. A rock gave out under my left foot and I stumbled. Unable to catch my balance, I fell and tumbled several feet down the hill.

"No stop!" Shafirgullah yelled at me.

I tried to get up but my chain was caught under the edge of a boulder. I stumbled again and didn't get up.

"I can't go any farther," I protested. "I can't."

Shafirgullah prodded me with the barrel of his Kalashnikov.

"Don't do that!" I told him. "It's not nice."

He looked at Khalid, who looked down at me and sighed.

"Come, we stop a little little up there." Khalid pointed farther up the hill. I followed his finger and saw nothing but a big mother of a mountain.

"We're going up there?" I asked.

He nodded. "Come." He came down and held out his hand to help me up. A small glimpse of the Khalid I knew. I took his hand, and he hauled me to my feet.

We continued hiking for at least an hour, straight toward the mountain. After a while, we came to an open area, where there was a creek. Khalid stopped, and he and Shafirgullah said a few words in Pashto before setting down their sacks. Shafirgullah opened his to reveal three blankets—two like the kind he had used in the hole, and one like my softer blue duvet. He gave one to Khalid, who was already wearing a jacket, and one to me. I laid mine out and sat on it, wondering if this was where we were going to spend the night.

Khalid brought out three boxes of juice from his pack and handed one to each of us. I hadn't even realized that I was thirsty. I drank the contents in one big gulp and wiped my mouth with the dirty sleeve of my kameez.

"Sit," Khalid told me, even though I was already sitting. He had spread out his blanket and was lying down, one hand on the other end of the chain that was fastened to me.

Shafirgullah had wandered away, and I could see he was washing his face in the creek. He spread his blanket in front of himself and got on his knees to pray.

Khalid's eyes were closed, and soon I could hear his deep breathing. Was he going to sleep for the night or was he just taking a nap? I looked over at Shafirgullah. He was still praying. I tried to lie down, but I couldn't get comfortable. The blanket was too thin to stop the rocks from poking into my back. And I was shivering. It was very cold, and I didn't have a coat. I looked down in the direction from which we came, and I could see the faint glow of the town kilometres away.

Then I looked up, and for the first time in three weeks I saw the night sky. It was clear and the stars were in the millions, like little pinpricks through which you could see the bright light of heaven. I could make out the Big Dipper, but it looked upside down to how I was used to seeing it back home. I thought I could also see the Milky Way, a hazy band of white light against the black sky.

Then I saw a shooting star, whooshing across the darkness, and just as I was about to make a wish, another one shot through my line of vision.

God, if you're up there, please help me. I don't know where they're taking me, but I'm scared, and I need you to keep me safe. I know you're up there. Please watch over me tonight. Please.

After about half an hour, Shafirgullah came over and roused his friend. Khalid woke up and rubbed his eyes. Shafirgullah motioned toward the mountain and Khalid told me to get up. I did, watching as the Afghans packed the blankets back into the hobo sack. We started hiking again, with only the moonlight to guide us. Rocks gave out beneath my feet. We kept climbing—higher and higher, until we came to the face of the mountain. The Afghans stopped, unsure of which way to go. I sat down and waited as they pointed to either side of the rock face. I must have been shivering because Khalid took off his scarf and put it around my shoulders, and I thought I saw another glimpse of the young man I had come to know. I was happy for the warm scarf. It was dark in colour and made of thick wool, and so big that I was able to wrap it around myself twice, layers of warmth I welcomed as the temperature continued to drop.

We hiked on for a long time, stopping once to smoke, although Khalid made us put out our cigarettes after only a couple of drags when he heard an airplane—he was afraid we'd be given away by their glowing orange ends. We kept climbing and climbing, and made it over the ridge through a small opening in the mountain wall.

I was exhausted but forced myself to keep up. Khalid and Shafirgullah had traded places, so now I was following Shafirgullah, and Khalid was behind me. I thought about running away—breaking from them and just running. It didn't matter where to, maybe back to the town we had come from. Or maybe this side of the mountain—there had to be another town not far away. I wondered what they would do if I suddenly darted. Would they chase me?

Shoot me? Should I try? Maybe three weeks ago, I could have out-run them, but now I wasn't so sure. My legs felt thin and weak, my lungs congested, like I couldn't get enough air down to them. I concluded after a few minutes that I wasn't going to be able to outrun either of the two Afghans. And I wasn't sure I wanted to face the consequences of a failed attempt at escape. So I continued to follow them. We kept hiking, into a valley, on either side two tall mountains, both taller than the one we had just scaled.

We headed for the mountain on the right and started up its slate slope. The shale was loose, and our steps were triggering minor rockslides. My legs were shaking, threatening to collapse underneath me, as I followed Shafirgullah's nimble footsteps from rock to boulder to rock. I slipped and fell some more, and was pretty sure I had bruised my left shin. I was more worried about my right knee, which isn't so good after years of wear and tear from running and skating. I should wear a knee brace while exercising, but I hadn't been, and I'd felt it after the Army Ten-Miler that Paul and I had run a few weeks earlier. Still, going up the mountain was better than coming down, and I tried to favour my left leg while we climbed.

I was now sweating underneath the thick wool scarf, so I took it off and stuffed it into the plastic bag filled with my belongings. The cold mountain air cooled me off immediately, and the sweat running down my back felt like rivers of cool water. It was getting harder and harder to breathe—the air had become cold and thin with the elevation. Khalid and Shafirgullah must have been in pretty good shape. They continued to scamper uphill, breathing almost normally, while I was—uncharacteristically—huffing and puffing.

The adrenaline from several hours before was now starting to wear off, and I was feeling more confident that I hadn't been marched out of the hole to be executed. Still, I'd have felt better if

I'd known what was going on, and Khalid wasn't telling me much. I'd stopped asking, knowing I wouldn't get an answer. At least not that night. As we reached the top of the mountain, Shafirgullah pointed to an alcove in the rocks. I followed him as he clambered up the loose shale at a great speed.

"Here," Khalid said. "We stop."

As I put down my plastic bag, my foot dislodged another rock. I watched it tumble about five metres down into a gulley. I've never really liked heights, and although I don't have a great fear of them like some people do, it suddenly seemed like a long way down.

Khalid and Shafirgullah were unpacking their sacks and spreading out the blankets. The space was small, too small for all three of us, so Shafirgullah climbed a little higher to where the rock jutted out, just a bit behind us but where we could still see him. He laid his blanket down and sat on it.

Khalid reached into his pocket and took out the small alarm clock that had been in the hole. I hadn't noticed that he'd taken it with him. I looked at the clock: it was almost one o'clock in the morning. We'd been hiking up this mountain for more than five hours, with a few rest stops.

I sat down, but the rock was so hard on my tailbone, it was hard to get comfortable. Shafirgullah lit a cigarette and tossed the package down to us. I was surprised at how relieved I was to have a smoke. After that hike, I needed something to calm myself. How strange that I had come to rely on cigarettes in such a short period. I could feel the addiction taking root again and it frightened me a little. I took a deep drag and vowed that I would stop the moment I was released.

"You like here?" Khalid asked me. I nodded, and told him I was happy to be out of the hole. He agreed. "That is not good place," he conceded. "But here—is not safe."

"What do you mean it's not safe?"

He waved his hand around and gestured at the scenery. "Look, anyone can see us here."

"But it's so much better to be out of that hole."

"That is safer place," he told me. "We no stay here long."

"How long will we stay?" I asked. "And where will we go if we do not stay here?" He didn't answer that, telling me only that he was waiting for a phone call the next day from Abdulrahman. I didn't want to assume anything, but I had a faint hope that the phone call meant we could be on the way to Kabul.

I looked around the large black boulder that shielded the alcove. The village from where we'd come was now a distant glowing patch of dim light. We had to be miles and miles away from the hole. I was amazed that from there, my kidnappers knew how to get to this spot, through the hills and the valleys and the mountains. I sensed it was a route they had taken before.

I thought it was further proof of why Afghanistan is sometimes referred to as the graveyard of empires. No one—no ISAF soldier, or US marine, or Canadian Van Doo—can navigate this terrain as well as a local. Afghans know this land like the back of their hands, and they know how to get around it without the use of a compass or a GPS. If my amateur gang of kidnappers could traverse the mountains like we had that night, think about what the Taliban could do. Knowing this terrain helped them to drive out the Soviets. And it was how they were going to fight back against the NATO coalition.

Shafirgullah reached into the white plastic bag and took out a box of juice and a piece of bread, which he ate hungrily. He downed the juice, and lay down.

"Sleep," Khalid said to me. "Sleep coming to me." He wrapped himself in his blanket and settled next to me, resting his head on a large flat rock. Shafirgullah got up and reached down for the end of the chain. He said something to Khalid, then fastened it to Khalid's wrist with a padlock. There would be no escape for me while my captors slept. The thought was vanquished before I was even aware of it.

"Good night," Khalid said and turned his back to me.

I shuffled around, but the rocks kept digging into my spine and tailbone. Every position I tried was uncomfortable. The rocks were hard against my head; there was a boulder digging into my shoulder; my knee was throbbing with pain. I finally gave up and just looked out at my surroundings. The sky was still a wondrous canvas of millions of points of light. Across from us was another mountaintop, backlit by the almost-full moon. I saw a small blinking red light—a satellite, perhaps—thousands of kilometres up in the sky. And then a flurry of shooting stars, one after another, their tails streaking across the dark curtain of night. It was possibly the most beautiful nightscape I had ever seen in my life. I was awestruck by the majesty of the hills, and the mystery of the night sky. I stared up into that sky for what seemed like hours.

I drifted off several times, only to be jolted awake by a rock digging into me when I shifted even slightly. I couldn't feel my fingers and tucked myself in even tighter under the scarf and blanket. My feet felt frozen. I must have been shivering as well, because at one point Khalid, half asleep, put half of his blanket over me. But I was happy to have the sky to look up at instead of the ceiling in the hole. I felt strangely at peace, like I was at one with nature and creation. I reached into my pocket for my rosary.

Dear God, I prayed silently, *only you could create such a beautiful sky, and all these stars. Thank you for giving me a glimpse of your amazing place. You who could create something so amazing are the only one who can free me from my captors. Please make this ordeal come to an end soon. But I just want to tell you that I'm thankful for tonight. Thankful that I'm not in the hole, and thankful that I am still alive. The rest is up to you.*

Thank you, God, for this moment I've had with you. It will stay with me forever.

Dearest M,

It's not even eight o'clock and I've already done the rounds of emails and have no idea how I'm going to fill the rest of the day. I hate to think of how much weight you've lost, knowing you can't afford to lose any. I think I'm down about five pounds. I also hope you're able to keep a diary, so that I will one day know what you're going through. Mostly I'm sure you've found comfort and inner peace in talking to God. I wish I could.

Poor Vanessa is really suffering today. I can tell by her overnight email. Her stomach is in knots, and I think she's drinking and smoking a lot. She says she sits in her office at work with the door closed and doesn't really care what people think. I'm beginning to rely on her notes for company, and the same goes for the rest of your friends.

By the way, the Canucks just came off a six-game road trip with two wins and four losses. Even Columbus beat them!

Miss you, darling.

xx

The birds were chasing each other down the slopes of the valley and over the hills, calling out to each other and anyone else within earshot.

I opened my eyes. It was barely dawn. The dark, star-speckled sky was now hued in bands of light blue, a soft orange glow at the horizon. Two large birds danced over the valley.

I sat up and rubbed my eyes, forgetting for a moment that I was still chained to my captor. My wrist felt like it was sprained. The chain had cut into my skin, which was red and raw. Khalid stirred but didn't wake. Shafirgullah was also still asleep, just above us. The alarm clock told me it was just after five o'clock. It was still extremely cold. I tucked my legs back under the blanket and stared out from the alcove. The jagged mountains jutted into the sky, huge shards of dark granite. Wisps of thin white clouds floated overhead. In the distance, a town was just waking up. From my obscured vantage point, it seemed like a fairy-tale town. I imagined it was already bustling with people starting their day: women preparing bread, children chasing each other through the mud streets.

Again, I felt a sense of peace. It was good to be outside, breathing fresh air and seeing this stunning scenery. It rivalled the view from the villa in Umbria my girlfriends and I had rented just a few months before for Maureen's wedding. Nestled in a hillside close to a tiny village, it had an infinity pool from which you could see the rolling green and gold hills and vineyards of the region. We'd spent our afternoons in the pool, a respite from the intense Italian sun. At the time, I thought it was the most beautiful landscape I'd ever see. Now, with the rugged Afghan countryside spread out in front of me, I was having second thoughts. *How ironic*, I thought. *This is not a view I would ever have seen if I wasn't here as a hostage.*

My captors were still sleeping soundly. I breathed deeply, enjoying the fresh air and relishing just being out, out in the open—almost forgetting again for a brief moment that I was a chained captive. I wished I could take a picture, and I closed my eyes and tried to sear the scene in my memory.

When I opened my eyes again and looked down, I blinked, because I thought my eyes were playing tricks on me. They weren't. At the bottom of the mountain opposite us was a man. He looked as tiny as an ant. And he was walking up the ridge of the massive hill. I followed him with my eyes for as long as I could. Sometimes he blended in with the rocks. He was wearing a hat, or maybe it was a headscarf, and he was making his way slowly up the mountain. I was fascinated. Where was he going? Where had he come from? Would he be able to hear me if I called out? But what would I say? Help? My kidnappers might kill him if he came over to us.

Khalid woke up. It was early for him, but he yawned and said he couldn't sleep because it wasn't comfortable. He fished around in his pocket for the key to the padlock so he could unlock himself from the chain. I reminded him that Shafirgullah had had it the night before. He nodded and shook his friend's leg to rouse him. Shafirgullah slept more and better than anyone I knew. My grand-mother used to say that people who slept well were lucky because it meant they had few worries in life. I think she was right. What worries did this young Afghan kid have? None. He had his tooth-brush, his gun, and no real responsibilities other than to make sure his hostage didn't try to escape.

Shafirgullah opened his eyes and rubbed them with his grubby fingers, like he did every morning I'd seen him. It's funny that I'd gotten to know their habits and routines. He was definitely more concerned about his appearance than any other Afghan man I'd met. Even here, in the middle of the mountains, he pulled a comb out of his pocket and ran it through his hair, he brushed his teeth with the stick contraption, and washed his face and forearms with the jug of water he'd carried up from the creek just below. After he finished, he offered me the jug. I put my arms out and he poured water into my cupped hands. I washed my face and scrubbed my hands. The cold water felt good. I felt like Pig-pen, the Charlie Brown character who is followed by a cloud of dirt. It had been forever since I'd washed. I didn't even want to think of how dirty I was.

Khalid motioned for Shafirgullah to hand over the key to the padlock, and he reached into his pocket, fishing around until he pulled out two. Khalid unlocked himself from me, and then took the other key to my wrist. He fiddled with it for a while and finally unlocked the chain from my wrist. It was a relief to have the chain off—a little more freedom than I'd had in a long time. Khalid got up and brushed off the dirt and some twigs that were clinging to his pants, then manoeuvred his way around the boulder. "Bathroom," he said as he disappeared into a crevice. I nodded, wondering where I was going to go.

Shafirgullah, having completed his ablutions, spread a blanket out and knelt down to pray. Khalid returned and splashed some of the water from the can on his face and hair. He sat down next to me and pulled out the package of cigarettes from his breast pocket. He lit one, handed it to me, and then lit another for himself. We smoked in silence for a while. I looked out at the ridge across from us again, squinting to see if the man was still walking. It took me a while to spot him, but I did eventually. He was almost over the peak. I pointed him out to Khalid. He couldn't see him and interrupted Shafirgullah's prayers to ask him if he could.

The two Afghans walked out to the edge of the cliff, staying behind a cluster of brown shrubs. They spoke quietly and pointed across the hill.

"Where is he going?" I called out to them. They didn't answer. I got up and stood next to them, squinting to try to find the man. He had disappeared over the peak.

"What is over there?" I asked, pointing in the direction of where he was walking.

No answer, so I tried to guess. "Kabul?"

Khalid looked at me and smiled. "Maybe Kabul."

"Is that where we are going?" I asked, my voice full of hope.

"Maybe we go. We wait here."

"How long are we going to wait here?"

"Maybe today. Tomorrow."

"I would rather be here than in that hole. I'm okay to be here." I estimated from the supplies they'd brought with them that they'd planned to stay here only a day, two at the most. Then what? Then hopefully I'd be back in Kabul, hopping into a hot shower to wash off three weeks of grime and dirt and blood.

I told him I had to go to the bathroom. He pointed to the area behind where we had slept, and so I took the roll of pink toilet paper they'd brought in the sack and ventured in that direction. Big boulders meant I had a little privacy from my captors. And it was cleaner than the trash can I'd been using for the last three weeks.

Free for a brief second, I was tempted to back out of where I was, into the side of the mountain. I would sit very still, hiding behind the big boulder just behind me—away from the two Afghans, who would no doubt come looking for me. I would make myself very small, and stay very quiet, until their search led them in another direction. And then I would get up and run as fast as I could down the hill and over the other side, until I found another village.

"Mellissa, where you?" I heard Khalid calling. Damn. He was probably afraid I'd do exactly that.

"I'm still going bathroom," I lied. I looked around for a place to hide. They'd be able to hear me if I started walking away now. I felt like I had no choice but to go back, so I got up and walked back to our little space.

Shafirgullah was pointing across the valley. I craned my neck to see what he was looking at, but I couldn't see anything. My eyes were dry and tired after three weeks of wearing the same contact lenses.

"There!" Khalid pointed something out to me. "Do you see?"

I could make out three people walking to the base of the mountain across the valley. From where we were, it looked like they were taking pictures of each other with a camera as they made their way up the mountain.

"Get back," Khalid told me, obviously concerned that we'd be spotted. Again I wondered what would happen if I yelled out. Would the people be able to hear me? They were quite far off in the distance, at least three kilometres, and I figured it wouldn't do me much good to call for help from here, especially standing next to my two armed captors.

I did as I was told. I sat back down on the rocks and waited. To distract myself, I stuck a straw into the top of a juice box and sipped. It was apple juice, which I was getting sick of, but it was still better than the sickly sweet, thick mango juice or the deep red pomegranate and cherry juices, which I feared would stain my teeth.

Shafirgullah stepped back as well, and ripped into a hunk of bread. He offered me a chunk and I took it. It was cold and chewy, but at least it wasn't sweet. I wasn't at all hungry, which was strange, given that we'd hiked so long to get to this spot, but I thought it best to eat something to keep my energy level up, particularly if we were going to make the journey to Kabul later that day.

"How far is it from here to Kabul?" I asked. I assumed it was in the direction that the people we had seen were walking, but I really didn't know.

Khalid scratched his goatee. "Maybe few hours."

"Is it over there? Over that mountain?" I pointed to the peak on the other side, over which the man earlier had disappeared.

Khalid shrugged and smiled. "Maybe." Of course he wasn't going to tell me. He was afraid I'd start heading that way myself.

"When do we go?"

"We wait here. Abdulrahman call us. Then we go."

I thought about what that implied. Would Abdulrahman give the go-ahead for Khalid and Shafirgullah to drop me off some-where, once they got what they wanted? Maybe that was supposed to happen today. It made sense. Once Khalid's father, or friend, or whoever he was in Pakistan was satisfied with whatever he got on his end, he'd send word to the people holding me that they could release me.

Did I trust them to release me? Who was to say that they wouldn't sell me to another group after they got what they wanted? Or that they wouldn't just kill me, because now I knew them; I could recognize them, and tell the police where they were holding me. Khalid had promised he wouldn't kill me, but could I really trust him not to? Was I being entirely naive about his real inten-tions? He had a commodity, and greed could easily overcome any sense of duty or promise he'd made to me. There were no laws here, no rules by which he had to abide. This was anarchy in its most primitive form. Khalid owed me nothing, despite his assurance that he wouldn't shoot me, and his promises to email me when I got back to Canada.

There was also Shafirgullah to contend with. I knew by now that Khalid could be influenced by his friend, and Shafirgullah struck me as the greedy one. I didn't trust him at all. His dark little eyes always seemed to be glaring at me. He was the one who had sunk the knife into me on that first day. The cut on my right hand was deliberate. He wasn't as kind as Khalid could be. He was simpler, not as smart, much less tolerant than his friend, and more likely to resort to violence, at least in my mind.

I was relieved that we couldn't really communicate, since it was getting harder for me to hide my dislike of him. And I had already sensed that he was getting a little sick of me, which didn't auger well if he had any say in the decision to release me.

I watched as he opened a package of cookies and started popping them into his mouth one after another. He threw the wrapper to the side and the shiny metallic paper caught the sun's light. Khalid chased after it and reprimanded Shafirgullah, pointing up at the sky. Then he turned to me and tried to translate. "This paper," he said, holding the foil wrapper in his hand. "It is . . . how you say . . ."

"Shiny?" I offered.

"Yes." He nodded, pointing up at the sky. "Airplane—they may see from sky." As if on cue, the sound of an airplane rumbled overhead.

"Get down!" Khalid ordered. I was already sitting, and he pushed my head down a bit farther. The plane's engines could be heard for a while. Not a fighter jet, but a commercial plane, probably one of the Afghan airlines flying out of Kabul's airport.

Khalid didn't want to take any chances, and wouldn't even let Shafirgullah stand until the plane was long gone.

"Khalid, they can't see us," I argued after the plane had passed. From ten thousand feet up, we couldn't be more than specks hidden in the landscape. It was just an extension of his paranoia that someone would find us.

"Yes, they see," he insisted.

I sighed. There was no arguing with him.

We waited all morning for the phone to ring. At one point, both Khalid and Shafirgullah took the batteries out of their phones and put them back in, to make sure they were working.

"Why don't you call him," I suggested. It was close to noon, and there was still no phone call.

"We wait," Khalid said, frowning. "Abdulrahman will call us."

The sun had moved directly in front of our spot, and it felt warm on my face. I shielded my eyes from it and looked down across the valley. Two people were walking up the other side. I could tell they were the same people who had been heading up the hill earlier by the colour of their kameezes. Except there were now only two of them instead of three. They were stopped, and it looked as if they were sitting on a plateau. They sat for what seemed like a very long time, and then one got up and walked off. The other person walked back down the hill. Again, I wondered who they were and what they were doing.

Shafirgullah was praying again, except this time he had a pocket Koran and was chanting directly out of it. It made me wonder if all those times in the hole he was just chanting the same thing over and over. I lit another cigarette and smoked half before stubbing it out and leaving the remainder on the rock beside me to smoke later.

Khalid was getting anxious. He kept looking at the alarm clock and then at his cell phone.

"Why don't you call him?" I prodded again. He sat for a while, then punched a number into the phone.

"Salaam," Khalid said. He spoke for a few minutes and then hung up.

"What did he say?" I asked.

"Nothing. He wait for phone call too."

I wondered if something had gone wrong. I surprised myself thinking this way. In the past, I had believed we shouldn't negotiate with terrorists or kidnappers because it would just encourage them to continue their criminal activities. Easy to say when you're not being held hostage. Still, whatever Khalid and his gang thought was going to happen today, it hadn't happened yet.

"How long will we stay here to wait?" I asked.

"Maybe one day. But we cannot stay here long."

"Why not? This is a better place than the hole."

"It is not safe. Someone may find us."

Shafirgullah had finished praying. He washed his hands with the last of the water in the jug. He said something to Khalid in Pashto and started walking down the hill with the empty container.

"He's going to get more water?" I asked. Khalid nodded.

I felt a rumble in my tummy, and a wave of nausea washed over me. I held my stomach, hoping it would pass. It didn't. It got worse and worse, and when I stood up, my head was spinning. I was sweating a cold sweat and my body started to shake. I barely made it around the corner of the boulder before I heaved and everything came out. I caught my breath just in time to retch again. I didn't even notice that Khalid had come behind me and had put his hand on my back. "Mellissa, you are sick."

I heaved again but nothing came out this time. Khalid was clearly worried. He led me back to the alcove in the rocks and we sat down. He patted my back. "You are sick, Mellissa."

I nodded. I really didn't feel well, and I could barely talk. Throwing up is a rarity for me. Something dirty had surely gotten into my system. A steady diet of packaged cookies and packaged juice wasn't all that risky, but the conditions around me were. Sanitation hadn't exactly been a concern for my kidnappers.

Khalid's hand was still on my back.

"I have to go home soon," I said weakly.

His thick brow furrowed and he rubbed his temples with his fingers.

"I've missed an important doctor's appointment already. I will only get sicker and you will not be able to find a doctor here who can help me."

He sighed and turned to look at me. Eye to eye. The Khalid I'd known for the last three weeks seemed to be back. "What you want me to do? It is not my choice," he said, somewhat apologetically.

"Tell me how to walk to Kabul from here. And just let me go. Please."

Silence greeted that request.

I pressed on. "If I get sicker and die, you will not get what you want—and your father or friend in Pakistan will just be angry. You can let me walk away and tell him that I died. It won't be your fault. And you know that letting me go home is the right thing to do. You don't want to keep me here for much longer. You know it's not right. You know I need to go home."

He was deep in thought. He knew that as my captor, he could also be my liberator. It was up to him whether I remained caged or whether I got to fly free. "If . . ." he started. "*If* I let you walk to Kabul, what will I tell my friend in Pakistan?" he said, ignoring my suggestion. "He will be angry with me."

"He is not your boss. You can make your own decisions. You're the one who took me, Khalid. You took me. Not him. It's not his choice. It's yours. You know the right thing to do is to let me go to Kabul. You know this."

He was still thinking, and lit a cigarette to highlight his pensiveness. I relit the half cigarette I'd left on the rock earlier.

"I take you. Yes. But my friend . . . he will be angry. With me. If you go, he might kill me."

"He won't kill you if you tell him I died. I was sick, and he didn't finish my case soon enough. It is his fault." I had to try to convince Khalid that he was in charge, not the man on the other end of the line in Pakistan.

"But—he will know you are not dying. You will tell police. You will tell about me. About Shafirgullah. And the newspaper will find out. And then my friend—he kill me." *This is probably true*, I thought. Nevertheless, I had to convince him that no one would find out.

"I promise you," I said earnestly. "I will not go to police. I will not tell police about you or Shafirgullah. I will just go to Kabul and then go to Canada. I will not talk to anyone. Not any reporters. No one. No one will know that you let me go."

Khalid scratched his goatee. I knew he was thinking about it. I reached out and took his hand.

"Please, Khalid. Please. It is the right thing to do. I am your sister. You cannot keep me here longer if I am sick. You know it is the best thing for me. I promise I won't go to police or tell anyone about you." He looked long and hard at me. "Please—just tell me how to get to Kabul and I will start walking. You know it is the right thing to do. I know you, Khalid. You know I need to go home. You know this has been too long."

I was pleading now, and he was listening. He looked torn—between his duty to his friend or father in Pakistan and meeting their criminal goals and his responsibility to his hostage.

"I need to go home to Canada, Khalid. My family, and my friends. They are so worried about me. They're suffering a lot too. Think about if Shogufa was in my place. You would want her home too, wouldn't you? You would be thankful for the person who freed her. Please, Khalid. Please help me. I need to go."

He took my hand and examined my scar.

"It is still hurt?" he asked. I nodded. He sighed. "I am sorry for you, Mellissa. I am sorry I take you."

"Then let me go, Khalid. Please, let me go."

He held my hand a little tighter and rubbed the back of it. He shook his head and sighed.

Shafirgullah, who was trudging back up the hill with a full jug of water, interrupted. He stopped short of where Khalid and I were sitting, aware, perhaps, that something serious was going on. Then he rushed over to us, speaking to Khalid in Pashto even before he reached us, gesturing frantically at something down below.

And in that instant, opportunity vanished. The two became engaged in deep conversation, Khalid was back into his role as head kidnapper, discussing something with his subordinate, and I was again his hostage, not someone he felt a tinge of guilt about. I bit my lip and tried hard not to cry. The phone call from Abdulrahman might still come, but the sun was starting to fade, and so were my hopes of being in Kabul by the end of the day. Khalid and Shafirgullah took a few steps away from me and continued their serious discussion, Shafirgullah looking back at me several times. I figured Khalid was telling him about our conversation. Shafirgullah kept shaking his head and glancing at me. Finally, Khalid walked back and sat next to me. I knew what he was going to say even before the words came out of his mouth.

"I am sorry. You cannot go to Kabul without me. I am sorry for you."

That fucker Shafirgullah had talked him out of it. I looked down at the little Afghan and glared at him. His beady eyes were mocking me again. I wanted to run over and push him off the cliff. Khalid had been thinking about just letting me go. I knew he had—I felt it—until Shafirgullah came back.

I sat there in stony silence. Khalid tried to reassure me. "Mellissa, I cannot let you go. You know—my friend will kill me. He will kill me if you are go." I didn't respond, just reached for the package of cigarettes and lit one. "I will call Abdulrahman. I call him now. Maybe I go to Kabul with you tonight."

I calmly told him not to bother. I knew nothing was going to happen that night, and all I wanted to know was whether we were going to sleep out in the mountains for a second night. He didn't know the answer.

For the next hour, we sat and waited. The afternoon was getting old. The days were getting shorter, and the sun would be setting soon. Across the valley, I could make out a figure walking slowly down the mountain. I kept looking and realized it was the same man I'd seen at dawn. He was carrying something on his back, but I couldn't tell what it was. Perhaps it was a basket, and I imagined that he had walked to Kabul or some other town on the other side of the mountain and was now bringing home food to feed his family for the next week.

The little hand of the alarm clock was pointing at four. Still no word. Khalid must have felt the same impatience as I did. He reached into his pocket, dug out his cell phone, and dialed a number—Abdulrahman's, I assumed, since he had been waiting for his call. The phone on the other end rang several times and then I heard the greeting. "As-Salaam Alaikum." A quick conversation followed, and I heard Khalid asking what sounded like the same question at least three times. Then he passed the phone to Shafirgullah and sighed deeply. He reached across me for the box of cigarettes and lit one. When Shafirgullah got off the phone, the two had a long conversation in Pashto.

Finally, Khalid turned to me and told me we had to go.

"Go where?" I asked. "Kabul?"

"No. We go back to the place."

"What place?" I knew what he meant, but I couldn't bear to think about returning to the hole after a day out in the mountains. It wasn't fair. If we could spend a day here, why not another?

"We must go now," he told me. "I am sorry, Mellissa. It is not safe here."

"But it is!" I argued. "No one saw us here today. No one. And this is a better place than in that hole down there. We can wait here. Maybe the phone call will come tomorrow." I was pleading again but didn't much care. I did not want to go back to the hole. I didn't.

"We go." There was no arguing. He and Shafirgullah started to pack up all the evidence of our being there. The empty juice boxes, the bits and pieces of cookie wrapper, and the blankets we'd used. I picked up the plastic bag that held my personal items.

The Afghans put their guns over their shoulders and told me we were heading down. I could do nothing but follow.

Going down was much harder than going up. I could feel my bad knee buckling under the strain. Those small rockslides we'd created heading up now threatened to take us down with them. Shafirgullah was a deft climber. He led us through a narrow path that ran straight down the mountain and zigzagged through some of the steeper cliffs, often having to wait until I picked myself up from a fall. We came to a big drop that I remembered from the night before. Khalid had had to give me a push up while Shafirgullah had held my arm to help me get my footing. Now I was looking down on it, and it was steeper than I remembered. Shafirgullah had already hopped down and Khalid was behind me, urging me forward. I jumped, and said a silent thank you to God when I didn't sprain my ankle as I landed. We continued to weave our way down as the sun made its exit to our left—west, I made a mental note to myself.

Suddenly, Shafirgullah whispered loudly, *"Dresh!"* and Khalid told me to stop and get down. I did as he said, and Khalid crouched between me and Shafirgullah. There was movement in the gulley just below us. I could barely make it out because it had gotten dark, but someone was there.

Then, just as I was wondering whether I should call for help, Shafirgullah stood up and started to laugh. Khalid stood up, and then motioned for me to do the same. "Do you see? Mellissa? Do you see?"

I couldn't see. See what? They were both pointing. I strained my eyes but still couldn't see anything.

"Quick—do you see?" Khalid repeated.

I squeezed my eyes shut, then opened them again, and I finally saw what they were pointing at. In the distance was a large dog—it looked like a coyote, though maybe it was a grey wolf—staring right back at me. I looked at him, or her, for a long time as if silently pleading for help. *Go and tell someone you saw me, if you can. Follow us back to the hole, and bring someone back to rescue me. You can pick up our scent with your nose. Follow us back and then go to the village and bring someone to find me. Please. Help me if you can.*

The dog stared hard at us from about thirty metres away, as if trying to figure out who we were and whether we were a threat.

I was still staring at it when a loud bang shattered the silence. The dog fled. Shafirgullah laughed and slung his gun back over his shoulder. I glared at him, but he didn't notice.

We continued down the mountain, stopping again at the creek for a break. I washed my face and my forearms and breathed in the fresh air, knowing that I would soon be confined in a dank hole again. I could see the town in the distance. We weren't far away now.

Again, I contemplated running away. Khalid might let me go, but Shafirgullah would shoot me for sure. It was dark, their assault rifles were probably not the most accurate, and I might be able to outrun them. I kept looking for my chance as we made our way back to the village. There wasn't one. Khalid was in front now, leading the way, and Shafirgullah and his gun were barely a step behind me. Finally, we stopped. We were very close to the town, and Khalid told me he had to blindfold me again. They did not want me to see where we were going and how we were going to get there.

I knelt down and let him tie the scarf around my eyes. I moved it a little so that I would be able to breathe and managed to create a little window over my right eye—the thin layer of scarf allowed me to see the world, albeit through the fuzzy, dark veil. Khalid took my hand and put it through his arm, and he guided me back through the grape fields and bumpy country paths. We talked almost the entire time, with the same exchange entering the conversation every few minutes.

"Khalid, you must help me get home to Canada."

"Inshallah, Mellissa, you will go soon. I am sorry for you this is not finished."

I told him it was nice to be away from the hole, even for a short time, and thanked him for taking care of me. I said he was nicer than his friend Shafirgullah, and he laughed.

"He didn't need to shoot at the dog," I said. "How do you say 'dog' in Pashto?"

"*Spay,*" he answered. "He was not shooting dog. He just shooting."

"Do you like *spays?*" I asked.

"Yes, I like. But Shogufa, she afraid of *spay.* You have a dog?"

"No, but I really want to get one. I love them." I vowed I'd get a dog someday. My friend Melanie and I had tried to share custody of a puppy a few years earlier when I lived in Toronto. Fudge was a little brown curly ball, and we loved him the same way divorced parents love (and raise) their children, but our work schedules made it almost impossible. We'd be sneaking him into work when we edited late, locking the door to our edit suite to hide him from the security guards. It was just too difficult, and he ended up in a good home with a co-worker, whose three young children doted on him.

I told Khalid about Fudge, and told him I'd get another dog someday, once I got home to Canada. He asked if I liked *pishos*—cats. I told him that my sister had two cats, but that I wasn't their biggest fan.

"*Dresh!*" came the call again from Shafirgullah, and we all sat down. Was someone walking nearby, and my kidnappers didn't want us to be seen? Eventually, we continued on, and I could sense that we were back in the town. Through the blindfold I could make out the shapes of mud houses and walls, and trees. We walked through some alleyways and I could just distinguish the abandoned house where I had been taken that first week.

"Sit here," Khalid ordered. I sat on the ground, still blindfolded. They left me there for what felt like a long time. It felt a little unsettling, almost like I was awaiting execution. Khalid finally returned and told me I would be going back to the hole. "I am sorry, but there is nowhere else to go," he said.

I nodded. "I know, Khalid, but can I ask you something? Will you not put me in the chain again? It hurt the last time, and I can't go anywhere anyway. Please?"

He didn't answer for a while but then said, "Maybe your foot only."

"No," I pleaded. "Please, I am not going to go anywhere. I promise. No chain."

I heard him take a deep breath. "Okay, Mellissa. No chain."

"Thank you, Khalid. Thank you."

"Get up," he said, guiding me by my elbow to the entrance of the hole. "Sit." Again, I sat cross-legged on the dirt ground. Through the blindfold, I could make out the outlines of what looked like a shed. My captors took some shovels from it and soon I could hear them digging.

"Come," Khalid said. He led me to the hole, and then he and Shafirgullah each took an arm and lowered me back in. Once down, I took off my blindfold and crawled back down the smelly tunnel. I had Khalid's lighter, the one with the small flashlight at the end, which I used to light my way.

The cave was still filthy, and it reeked. My backpack was where I'd left it. I shook out the blue duvet. A big spider was sitting on my pillow. I squashed it with my foot.

I sat down and waited for the sound of digging to start. There was no juice, no cookies, no bread. I wondered what they'd do. Someone was coming down. Khalid, maybe? Was someone going to stay with me now that the endgame might be near?

"Mellissa."

It was Shafirgullah. He had supplies. A plastic bag, black this time, with the juice boxes we hadn't yet finished and the remaining cookies. But he had something else. The thick metal chain, which he started to wrap around my ankles, fastening them with the padlocks that had just been removed the day before.

"No!" I shouted, but he continued.

"Stop, Shafirgullah! No! Khalid promised me no chain! Stop! That is too tight!"

"I sorry," he said, shaking his head, "I sorry." He brought the chain to my left wrist this time, and I protested, complaining it was too tight. He loosened the noose, and then put the padlock around it.

"You don't have to do this, you know," I said, knowing that he wouldn't understand. "It's not like I'm going anywhere. How would I get out? What are you afraid of?"

"I sorry, Mellissa," he said, before scampering into the tunnel and out the shaft. The sound of digging started. And soon I was covered in a shower of dirt and dust, chained to myself once again, in the exact same place I had been just a few days before. Only now I was a lot less optimistic that the end of my nightmare would come anytime soon.

Oh dearest M,

I can't believe we have to endure another Friday like this. I scrounge for any hint that we are getting closer to your release. It is very quiet on the streets. The day when good Muslims go to the mosque to cleanse their hearts, I have visions of your kidnappers doing the same.

xx

I was angry. Angry at Shafirgullah for putting me back in chains. Angry at Khalid for not telling him I didn't need to be chained. Angry at myself for actually thinking I might be in Kabul that night. But who I was really angry with—and this surprised me—was God.

How could you let this happen, God? I've been doing nothing but praying and praying and praying. Every hour on the hour. Even on the mountain, I didn't miss a decade of the fucking rosary. Why aren't you listening to me? Why aren't you hearing my prayers? What more do I have to do to get you to hear me?

I threw the rosary on the blanket and stared at it. I decided to go on another prayer strike and see what happened. How could it be any worse, anyway, than what was already happening, or not happening? I looked at the filth that surrounded me and I was beyond disgusted. The trash can that had been my toilet hadn't been emptied in days. Empty juice boxes, cookie wrappers, stale dirty bread, and cigarette butts littered the place. I felt like I'd been dumped in a garbage bin and left to rot with the refuse.

Look at this, God. Look at me. This is ridiculous. How much longer do you want me to stay here? Why would you want me to stay in here any longer than I already have? How could you let me stay in here? How could you let this happen? I've been begging you to help me for the last three weeks. Why aren't you listening to me? Do you even exist? Or am I just praying to some phantom entity that's a figment of society's imagination?

I stopped. It would not be a good time to doubt the existence of God—not when I needed him to help me. As angry as I was, I still needed help.

The lamp was fading. The batteries were probably dying, but I knew there were new ones somewhere. I fished around in several of the plastic bags trying to find them. They were in the same bag as the cookies, alongside three unopened packages of fruit cremes. My kidnappers had put the alarm clock back in the bag, and I took it out. It was just after ten o'clock. It was Wednesday, November 5, and the night after the US presidential election. I wondered what had happened, and hoped that America had made the right decision. Maybe President Obama would find a way to win the war in this country and give Afghans some hope for a better future. I remembered my plans to have an election party to watch the returns. Two elections in two countries and I'd missed them both. Along with countless other events, I was sure. I felt like I was missing out on life. On *my* life, and everything that was happening in the world. For all I knew, Osama bin Laden could have been found by now and NATO troops were pulling out of the country. Anything could have happened in the last month. Life and the world were passing me by and I couldn't do anything to try to catch up to it. I was stuck in a dark, putrid hole in the middle of nowhere.

Stop it, I told myself. *Stop feeling sorry for yourself. You could be much worse off. Your kidnappers have at least left you food and drink. You're not starving, and you're not in pain, save for your stab wound and the pain in your stomach. And once this is over, you get to go home to Canada, where you have a pretty good life. You have nothing to complain about.*

I lit a cigarette and smoked the whole thing. And when I finished it, I lit another. There was almost a full package left, and I didn't really care anymore about running out. I'd just ask for more when someone came to check on me. *If* they were going to come check on me. They had to, didn't they? Someone had to. Or maybe they didn't and they were happy to leave me alone for a few days. I thought better of lighting another smoke and stuck a straw into a box of apple juice instead.

I felt completely, hopelessly alone, though I tried to remind myself that I wasn't. People were looking for me, talking to my kidnappers to try to get me released. The military was probably also looking for me, and maybe it already had an idea where I was. And perhaps there would be another opportunity to escape at some point. One way or another, I would be home soon, and I would never, ever again have to drink out of a juice box, or eat fruit creme cookies, or pee in a trash can.

I had absent-mindedly been playing with the chain around my wrist, and now realized that Shafirgullah had tied it looser than Khalid had before. I was able to slide my wrist out of the loop— my left hand was free. I took off my sneakers and tried the same thing, but the chain around my ankles was too tight. Still, I was happy to have the free use of both arms. I took it as an omen that true freedom would come soon.

I pulled out my notebook and wrote down on a fresh page, *I will be home soon*. Then I flipped the page, realizing it had been a day since I'd written anything.

Hi dear P,

I will be home soon. I just spent an incredible twenty-four hours in the mountains of northern Afghanistan. My kidnappers dug me out of this hole last night, and for a while, I was very scared they were going to shoot me, but instead, we went on this long hike. Up this big mountain, and I thought I wasn't going to make it to the top. But once we did, it was the most amazing view of the stars— and the Milky Way—and even shooting stars. It was so beautiful, P. I wish you could have seen it. Maybe you did, from wherever you are tonight.

We stayed up on top of the mountain all day, thinking that we'd get a call, a signal that it was time to take me back to the refugee camp in Kabul, but it never came.

So tonight, after waiting all day for that call, Khalid and Shafirgullah took me back down the mountain. And put me back in this hole. At least this time, I managed to slip my wrist out of the chain, so I have two free hands.

It's the little things, huh? I still don't have any idea when this nightmare might end, but I hope it's not much longer. Maybe you know more than I do these days, because I am truly in the dark. I'm just trying not to get despondent, and remember that you're looking for me. You and everyone else.

I'm just so sorry for everything I'm putting you through. I can't imagine how hard it must be on your end.

I'll be home soon, P. Love you.

xox

I must have dozed off, for I woke up to see the small hand of the alarm clock pointing to six. It was morning. The long hike of the last couple days had tired me out, and I was grateful to have slept through most of the night. My legs were aching from the lactic acid that had built up in the hours after the long walk down the steep mountain. I stood up and stretched my right leg against one of the walls. I bent my head down to meet my knee and stretched. Then I switched legs, almost losing my balance. I felt like I'd just run a marathon, and I guess I shouldn't have been surprised. I'd been sitting in almost the same position for three weeks, without even being able to walk, and then over the course of twenty-four hours I'd hiked for kilometres, up and down a frigging mountain. Still, I was a little disappointed that I wasn't in better shape, and that my body didn't seem to be able to cope with these sudden changes. I sat back down and rolled up the bottoms of my pants to my knee. My once too-big calves were about half the size of what I'd last remembered. And the tops of my pants were very loose.

I'd worn the Afghan pants my kidnappers gave me over my hiking pants, and both were now on the verge of falling off. I pulled them up, and I could feel my ribs jutting out. I ran fingers up and down my rib cage and counted my ribs—*one, two, three, four, five, six.* How much weight had I'd lost over the last few weeks?

I've never been fat, but I've struggled with a little chubbiness over the years, mostly because I eat more than anyone else I know. I figured I could lose up to five kilograms, but because I exercise on a regular basis and am in pretty good shape athletically, I'm not obsessed with weight loss. I laughed a little. How ironic that I might finally have lost the weight I'd been wanting to, but it required being kidnapped and fed nothing but juice and cookies for almost a month.

A month. I'd been here almost an entire month. A month out of my life, a month that I'd lost forever, that had been stolen from me. How could time pass so slowly, day to day, hour to hour?

Four weeks was too long. Too long to be held hostage in a hole, and too long to be away from my family and friends. It felt like forever since I'd had a decent conversation. I was tired of the circular discussions I'd been having with my kidnappers, and I was tired of talking to myself. I longed to pick up a phone and call someone, to open my inbox on my laptop. I was sick of being alone.

But I wasn't entirely alone. Another big spider—it looked like a daddy-long-legs—was crawling toward me from the entrance. I hate spiders.

This spider was about the size of a loonie, not including its very long legs. I took off my shoe and whacked it. Its legs curled up and it stopped moving. I picked it up with my fingers, something I never would have done if I had been at home. (I'd use a piece of thick paper towel to pick it up and throw it in the garbage.) The thing had started to move a little again, and I was determined to stop it. One by one, I picked off its long spindly legs, until all I had left was the body. It was almost as though I was getting back at every mosquito or spider that had bit me and made me swell up. Then I put it down on the ground and held Khalid's lighter to it. The smell of burning spider permeated the air.

I picked up the English books Shafirgullah had been reading, ripped out more pages, and burned them as well. But, as before, the dampness prevented them from fully catching on fire. I stared at the glowing embers and wondered how I would spend the time. And how much time I'd have to spend before someone came back. I had only enough cookies and juice to last a couple days.

I flipped open my notebook and reread some of the letters and notes I'd written that first week in captivity.

October 13, 4:30 p.m., eating two chocolate cookies. I suppose this will be dinner.

October 20, 6:15 a.m., Grandma's birthday. Lots of noise outside last night—possibly a firefight.

October 26, 9:30 p.m., Khalid called Shafirgullah to confirm he wasn't coming tonight.

I reread all the letters I'd written—to Paul, to my friends, to my parents. I could see the times I had been hopeful, and the times I had not.

Suddenly, I heard footsteps. *Clomp, clomp, clomp, clomp.* Someone was walking overtop of the hole. I stood up and looked up the pipe, which I knew was futile, but at least I'd be able to call out if I decided I needed to.

"Mellissa!" I heard. I thought it sounded like Abdulrahman.

I was about to answer but then remembered I wasn't supposed to respond to my own name.

"Khalid!" I heard a few seconds later. "Khalid!"

"Yes? Abdulrahman?"

"Yes, Mellissa, hello. Can you hear?"

"I can hear you. Can you hear me?"

"Yes, I hear. Okay. Tell me what is your sister's favourite hockey player?"

My sister's favourite hockey player? Another proof-of-life question. They had to be getting them through Vanessa. The answer was easy.

"Trevor Linden!" I yelled.

"What?"

I yelled it again but it was still lost on the fat Afghan.

"TREVOR—T-R-E-V . . ."

"T-R-E-B . . ." he repeated.

"NO! Not B! V!"

I made him repeat the spelling to me until I was satisfied with it. And I made him put down the number 16, which was Linden's number, so there could be no mistaking. But I didn't want him to go just yet. I told him I needed more batteries for the *tsiragh*, and that I was running out of juice boxes. Oh, and I also wanted more cigarettes.

"Okay, okay," he called down. "I bring for you."

"Abdulrahman!" I had one more question. "When do I go back to Kabul?"

"In two days, inshallah. *Saba, saba.*"

"Are you sure?" I asked, knowing that he wasn't, but I wanted to see how he'd respond.

"Inshallah! I go now. Goodbye!" And he was gone.

That was the third proof of life, a sign that my captors were still talking to whoever was negotiating for me, and it made me feel a little better that the process was still in play.

Trevor Linden. The one-time captain of the Vancouver Canucks, he was the most popular player ever to wear the team uniform. With his dark curly hair and nice-guy demeanour, he had been the heart-throb for a generation of female Canucks fans, my sister included. She had all the incarnations of the team jersey with the number 16 emblazoned on the back, which she'd wear proudly whenever she was at a Canucks game in Los Angeles or Anaheim.

Hey V,

I hope you're doing okay over there. They asked me who your favourite hockey player was today, and I almost laughed. I had to explain to them what hockey is, and here is one of my kidnappers asking who your favourite player is. I thought that was pretty funny.

I know you're probably dealing with a heck of a lot—with Mom and Dad and the CBC and everyone else. I hope you're managing and hanging in there. I feel terrible that I put you down as an emergency contact because I can't imagine the phone call you would have got in the middle of the night from someone telling you I've been kidnapped. I'm so sorry, but I never thought this could happen. You shouldn't have to be dealing with all this when you've already got enough on your plate.

But I wouldn't trust anyone else to take care of stuff for me, and I hope I'll be out soon enough and can make it up to you. I'll take you to a Canucks game maybe! Although you get to enough of them down there as it is.

If you're reading this, and something's happened to me, just know that I've made you the beneficiary in everything. It's the least I could do, right? There should be enough to pay for everything that needs to be paid for—like my massive Visa bill—and some left over for you to do what you want with.

I love you so much. Hope you're taking care of yourself. I'm glad I got to see you before I came here—I just wish we'd had more time.

See you soon, hopefully.
M

I was glad that I'd been able to see my sister before I left for Afghanistan. She had been in Toronto for the international film festival, and we'd spent the night with Jen and Paul at the bar of the Drake Hotel, on Queen Street. I hoped they were all leaning on each other now and helping each other get through whatever hell I knew they were enduring. A fresh wave of guilt came over me. The pain and anguish and worry I was causing everyone at home was something I didn't want to think about. It scared me and had the potential to paralyze me, so I'd been trying hard not to dwell on what my parents must be suffering, or what my sister might be thinking, or how my friends might be coping.

I looked down at my hands and noticed they were a dark shade of brown, and there was a thick layer of dirt under my fingernails. I looked through my makeup bag and found my nail clipper. I used the tip of the small nail file to dig out the dirt from underneath each of my nails. Soon, I had a small pile of dirt in front of me. I rubbed my hands together hard, and noticed that thin ribbons of brown grime were forming as I rubbed. I rubbed the back of my left hand with my right middle finger and a ball of brown goop formed underneath my finger. And it was the same everywhere. My forearms, my neck, behind my ears, my chest. I was covered in it, and was suddenly obsessed with rubbing it all off. I hoped I wasn't losing my mind, but I kept rubbing and rubbing, until I had a pile of brown dirt balls in front of me. I threw them all toward the door, and they scattered among the cigarette butts and rocks on the ground.

Shafirgullah had not left me any water, so I couldn't even rinse my hands after that nasty exercise. I thought I had some hand sanitizer with me, forgetting until I started digging in my knapsack that

I'd already been through that routine. It wasn't there. Abdulrahman must have taken it when he brought my bag down from the mountain on that first night. Maybe I really was starting to lose my mind. Too many hours spent talking to myself, going back and forth and forth and back over possible scenarios and why they might or might not happen. Too much time spent repeating the same phrases over and over again, talking to kidnappers who didn't understand what I was saying. Too much time spent by myself wondering and waiting and twiddling my thumbs. No wonder I was starting to lose it. Any sane person would, wouldn't she?

I looked down at the rosary I'd vowed not to pray with again and picked it up. I didn't have much of a choice, did I?

Oh my God, I am heartily sorry for having offended Thee, and I detest my sins, because I dread the loss of heaven and the pains of hell . . .

Funny that the Act of Contrition would be the first prayer to pop into my head at that moment. I had planned on starting with the Hail Marys, but for some reason, the Act of Contrition just came to me.

But most of all because they offend Thee, my God, Who art good and deserving of all my love. I firmly resolve, with the help of Thy grace, to confess my sins, to do penance, and amend my life.
Amen.

I'd last been to confession in Italy, when the girls and I had taken a day trip to Rome before Maureen's wedding. We were in Vatican City, and they were heading to the Vatican Museums, but I wanted to go to confession instead. The only time I ever went to confession anymore was at St. Peter's Basilica. A special occasion.

The priest in the confessional told me to say the Act of Contrition, and for a second, I couldn't remember it.

"Look down," he told me, and that's when I noticed it was written right there, where my elbows were. It was obvious that I didn't go to confession very often.

My mother used to remind us around Lent before Easter, and Advent before Christmas, that we should make a confession before the major feast days. My sister and I are both somewhat lapsed Catholics, and neither of us had been to confession regularly since high school, when priests would come to our school for penitential services.

Maybe, I thought to myself now, the Act of Contrition came to me because I was about to be released soon. A big feast day *was* just around the corner.

Okay, God, maybe you are listening to me. Maybe you're hearing me after all. I'll come off my prayer strike, and you can prove to me that you've been listening all along. I'm beginning to think, after all, that you are the only one who can help me out of here. So please make it happen soon. Please hear my prayers.

And then I started again, praying the rosary, and the one prayer that I must have said thousands of times over the last four weeks.

Hail Mary, full of grace,
The Lord is with thee.

I was sitting with my girlfriends by the infinity pool at our rented villa in Umbria, and we were drinking beer. The girls looked worried. I can't remember what we were talking about, but my friend Angela put her hand down firmly on the arm of her deck chair and declared, "This weekend! It's going to happen this weekend! It will be over this weekend!"

I sat up, confused as to where I was. Where did everyone go? Where was the pool? A beam of light illuminated a small patch of wall across from me. And then my heart sank as I realized I had been dreaming. I wasn't with my girlfriends in Italy. I was still in a dark, disgusting hole somewhere in northern Afghanistan.

What a strange dream. It had felt so real. I could see all my friends as they were the summer before, sitting by the pool and talking to each other, faces illuminated and skin darkened, kissed by the Umbrian sun. What was Ange talking about? I looked at the clock—it was almost six o'clock. Damn if I couldn't get a break and sleep for a few more hours. Six in the morning, Saturday, was about nine o'clock Friday night in Toronto, and I imagined that my girlfriends were gathering somewhere over drinks, talking about their week—and probably worrying about me. At least they were together, and I knew they would be drinking copious amounts of wine. Another day, another week had passed with no news of me. Or maybe there was news. I thought about my parents, and my sister, and how helpless and far away they must be feeling, hope ebbing and flowing with the dawn and dusk of each day.

Not unlike what I was experiencing in my hole. My emotions rode the same wave almost every day. I'd wake up and wonder if this would be the day. Anticipation would start growing by the hour, peaking around six in the evening, when it was dark, because I knew if I were going to be dug out, they would come at night. Then between six and eight, I would be on high alert for any sound, any hint, that my kidnappers were coming to take me back to Kabul. Nothing would happen, and by nine o'clock I would be despondent, resigned to another night in the hole, disappointed that yet again I was still here, and freedom was only a dream. And this pattern would start all over again as soon as I woke up.

This dawn was no different. It was Saturday, November 8. Three nights had passed since my kidnappers returned me to the hole after our mountain hike. Exactly four weeks before, I was in my work tent in Kandahar, packing a small bag to take for my flight to Kabul. Paul had walked with me to the tent—we'd gone to the gym on the base that morning, and I had to pack the camera and my computer, and my radio equipment. The public affairs officer was going to take me to the civilian airport for my Kam Air flight to the capital. I should have been home by now, my five-week assignment in Afghanistan over, and organizing my move to Toronto from Regina.

I sighed and was just about to turn to a fresh page in my notebook when I heard footsteps. It was early for someone to come by, but Abdulrahman had come this early before, when he was asking the proof-of-life questions.

"Mellissa." He called my name a couple more times, and it occurred to me that he might have forgotten what I was told about not answering to my name.

"Khalid!" he called down, finally realizing his mistake.

"Yes, Abdulrahman?" I stood up and shuffled my chained feet over to the pipe hole.

"*Saba*—tomorrow—we go Kabul. You and me go."

"What?" I asked. "Tomorrow? Are you sure? Where's Khalid?"

"Khalid go too. You, me, Khalid."

"Are you sure?"

"Yes," he said. I could hear him stuffing something into the pipe. Two batteries for the lamp, four boxes of juice, and two packages of cookies fell into my hands. If I was leaving tomorrow, why was he giving me more supplies?

"Okay?" he asked.

"Cigarettes!" I called up. I had only two more left in the package Khalid had left me.

"No cigarette," he said.

"Come on, Abdulrahman. Please! Cigarettes!"

A few seconds later a package came down the pipe. It was stuck somewhere in the middle, and I had to shuffle back to get my pen to dislodge it. The package landed on the floor and when I picked it up, I saw that it had been opened and was missing a few smokes. Still, better than nothing, I thought.

"Thank you," I said.

"*Saba*, Kabul," he repeated.

"Okay. In the morning or in the evening?" I asked, knowing the answer but hoping he would say morning. He didn't respond right away, and I repeated the question.

"Afternoon," he called down. Afternoon? I assumed he meant late afternoon—early evening, after the sun had set.

"I go now. Goodbye!" He was gone as quickly as he had arrived, leaving me with more questions than answers. I desperately wanted to believe that Abdulrahman was right, but I had been disappointed too many times. Still, I thought he sounded like he knew what he was talking about. Maybe there was something happening I didn't know about. Something that meant my release was imminent. Maybe Ange in my dream was right, that it all would be over this weekend. Tomorrow night meant only thirty-six more hours in the hole. *I can handle that*, I thought. *It's not too much longer.*

I pulled out the second-to-last cigarette from the old box and lit it. But after only two drags, I didn't feel like smoking any more. I was tired of the taste, and I could feel my lungs weighed down by the nicotine in my system. I didn't want to smoke any longer, even if it did help me pass a few minutes of every hour. I put the cigarette out against the wall behind my pillow and watched the ashes crumble to rest on top of my backpack. I brushed them off.

With my legs chained together, I couldn't even do my standing stretches, so I lay down and did a few leg lifts, lifting the heavy chain as well. I was tired after just ten, so I lay down and started to do sit-ups. This I could do. And I counted. Up to ten, down to zero, back up to ten, until I did three hundred and could do no more. Not too shabby, considering that I was probably in the worst physical shape of my life.

I flipped to a new page in my notebook and jotted down a few notes from the morning.

November 8, 6:30 a.m., Abdulrahman stops by—drops off cookies and juice—says we are going to Kabul tomorrow evening.

I reread what I had just written. Tomorrow might finally be freedom day. I had to remind myself that this could once again end in bitter disappointment, but something in Abdulrahman's voice suggested that he wasn't making it up this time. Or at least that's what I wanted to believe.

I counted down the hours as I'd pretty much been doing for

the last four weeks: I prayed the rosary at the top of the hour and then wrote for the rest of the hour. Noon came and went, and I ate two cookies with a sip of juice. Then it was two o'clock, then four o'clock—night would soon fall. *My last night in this hole*, I thought, even though I tried not to let myself believe it. I'd said that enough times now to know that there was always, always, another night. I was getting used to tomorrow coming, and passing, and looking forward to another tomorrow, hoping it would finally be the day. I wasn't going to let myself be disappointed again. Instead, I distracted myself with my pen and pad.

Dear P,

Abdulrahman said I'm going to Kabul tomorrow afternoon. I know he's said it before, but he seems to know what he's saying this time.

The thought crossed my mind that my idea of going to Kabul might not be the same as his. I'd been saying it as a euphemism for being freed, but it now occurred to me that my kidnappers might be taking me to Kabul to be handed over to someone else. I refused to let myself go down that path. It was too scary.

You'll be happy to know that I've stopped smoking for the time being. I took a puff this morning, and I couldn't smoke anymore. Maybe my lungs are trying to tell me something—that I need to stop if I ever want to start running again.

I'm not sure where you are. Maybe you needed to leave Afghanistan after so long, and if you did, I wouldn't blame you. It's not a great place to be hanging out and waiting. I just hope that wherever you are, you know I'm thinking about you, and that "talking" to you all the time has saved my sanity while I've been here. I'll be okay, and so will we. I promise I'll make this up to you when I get home. I can't imagine what you've been through the last four weeks. I am so, so sorry.

xox

Sure, I wanted to get the hell out of the place desperately, but more than that, I wanted to stop the pain I was surely inflicting on those closest to me.

Don't worry, I said to myself. *It's your last night here and this time tomorrow, you'll be on your way to Kabul, where you can tell everyone you're okay, and you're sorry for everything you put them through.*

I was about to write more when I thought I heard footsteps. Not just one person's, but several sets. My heart started pounding. Voices too. Impossible. It was just after seven in the evening, and I didn't expect anyone until the next afternoon. I was settling in for what I wanted to believe was the last night in the hole. The footsteps were loud, and soon they were right overhead. Could it be police? Or just nearby farmers?

"Mellissa!" It was Abdulrahman, again forgetting that I wasn't answering to my name.

"Khalid!" Another voice—the real Khalid—or, at least, the man I knew by that name—was calling down.

"Yes?" I responded.

"We go. We go now!" Abdulrahman again.

"What do you mean? You said we go tomorrow!"

"No, we must go now!"

"To Kabul?"

"Yes!"

I felt like I was having an out-of-body experience, and I could feel my extremities going cold. The adrenaline started flowing and I looked around me at the garbage can that had been my home for the last month. I packed everything into my backpack—my notebooks, makeup bag. I shoved the cigarettes and lighter in my pocket, and patted the lower pocket of my hiking pants to make sure I still had my passport, ID, and credit cards.

The sound of digging started, and dust started falling like rain into the hole. I covered my head with my scarf and sat down on the duvet. They lifted the cover to the hole, and I heard two thumps. I fiddled with the chain and slid my left wrist back into it.

Khalid and Shafirgullah were making their way toward me down the tunnel. They each had a flashlight.

"Mellissa, Kabul!" Shafirgullah said. I wasn't sure if he was mocking me or if he was serious.

"Khalid, what is happening?" I asked. His brow was furrowed. He was fumbling in his pocket for keys to unlock the padlocks that held the chain to my legs and my arm. He managed to unlock all three this time.

"What is happening, Khalid?" I asked again.

"We go—now!" he shouted. I put my shoes on and grabbed my backpack.

"No, you leave that!" he ordered.

What? He wasn't going to let me take my backpack? "But my notebooks are in it! My wallet, all my stuff!"

"No." His voice was low and serious. "You leave. Your books—for me. You take wallet. Passport. That is all."

"No! You said I could have my notebooks! You bought that notebook for me, Khalid!"

"No, I bring for you so you can write. What you write—is mine now."

I couldn't believe he wasn't going to let me take my diary and letters. I was suddenly afraid that I wasn't going to Kabul after all. What if I was going to a new group of kidnappers? That thought sent a chill up my spine. This was the moment I'd been waiting for—but I knew in the back of my mind that going to Kabul wasn't a guarantee that I was going to be freed.

"Go, quickly!" Khalid pushed me toward the tunnel. Shafirgullah had gone ahead. I looked back. Khalid was gathering everything else. My knapsack, the remaining packages of cookies and boxes of juice.

I hurried up the tunnel on my tummy and my elbows, hitting my head when I got to the end. I stood and looked up. There was a crowd outside, around the shaft opening. Khalid came up behind me and lifted me up by the legs. Someone grabbed me and set me on the ground.

"Sit!" said Abdulrahman. "Mellissa, yes! Sit!" I did as I was told. Soon Khalid scrambled out of the shaft. "We cover your eyes now," he told me. He tied my dirty black scarf tight around my eyes.

"Ow!" I complained. "It's too tight!" I reached up to my face and rearranged the scarf so that I could see a little through a space just above my nose. I looked around as best I could. I saw fat Abdulrahman to my left and Khalid to my right. Abdullah was there, and so was the guy with the lazy eye, who I had not seen since the first week. There were at least two others I didn't recognize. I heard Shafirgullah say something in rapid Pashto, then felt the barrel of a gun at the back of my head, just above my neck. My blood froze. Had my kidnappers taken me out to execute me?

"Khalid," I said softly, my voice quivering a little. "What is going on?" I reached out for his hand, but he brushed mine away.

"We are angry!" he yelled. "We should kill you now!"

I was paralyzed. Maybe freedom meant death.

"We angry!" said Abdulrahman. "But we must walk! Come!"

The fat Afghan grabbed me roughly by one arm and started leading me away from the hole. Khalid was walking next to me, and walking quickly. We were rushing, definitely in a big hurry. Someone was talking on a cell phone.

We walked in the opposite direction from where we'd come when we returned from the mountain a few nights earlier. At least that was my sense from what I could see, given the blindfold, for I really had very little sense of direction. I could make out houses, and mud walls, and trees. They were rushing me along, and I was struggling to keep my balance. I could tell we were on the outskirts of the town, and I saw more trees ahead. The ground was bumpy, and I assumed we were in a grape field. We kept walking, Khalid propping me up whenever I lost my balance. I fell several times, and each time I'd feel the barrel of a gun at my head, signalling me to get up immediately.

We entered a wooded area outside the town. Someone said something in Pashto, and Khalid pushed my shoulder down. I sat down, along with everyone else, so that we were sitting in a circle on the ground. I could saw Abdulrahman rooting through my knap- sack—for about the tenth time. He pulled out my notebooks and flipped through them. Someone lit a cigarette, and I asked for one as well. Khalid lit one and put it in my hand. I promised myself it would be the last cigarette that would touch my lips and then I took a deep breath and blew out a stream of smoke. Khalid was also smoking, and so was the guy with the lazy eye.

"I'm cold," I told Khalid. "How much longer are we walking?"

He sighed. Maybe one hour, he said, maybe two. Khalid put a coat on me. It was a large green camouflage jacket, so big that the shoulders drooped over my arms. Still, it was better than nothing. The night was young, and it would only get colder.

Someone was talking on a cell phone just beyond the circle. He called out something and Khalid told me we had to get up. "We must go," he said, yanking me to my feet. Shafirgullah followed, and I could feel the barrel of his gun in my back. I got up and allowed myself to be led, up and down and through more grape fields, walk- ing at one point along a ledge of some sort with a shallow drop down to what looked like a field with a house in a distance.

We finally made our way to a paved path of some sort. I sensed that we had lost several of our entourage.

"We are angry," Khalid said to me. "Tell me why we not kill you now?"

"Why would you want to kill me?" I was completely confused.

"Because! I am getting nothing from you!" Getting nothing for me? He wouldn't release me for nothing. Was he trading me to someone else?

"What? You are lying," I challenged him. "You are lying. You wouldn't be letting me go without getting something for me."

"We get nothing for you, do you hear me?" He was almost yelling now.

"I don't understand. Then why are you letting me go?" I asked this mostly because I wanted confirmation that I was being released.

"I should not promise not to kill you," he said bitterly. "I get nothing now."

I still didn't understand what was going on but decided it was probably better not to ask too many more questions.

After several minutes on the path we stopped, and they took off my blindfold, satisfied that we were far enough away from the hole that I would not be able to recognize the route back. Hell, I didn't want to know how to get back, I was so happy to leave it.

It was a clear night, not as spectacular as that night up on the mountain, but the air was crisp and the moon was high. We were on a narrow path lined on the right with trees that had shed their leaves, and to the left were hills, quite a distance away. Ahead, I could see more hills and several spots of light—houses, I presumed, set into the slopes.

Khalid still held onto my elbow, even though I could see, and guided me as we continued walking. "Mellissa," he said quietly after a little while. "You do not hate me, okay?"

"Hate you?" I asked.

"Do not hate us. Okay?"

"Why would I hate you?"

"Because we take you. We hurt you. I sorry you were here so long, Mellissa."

"I don't hate you, Khalid. You do what you do for whatever your reasons are. I'm just sorry for you. You live in this country that is torn apart by war."

We kept walking, and he looked at me. "You not angry with me?" he asked.

"No," I said, "I'm not angry. I forgive you." The words came out of my mouth before I'd had a chance to think about them. But I realized I'd forgiven him a long time ago, almost from the first week. It was true. My kidnappers were just a gang of simple thieves, trying to survive the only way they knew how, caught between the Taliban and the police. It wasn't right what they did, by any means, but it wouldn't do me any good to hold a grudge, or to be angry, or forever resentful of what they had done to me.

"You not hate me?" he asked again.

"No, I forgive you," I told him.

It was just the four of us now, walking this path through the Afghan countryside. Abdulrahman walked ahead, and Shafirgullah followed behind. We came upon a construction site where it looked like a road was being built. I thought it must be the one they had told me about the first week, being built by Chinese workers.

All of my kidnappers were armed, alert, and at the ready, should someone or something pop out and surprise us. Shafir-gullah ran ahead and jumped into the construction site, looking around before waving us over. Abdulrahman said something in Pashto, and the two of them pointed to a house in the distance. It was lit, but far enough away that whoever might be inside would not be able to make out four lonely figures making their way across the landscape.

We continued on. It was getting colder, and Khalid seemed concerned that I was becoming tired. We stopped for a while, and Abdulrahman made a call on his cell phone while Shafirgullah guarded the perimeter around us. Abdulrahman finished his call and gave us the signal to continue walking.

"Mellissa," Khalid said. "When you go to Kabul, you not tell police about us, okay?"

"I'm probably not going to see any police," I replied.

"They ask you who take you, you tell them—Khalid. Okay? No Abdulrahman, no Shafirgullah, okay? You say 'Khalid,'" he instructed.

"Khalid isn't your real name, is it?" I asked. He didn't respond, but I knew he wouldn't say it was okay to tell the police I was with "Khalid" if that were his name. "What's your real name? Hezbollah?" I pressed.

"You just say 'Khalid.' You understand?"

"Okay. No Abdulrahman. No Shafirgullah. Just Khalid."

We were now walking up a small hill on the paved road. I could see the faint outlines of a house on our right, a dim light the only other hint of its presence in the dark. I wondered if there was electricity out here, or if it was just a candle. I wasn't sure if there was even electricity in the town we had come from.

"Are you really going to email me?" I asked Khalid. He turned and looked at me. The man who had taken me from the refugee camp four weeks earlier suddenly looked like a young boy.

"I will not forget you, Mellissa," he said.

I felt a strange sense of calm as we continued walking. I wasn't sure where we were going or who we would be meeting, but Khalid's earlier instructions suggested that they were taking me somewhere

where I might come into contact with the police. Maybe today really was freedom day after all. I still didn't want to get my hopes up, just in case I was being handed over to some other group, but either way, I felt at peace. If, at the end of the walk, I would be handed over to someone else, I knew in my heart I was ready for it. If I was being released, I was more than ready to go home.

I wondered, though, if the authorities would try to arrest my kidnappers. Wouldn't they be afraid of turning me in if the police were involved? Would there be a confrontation? A shootout? No, impossible! They knew what they were doing. They would not let me go if they were afraid of walking into a trap.

I was just wondering how this was going to work when Shafirgullah cocked his gun and motioned for us all to get down. Khalid pushed me to the ground, and then forced me to crouch behind a bush.

"What's wrong?" I whispered. He put his finger to his lips. What were my kidnappers afraid of running into? If I was being handed over for release, they would be wary of running into other groups, like the Taliban.

I watched from my spot behind the bush as Shafirgullah and Abdulrahman checked the area around us, their guns cocked and ready. A few minutes later, Abdulrahman gave the all-clear and we resumed our trek.

In the far distance—kilometres away, I could make out what looked like a city. I wondered if it was Kabul. It was impossible to tell because it just looked like a glowing speck off in the distance. Although our pace had slowed, Khalid was still holding my arm. Shafirgullah was now walking behind us, Abdulrahman in front.

The path that we were walking on had morphed into a road wide enough for vehicles, with an embankment on one side. Through the darkness, I could make out a black SUV. And then

I saw them. Lined up on the embankment, dark figures—men in black with guns—two, three, four, five, six— I stopped counting.

Abdulrahman came to a standstill. Two men stood in front of the SUV. One wore a turban, the other a dark suit. The fat Afghan cocked his gun, and one of the men waved him away.

To my surprise, Abdulrahman then greeted the men with a hug. "Salaam," he said.

"Salaam," they answered.

The men exchanged a few words, then the one in the suit gestured toward me. Abdulrahman turned to Khalid and me and motioned for us to come to him. Again to my surprise, Khalid let go of my arm and pushed me forward.

"Go! Goodbye!" he said.

I couldn't move. I tried holding onto Khalid's hand, but he pushed me away toward Abdulrahman.

"Goodbye, Mellissa! Go!"

I took a tentative step forward. Abdulrahman was still waving me over. I took another step. Impatiently, my captor stepped back and grabbed my arm, hauling me toward him and the two men.

"Hello," the man in the suit said to me.

"Hello," I replied. "Who are you?"

His English wasn't good. Abdulrahman answered that his name was Haji Janan. "He is an important person," the fat Afghan said in English, and then translated that into Pashto for the others. They laughed, and Haji Janan took my hand. "We go," he said, leading me to the waiting black SUV.

I looked at Abdulrahman and then to Khalid, who had stepped farther back.

"You go," Abdulrahman said. "Kabul!"

Haji Janan opened the passenger door to the SUV. I climbed in, and he followed. The man in the turban got in the other side, so that

I was sitting between them. The driver started the engine. I could still see all those figures, standing on the embankment, dressed in black and holding rifles, poised and ready to shoot. And as we drove down the hill, I saw that there were dozens of them lining the road—for at least a kilometre or two. Plus about a dozen other SUVs on the side of the road, which, as we drove past them, pulled out and followed us.

I turned to the man in the suit. "Where are we going?" I asked.

He didn't seem to understand.

"Are we going to Kabul?" I tried again.

This time, he recognized the word "Kabul" and nodded. "Yes! Kabul!"

It was what I had been waiting for. I didn't know whether to laugh or cry.

The two Afghans on either side of me were speaking to each other and laughing. The man in the turban pulled out his cell phone and started making calls, speaking in loud, excited Pashto.

I suddenly realized I had to call someone. I asked Haji Janan if I could borrow his cell phone. He happily handed it to me. His screensaver was a drawing of a red rose.

"Call anybody!" he told me.

I punched in the numbers for Paul's Afghan cell phone.

No answer. How could that be?

I tried again. Maybe I had dialed the numbers wrong. Still no answer. Maybe he'd left the country.

I tried a third time. No answer. Where was he? I had to call someone, had to let someone know that I was free and alive.

Haji Janan took the phone back and made a quick call. I could hear a man's voice on the other end of the line. He handed the phone back to me when he was done.

"Can I dial long distance?" I asked.

"Call, call!"

I punched in the numbers most familiar to me—the ones I'd been dialing for more than thirty years. I could hear faint ringing, and I tried to adjust the volume. After three rings, I heard a voice.

"Hello?"

"Hi, Dad. It's me."

There was a pause.

"Mui?" he asked, using my Cantonese nickname.

"Hi, Dad, it's me. I'm okay. I'm so sorry, Dad. I'm so sorry. I'm okay. I'm on my way home."

Epilogue

It's been months since that night in Kabul, and I'm back in my happy place in Kelly's condo in Tofino. I've been back at work as a journalist for the CBC for a while, and I've been surfing and savouring my freedom, but the memories of my time in the hole are still vivid and sometimes haunt my dreams. Which is one of the reasons why I decided to write this story.

I was taken that night to the office of the head of the Afghan National Directorate of Security, Amrullah Saleh, who greeted me by telling me that not a penny had been given to my kidnappers in exchange for my freedom.

We spoke at length in his office, surrounded by his aides, as we waited for the Canadian ambassador to come and get me. He asked me to describe my kidnappers, and where I had been held (as it turns out, the village was Maidan, in Wardak province). He nodded knowingly as I spoke, and I could tell he knew who they were. I later found out that he had arrested the mother, the brother, and the sister-in-law of Khalid's "friend" or father in Peshawar, as they were trying to cross the border into Pakistan. They were thrown in jail the day that Khalid came to put the chains on me. It was a straight trade: my kidnappers released me in exchange for the authorities' guarantee that the mother would be released from prison simultaneously.

The Afghan president, Hamid Karzai, called me while I was in Saleh's office to tell me how happy he was that I had been released. Like Saleh, he reiterated that not a cent had been paid for my release. Prime Minister Stephen Harper also called me later that night. I don't remember much of that conversation, but I do remember congratulating him on his election victory.

To my great dismay, I was told that Shokoor and his brother had been arrested and jailed, the only suspects the Afghan police could come up with in my disappearance. It was the most ridiculous thing I had ever heard, that our trusted colleague was a suspect, especially after I'd been so afraid that my kidnappers would hunt him down while I was in captivity. The Canadian ambassador at the time, the wonderful Ron Hoffmann, was trying to negotiate Shokoor's release, and I didn't want to leave the country until I knew that he was okay, but his freedom didn't come until two weeks after mine.

The ambassador opened up the embassy to me—and to Paul, who was still in Kabul waiting for my release. He met me at the embassy that night. It turned out that the negotiators wouldn't let him answer his phone that last day. Even though the Afghan authorities had agreed to release the mother of Khalid's "friend" or father, the people who were holding me were still trying to squeeze the negotiators for money. They called several times, threatening to kill me unless they got it.

I learned that the CBC had set up a negotiating team in a local guest house. Jamie Purdon, my immediate boss, flew in from Toronto, as did Margaret Evans, the talented and experienced CBC correspondent from Jerusalem. There was a team from our security firm, AKE, and the CBC had brought in a second security company as well—the British-based Control Risks, who specialize in kidnapping and ransom. The group in Kabul communicated on a constant basis with a team at CBC headquarters in Toronto, who were set up in a boardroom dubbed the "war room," which was staffed twenty-four hours a day for the twenty-eight days I was gone.

Paul and I spent three days at the embassy, trying to decompress. Ron's cook, Linus, made me cheeseburgers and taught me how to make mantu, the delicious meat-filled Afghan dumplings, which I ate hungrily.

There was a contingent from the RCMP to meet me as well. The kindly Al McCambridge had the difficult job of debriefing me about my experience, and then escorted us out of the country on a Pamir flight to Dubai days later. My sister and Kelly flew to Dubai to meet me and take me back to North America, where I would be reunited with my parents. I'm still amazed at how strong they were through their ordeal.

My last image of Afghanistan was through that airplane window. I remember looking down at the mountains as we flew south, wondering if that was the peak where we had hiked to that night, and what my kidnappers were doing at that moment, where they were. As the plane climbed higher, I thought about the soldiers down there who were still fighting the war, still trying to make a difference. I wondered what had happened to the little girl in the pink and black scarf I'd met outside the PRT in Kandahar.

And I hoped I would be able to come back someday, to what might be a better, safer place, not just for me, but more importantly, for children like her.

Acknowledgements

To my editor, Jim Gifford, whose patience and steady guidance helped me through a long and at times difficult writing process, my eternal gratitude. Your insight and talent are evident throughout these pages. And to my copy editor, Judy Phillips, for your critical eye and strong sense of story. Thank you for making me a better writer.

To Perry Zimel, my manager, my dear friend, who took care of so much for me when I returned, I cannot thank you enough. You are right. There is a reason for everything.

To family—my sister, Vanessa; and my parents, Joyce and Kellog—I am humbled by your strength and courage and love, and I cannot thank you enough for what you endured because of me.

To my amazing friends—in particular, Kelly McClughan, Jen Barr, Kas Roussy, Marie Morrissey, Angela Naus, Maureen Taylor, Jen and Brian Burke, Denelle Balfour, Stefani Langenegger, Coreen and Mal Moore, Shelley and Gerry Thue—you were my pillar of strength for four weeks, and you continue to be there for me. I am lucky to be surrounded by so much love.

To the "war room" at the CBC in Toronto, and everyone who worked tirelessly for my release, thank you for your dedication, your long hours, and all those sleepless nights. A special thank you to Hubert Lacroix. Your generosity and caring toward my parents while I was gone will never be forgotten.

To Paul, who lifts me up and gives me so much, and who inspires me to be better every day, you have lived this story a thousand different ways. I would not be here, and this book would not have been written, without you.

And to the members of the Canadian Forces—those who've come home, those who haven't, and those who continue the mission in Afghanistan—and their families, you are all the true heroes. You inspire and remind us every day that the world *can* be a better place. We cannot thank you enough for your sacrifice.